Understanding Management Software

Andrew Leigh
B.Sc., M.A., MIPM

MACMILLAN

in association with

the Institute of Personnel Management

First published 1985

Published by
MACMILLAN EDUCATION LTD
Houndmills, Basingstoke, Hampshire RG21 2XS
and London
Companies and representatives
throughout the world
in association with
the Institute of Personnel Management

Photoset by Parker Typesetting Service, Leicester
Printed in Great Britain by
Camelot Press
Southampton

British Library Cataloguing in Publication Data

Leigh, Andrew
    Understanding management software.
    1. Management—Data processing
    2. Microcomputers——Programming
    I. Title   II. Institute of Personnel Management
    658'.05425   HD30.2

ISBN 0–333–40946–9

Understanding Management Software

Other business computer books from Macmillan

Planning for Data Communications
  J. E. Bingham and G. W. P. Davies
The Ultimate Software Selector for Business Micros
  Federation of Micro System Centres
Introduction to Local Area Computer Networks
  K. C. E. Gee
The Computer Handbook: A Businessman's Guide to Choosing and Using Computer Systems
  Charles Jones
Security of Computer Based Information Systems
  V. P. Lane
Understanding Microcomputers
  Dennis Langley
Dictionary of Information Technology
  Dennis Langley and Michael Shain
The Microcomputer Users' Handbook
  Dennis Langley and Michael Shain
Dictionary of Microcomputing (third edition)
  Charles Sippl

Other Macmillan computer books of related interest

Advanced Graphics with the IBM Personal Computer
  Ian O. Angell
Advanced Graphics with the BBC Model B Microcomputer
  Ian O. Angell and Brian J. Jones
Interfacing the BBC Microcomputer
  Brian Bannister and Michael Whitehead
Sorting Routines for Microcomputers
  Angus Barber and Keith McLuckie
Assembly Language Programming for the BBC Microcomputer (second edition)
  Ian Birnbaum
Micro-Maths
  Keith Devlin
 Microchild: Learning through LOGO
  Serafim Gascoigne
Using CP/M
  Peter Gosling
A Science Teacher's Companion to the BBC Microcomputer
  Philip Hawthorne
Microprocessors and Microcomputers – their use and programming
  Eric Huggins
Operating the BBC Microcomputer: A Concise Guide
  Graham Leah
The Apricot Computer System
  Del Morgan *et al.*
Microprocessor and Microcomputer Technology
  Noel Morris
Using Sound and Speech on the BBC Microcomputer
  Martin Phillips
File Handling on the BBC Microprocessor
  Brian J. Townsend
Computer Literacy: A beginners' guide
  Vincent Walsh
Good BASIC Programming on the BBC Microcomputer
  Margaret White
Mastering Computers
  G. G. L. Wright
Mastering Computer Programming
  P. E. Gosling
Mastering Data Processing
  J. Bingham
Mastering COBOL
  R. Hutty
Mastering Pascal Programming
  E. Huggins

To Aiden and Darion

Acknowledgements

This book would not have been possible without the help of the following, to whom sincere thanks are offered:
Fiona Murchie of IPM who kept my spirits up when times were difficult;
Jon Finegold of Macmillan Education; the staff of The London Borough of Croydon Reference Library; James Blackledge of Pulsar (UK) who provided a substantial number of software packages; Doreena Ward of ACT (UK) Ltd; ACT (UK) for assistance with purchasing an Apricot PC; MBS Data Efficiency Ltd for assistance with purchasing a Taxan/Kaga Printer; Business Simulations for use of *Cardbox Plus* in preparing the bibliography; Sapphire Systems for use of *DataMaster* for keeping track of all the software products and preparing the index; Raven Computers for use of *Grammatik* for checking the grammar of the text; Caxton Software for use of *Brainstorm* for miscellaneous creative purposes; Keith Mackay for helpful advice; Mary Davis for occasional clerical help; Sharon Behr of the IPM who kindly suggested the title; the producers and suppliers of the various software products mentioned throughout the book and finally my wife for her constant, enthusiastic support and tolerance for a husband who goes to work as a manager during the day, and comes home and starts work all over again.

Contents

Part One

Introduction

So many computer publications are available that to inflict another on the world warrants at least a brief explanation. This is the sort of book that, as a working manager, I would have liked to have been able to buy for my own uses. Since it did not exist, I decided to write one for my fellow managers, more than a few of whom have confessed their wish to turn the microcomputer into a personal working tool.

Evidence in both Europe and America confirms that despite the growing number of microcomputers sold, their use as personal management aids is more restricted.

Many managers have made the microcomputer into a personal working tool. But few have the time or inclination to go further and write a computer book from a management perspective. Sensibly, they leave that chore to consultants, journalists, computer scientists, and the odd manager like myself who, strangely, enjoy both managing and writing about it.

Holding down a line management role and using this perspective to develop a book that other managers might find helpful was certainly more demanding than I originally anticipated. But I hope the effort proves worth it and provides a stimulus to those of my colleagues who are in the same position that I was a while back.

Understanding Management Software is for managers who have not yet made the leap from broad-based appreciation of what computers do, to employing the microcomputer in the office for their personal use, not merely as part of some large office system.

Part One introduces the main areas which you will need to consider when thinking about choosing management software. Part Two tackles the problem of what to buy, using the know-how from Part One.

It is said that a new software product for the IBM Personal Computer is written every day of the year. Even informed managers might quail at making sensible selections from the enormous range of products now available.

Thus in Part Two you can read about 30 mainly well established products that have been selected for you because of their potential as management, as opposed to routine office, tools.

Having tried and used each one I commend them as worth investigating, should you be contemplating the purchase of software for your personal office use. These product reviews should help to narrow down to manageable proportions the burgeoning variety of available products so that you can develop your own final short list.

Hopefully, the material conveys the nature and potential of these packages. But for evaluations in depth, it would be advisable to refer to the kind of detailed appraisals published by specialist magazines.

All the products in Part Two work on an IBM Personal Computer but were in fact tested on an Apricot. The latter has held its own with the IBM PC in Britain and for this reason was used for this book, despite the narrower range of available software.

A MICROCOMPUTER, PLEASE

Many managers who are keen to experiment with and use the personal computer on their own desk have difficulty in persuading their organization to let them do so. Frequently this is because they cannot present a sufficiently impressive and cost-effective case for such an expenditure. Unfortunately, it is also occasionally due to the reluctance of those who should know better.

A recent glossary of computer terms, for example, defined an in-house computer department as 'a group of people who are dedicated to ensuring that microcomputers never enter the building'. Thankfully, that has not proved true in my own local authority. Once I had expressed a wish for a personal business computer to 'learn on' it was supplied and various benefits have flowed as a result.

I endorse such an approach and would recommend it to other organizations which perhaps demand too much of their busy line managers in expecting them to produce elaborate justifications in support of providing a personal microcomputer.

The more imaginative approach taken by a Unilever subsidiary sums up the right philosophy, as expressed by a senior operations manager, 'If someone has a sparkle in their eye and enthusiasm, then give them a micro computer'.

I am not advocating that microcomputers should be dispensed like giveaways in a packet of corn flakes. Certainly some case must be made to justify a line manager having a personal computer. *Understanding Management Software* should help such managers to present brief but informed proposals, not so much for a computer but for the more crucial software that underpins it. In turn, that should enable sensible proposals to be made for using a personal computer without making exaggerated or ill-informed claims.

The contents of this book can be found scattered in many magazines and allied publications. There are some excellent journals, like *Which Computer?* or *Apricot User* for example, which try to educate new readers and help them to get to grips with the bubbling, ever changing computer scene.

But books *by* managers *for* managers, that bring together the key aspects of using management software, are less common, hence the justification for *Understanding Management Software*. If you want a computer expert's view of the software field then look elsewhere; if you want a manager's view then I hope that this book will meet your needs.

1 Coping with the Jargon and Some First Principles

Something curious happens to even the most sane and practical person on becoming involved in computers. Inexorably, and despite their protests to the contrary, they start talking in a different language to you! It is certainly something that you will have noticed. You are probably almost reconciled to learning some of the jargon too.

As a practising manager you will also by now have concluded that if you are not going to retire within the next couple of years then you will probably have to get to grips with the computer.

Maybe you have been on one of those so-called 'computer appreciation' courses. If so, it is likely that you came away appreciating how clever the people were who did the talking. Whether you even touched the keyboard of a machine is highly doubtful. Or perhaps you are a manager with a computer on your desk or close by your office, but – like many others – you secretly know that it has become an expensive paper weight.

Incidentally, the number of computers installed but seldom used is enormous and growing daily. Not because the managers owning them are incompetent, but because they have discovered the hard way that to make the computer really help them do a better job demands far more than they originally anticipated, in effort and above all personal investment of time.

WHY DO YOU NEED A COMPUTER?

Managers who fail to use the computer as an effective personal tool usually do so because they start from a position of great uncertainty about how it might enhance their daily work. We must also distinguish between the computer used as a tool around the office and one which is your personal helpmate. This book is concerned with the latter situation.

Work styles differ radically between people so there can be no clear-cut promises that the computer will make you a better manager. But developments over the last few years suggest that you can expect a range of benefits:

- better and faster access to useful information for thinking about your job, particularly when making decisions or solving problems

- help with thinking through what you are doing and why

- a tighter grip on what is going on under your control

- elimination of time wasting activities
- a more creative approach to taking action
- new and more satisfying ways of working
- less dependence on others for certain kinds of help
- improved communications between managers

More specific payoffs are outlined in the later chapters and in Part Two. The cost of these gains will become apparent throughout the book. One particular price that must be paid immediately though, is to overcome the jargon hurdle.

Even computer experts quail at the sheer quantity of jargon in their specialism. But as far as you are concerned you can stick to a simple principle:

> if you do not understand, it is they, not you who have the problem.

Underlying this principle is the requirement to be utterly ruthless about asking for an explanation and for help. If you are one of those people who like to appear confident all the time and pretend that you know it all, then the computer will be bad for your ego.

The most experienced experts constantly have to keep asking questions to find out what on earth is going on. If, while trying to come to terms with the computer, you meet a salesman, a trainer, a fellow manager, in fact anyone who makes you feel confused and anxious about finding out precisely what you need to know, avoid them. They will do you more harm than good.

With the explosion in the number of computers, their power and their uses, has come a new complexity in our language. Nowadays there are computer dictionaries, glossaries, handbooks and guides just so that the experts can keep track of what it all means. So why be worried if you too feel a bit in the dark?

However, *you* possess a particular and enviable form of power which you can exert in this complicated computer world. You are a practising manager, with responsibilities for staff and resources. No amount of gobbledegook and wasted hours at a computer keyboard are justified if the result does not clearly help you do your job better.

It is impractical to list all the words and ideas that you are going to need. Some you will know, others will be vaguely familiar, but turning out to be different to what they seemed at first.

Because this book is not about the computer itself – the hardware – and focuses instead on what you need to make any computer useful to you, there are a few words and ideas that are worth clarifying right at the beginning. You will not be able to avoid these if you are ever going to turn the computer into an effective personal tool.

Like any language, if you use the wrong words you're likely to be misunderstood and that is particularly true in respect of computers. What matters even more than the jargon words are the particular ideas or concepts behind them. Thankfully, from a manager's standpoint, there are few such basics that need to be mastered to make a meaningful and satisfying start on the road to using the computer profitably.

COMPUTER BASICS

First, what do you really need to know about the computer itself, that is the physical boxes, screens, keyboards and so on that make up what is called hardware? Do you really need to know anything at all about what is actually inside, beyond endless quantities of wires, circuit boards and things that we've all learned to call microchips?

One glance at the computer magazines will convince you that learning about the hardware itself is a joke. As a busy manager have you really got time to investigate:

820Kbytes floppy disk
central processor with 256Kbytes
160 cps printer
exchangeable cartridge back-up
multibus expansion cards
multi-user performance
six times faster than MP/M
VT100 compatibility

and on and on and on!

All these facilities are useless if you do not really understand what they mean, or if you have no initial idea what results they are meant to achieve. Nor will you ever find out, if you spend your time trying to unravel how the computer functions, instead of attempting to make sense of where it might fit into your job.

There is at least one essential concept that will safely guide you on your journey through the computer maze. This is that the computer is really a gigantic filing system, able to store away apparently endless quantities of information as numbers, words, characters and so on. It can also find them again quickly and, with the help of various other bits of equipment, do amazing things in the way of shuffling the information around for your benefit.

To get even more basic than a giant filing system, computer experts will tell you that the machine is really just a jumbo box of minute electrical switches that are continuously set and re-set in different patterns. These patterns can eventually be interpreted into words, numbers, pictures and even sounds.

What control the filing system or what set the switches in a particular pattern, are instructions from you the user. These instructions (*programs*) give the computer a course of action to follow. These non-physical instructions and data are contained in and carried by the computer's electronic circuitry. As they contrast to the hardware that you can touch, these instructions or programs are generically called *software*.

Instant history

Software began not in the laboratory but in the sooty factories of the Industrial Revolution. Back in the mid-1700s weavers had to remember which strands of coloured wool should be looped over each other to produce different patterns of cloth. To help jog their memory, a system of cards with holes in was devised. It was not long before a trouble-maker called Jacquard invented a power loom with a device for reading the cards automatically.

The cards went in, the cloth came out, and away went the jobs. Thousands of unemployed weavers rioted and nearly killed poor Jacquard who had thought that he was doing the world a good turn. In fact he unwittingly caused more trouble than he ever imagined.

Across the English Channel, Jacquard's brainwave triggered another one. Charles Babbage, whom everyone now calls "the father of the computer", took the idea of punched cards with their instructions about which piece of coloured wool to use next, and turned it into a set of instructions for a machine that would read and add up numbers. The punched cards not only told the machine what numbers to use, but the pattern in which they were to be handled, that is, how the numbers should be manipulated.

It all sounded exceedingly clever but Babbage never actually built his machine, although later other people did. Thus we arrive at another principle which you will find worth remembering:

> do not believe what you are told about a computer or the software, say, 'Show me!'

Because of the ease with which it is possible to baffle and confuse people about software and what it will do, the golden rule is never to take anything for granted. Always insist on seeing a live, practical example that you can understand and under conditions which will be discussed later.

Babbage's idea sparked another in a man called Hollerith. He adapted the punched card to handle census information and cut the time needed to produce the result from eight years to just over two. He sold his card operated machine to process information in a growing number of other ways: railways kept track of their freight statistics, tool manufacturers calculated their costs and managed their stocks, wholesalers kept track of their goods, sales, salesmen, customers' orders and so on. Hollerith and his company did well. Later it changed its name and you frequently see it around today, it is IBM.

A combination of World War Two, a college professor in Massachusetts plus IBM, led in 1939 to the world's first automatic computer, which blew everyone's minds with the sheer amount of noise that it made. Although it could only perform five to ten instructions a second it relied on an important principle. It used electrical switches to set and re-set the endless quantities of patterns needed to hold information, store it somewhere, manipulate it and, when necessary, churn it all out again.

Although computers have obviously developed considerably since the late 1930s they still, in essence, rely on patterns of electrical switches, though the latter have become almost invisibly small and without any moving parts.

That your computer is just a giant filing system or a set of switches, can be a misleading idea. Be careful that you do not react by becoming somewhat contemptuous of the whole business in the light of this revelation. The computer remains the most powerful tool at your disposal that has come on the management scene for centuries and that is certainly not to be dismissed lightly.

THE PC

The reason that you are reading this book is the emergence of the personal computer or as the jargon merchants love to say, the PC. The PC has made us all sit up and take notice because it brings the power of what used to be the exclusive preserve of the computer experts right onto our desks.

To the increasing dismay of a diminishing band of acolytes who like to keep the rest of us bemused and dependent on them, the PC only needs us, the users, to love and care for it. No longer are you, the manager, utterly and hopelessly dependent on a group of clever (but usually out of touch) specialists who have little idea about what your job involves or how to help you do it better. You can now directly turn the power of the computer to your own use and there are plenty of people around who can ensure that your questions are answered and that the machine becomes a practical management tool.

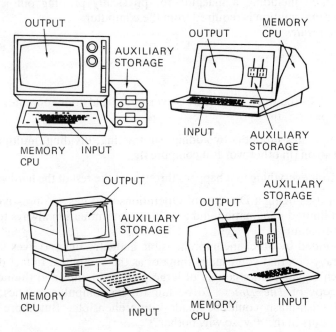

Figure 1.1 Some typical arrangements of hardware, excluding printers and other add-on devices

You will have seen and heard enough of computers to know that they come in a variety of shapes and sizes with a confusing array of add-on items for which you will doubtless pay extra.

The personal computer that most managers will use can be described simply. You do however, need at least a basic understanding of what the various bits do.

There are five main parts of your personal computer.

A microchip which is the 'brain' of the computer and directs how information shall be handled:

- the *central processor unit* (CPU)

A machine (auxilliary storage) to enable you to record and keep information which would otherwise be lost when the computer is switched off:

- one or more *disk drives*

An input machine for typing in instructions and information to the computer:

- The *keyboard*

A television style screen to help the computer communicate with you and for seeing its output:

- The *visual display unit* (VDU)

To these four components it is also desirable to add various other devices (*peripherals*) including a machine for physically printing out a copy of whatever information is required from the computer:

- The *printer*

The CPU

The CPU does the work and controls everything that your computer does. To be more precise, the CPU

manipulates numbers by adding, subtracting, dividing, multiplying and so on (in other words it computes);

controls everything that happens throughout the rest of the hardware.

Think of it as being a Director of Operations who has an obsessive eye for detail, a limited imagination and a ruthless determination always to stick to agreed procedures.

Surrounded by other incomprehensible gadgetry the CPU lives inside the main heavy box that you usually think of as the computer. In fact the CPU is not much bigger than a couple of large postage stamps and thinner than a folded copy of *The Times*. To be fair to the computer fanatics, all that internal mish-mash could be made comprehensible. But there are not enough hours in the day, so why bother?

Through your general reading you will have realised that computers have a *memory*. This is one or more microchips wired into your central processor. Memory capacity governs how many patterns the computer can handle at any one moment of time, which in turn mainly governs how much information it can deal with simultaneously.

What separates the personal computer that managers use these days from all kinds of pale imitations in the popular hardware stores is memory. It is more than enough, at this stage, to be able to relate memory size to some understandable baseline.

For some time the most popular home computers which you could buy in the average retail store cost around £100 and had a 64K memory. The K stands for *Kilobyte*, that is about 1000 bytes. You can think of a byte as roughly equivalent to a single character or a letter. A memory capacity of 64Kbytes may sound plenty, but in fact it is only equivalent to around 12,000 words, or roughly a quarter of a slim paperback.

By contrast, the average business personal computer will have anything from 128Kbytes to 256Kbytes of memory. That may seem impressive but it is only about the same as this whole book. Complicated computer instructions and the creation of large documents or reports can soon absorb this capacity.

There are all kinds of computer memory and once again you can quickly experience that sinking feeling if you start delving too deeply. Inside your computer there are two main types of memory chip.

Memory is the equivalent of an empty filing cabinet which you, the user, can fill with information. Thus when starting the computer you might see a message on the screen saying that there are 512K of memory currently free for use. This is:

- random access memory (RAM)

The main other type of memory already contains information for use by the central processor and you the user cannot change the contents. This is:

- read only memory (ROM)

An important difference between these two types of memory is that when you switch off the computer, anything stored in the random access memory vanishes into oblivion. Think of the filing cabinet contents as simply melting away into grey mist.

Incidentally, it is called 'random' because the memory is arranged like a staff notice board. You can read anything that is posted there, in any order. You do not have to read one notice after the other until you reach the one that you want. Similarly, when you play a record by starting the stylus on a track somewhere in the middle of the record this is random access.

Read only memory holds permanent instructions to the computer, such as how to start once you switch the machine on. The user cannot read any data into ROM. But like RAM, the computer has random access to the contents.

ROM is equivalent to a filing system frozen in a block of ice, or the patterns talked about earlier, captured for ever on film. There is no way that you can directly influence the ROM, short of tearing out the micro chip or blowing up the computer.

To make things suitably confusing though, computer experts will smile knowingly at this admittedly simple description and immediately tell you about different versions of ROM and RAM that turn into one another or worse. But as a manager you can safely smile back and say you are 'rather busy right now'.

ROM and RAM are important to you only because the more memory you have at your disposal, the more instructions can be handled within your computer. Well-produced software, for instance, uses the minimum amount of computer memory possible and making the software 'talk' to you in a friendly way is a voracious user of memory.

Computer wizards say that no matter how much memory you own it is never enough. What they forget is that most managers seldom personally have time to do anything elaborate with the computer. If there is a reasonable amount of memory available for the software to work properly the rest tends to be a luxury.

If you have between 128Kbytes and 256Kbytes of memory in the RAM part of your computer, which is the capacity of a business personal computer, you will usually have enough for most jobs. Some complex, multi-purpose packages like *Symphony*, or *Open Access* and certain databases though, may be more greedy for memory.

Much the same reasoning applies to another esoteric aspect of personal computers, namely how much of their internal memory is available to be used by your selected software. Computers are graded as 8, 16 and 32 bit machines, which in practical terms says something about what happens once your software reaches the hardware. The higher the bit rating, the more memory the CPU can address and hence use for your software.

In theory, the higher the bit rating the faster data can be shuffled around, but in practice there may be other factors that make such a definite relationship between bits and speed not always consistent.

Summarising the advantages of both 8 and 16 bit machines leads to these conclusions.

8 bit
Vast choice of hardware
Enormous selection of available software
Uses the most commonly known operating systems (see Chapter Two)
Masses of relevant and available supporting literature

16 bit
Speed at which data is handled internally can potentially be twice as fast
Amount of memory usable for your software can be several times larger
Better multi-user facilities
Calculation speeds up to 4000 times faster for some applications
Greater overall speed and flexibility

There is little point in becoming too involved in the debate over whether to have an 8 or 16 bit machine as you may never even notice the difference. Some software that runs on 16 bit machines in fact works even slower than on a comparable 8 bit machine because it was originally written for the latter. Even though the vast majority of installed micro computers are 8 bit machines, new purchases of personal computers for businesses and other organizations are nevertheless tending to be 16 bit machines.

Disk drives

One or more disk drives are built into the heavy box which one thinks of as the computer and it usually has slots at the front, or occasionally at the side.

The disks which you load into the drives are really the computer's external memory, as opposed to the internal ones discussed above.This is why they are sometimes called *auxilliary storage* in the computer jargon. You insert the disks much like loading a cassette tape recorder and usually, as far as you are concerned, the computer takes over at this stage.

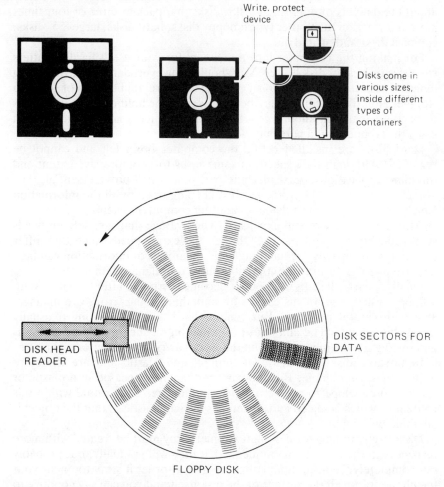

Figure 1.2 Disk sectors and different sized disks

Disks have information recorded on their surface which is divided up into tracks like grooves on a record. The tracks are separated into sectors. The read head of the disk drive can move to a particular sector on a track and find or add information.

Information can be relocated, erased and the disk re-used. As with audio records or video tapes, computer disks can come prerecorded, not with music or films, but with instructions for your computer's brain, the central processor. Other disks arrive entirely blank and cannot be used until you make them ready for the computer.

You can also prevent material which is recorded on them from being erased. This is done in various ways, such as covering or uncovering a notch at the edge of the disk, or by sliding a small tag up or down in a groove.

So disks are the way that information can be retained once the computer is switched off and its internal filing system suffers amnesia. Disks are a whole world of their own. Like hi-fi, enthusiasts will bend your ear interminably about the delights of dual-sided disks, disks that pack in three or four times more information than other types, floppy disks, hard disks, large 8.5″ disks, compact disks and on and on.

For making the computer into a real tool for your use it hardly matters what size or kind of disk is used. You should, however, definitely avoid using tapes or cassettes as a main form of using software applications or for data storage. Non-disk facilities may be appropriate for holding large quantities of back-up material, though few managers will need such facilities when using the computer as a personal tool.

Hard disks are installed within the computer box itself and cannot be removed. Although they speed up some tasks to an impressive extent and for some applications, particularly in personnel, may prove essential, they also cause considerable problems. Just keeping track of all the information which accumulates almost demands another computer system!

Also, hard disks are still expensive. The average manager seldom needs such a facility for personal use, though the extra speed which they offer together with capacity for handling large quantities of information can be a decisive factor in turning the computer into a useful management tool.

Finally, nearly all disks wear out or become corrupted after long use. With a floppy disk the problems caused by something going wrong are manageable with careful planning. But when a hard disk goes wrong it usually means big trouble. The amount of information on such a disk is enormous and sorting out the mess once something goes awry is a computer nightmare.

Removable disks are made of thin, coated plastic and are therefore floppy, hence the name. But they are permanently encased in a plastic or cardboard envelope to protect them from damage. They rotate within this container, which is sealed and sometimes of rigid plastic so that the object is anything but 'floppy'.

Disks are your new form of filing cabinet. They must be treated with more respect than the old steel monuments that they will gradually, but probably not completely, replace. Spill coffee on a disk, or let it stray too near your telephone, or touch the surface of the disk itself and you can say goodbye to your precious data. Worse, if one of your expensive preprogrammed disks is damaged in this way it could prove expensive and inconvenient.

So the first thing to learn in taking charge of your computer is the absolute necessity of making a copy of your disks at regular intervals. You should make at least two (some people say three) copies of each of your master software disks. One set is for everyday use and the other one or two are for back-ups when the daily copy springs a leak or you do something stupid like erase all the information on it! Never use the originals of your preprogrammed disks; they should be copied and then stored in an absolutely safe place.

Some experts argue that it is essential to store software master disks in a fire-proof safe and this may be a sensible precaution. On the other hand, it is worth checking on the cost of insurance as this may well be cheaper than buying an expensive and cumbersome hunk of heat-resistant metal. For your data disks though, insurance may be no substitute for the disaster that complete loss can cause.

Dire warnings are rightly issued by the experts that you must know the rules of disk care. Probably in a few years disks or whatever comes along to replace them, will be made totally damage proof, but at present they remain vulnerable to:

> dust, smoke particles, liquids, touching the recording surface,bending, heavy weights, magnets, any source of magnetism, uneven temperatures and direct heat sources such as radiators, electric fires, sunlight and being left in the computer when you switch it on or off.

Thus you will soon become fanatical about making copies (*back-ups*) of your disks, which only takes half a minute or so. You can delegate this, but it is best kept under your own tight control. After all, disks are as easily erased as copied.

An irritating technicality that you will need to master is how to prepare disks for use on your computer. The blank ones need to be given the equivalent of filing cabinet labels so that the computer can find its way around, like using a road map.

This process of preparation (*formatting*) is simple and quick but with many disks can become a bore. You can safely delegate this job once you are sure that the person can press the right buttons and will not mistakenly try to process one of your other disks which you have laboriously filled with important information. If you reformat a disk it rubs out everything!

Preprogrammed disks may need the information on them rearranged in some way and this is where you can run into a real road block. To reorganize (*install*) the disks so that they are suitable for your particular computer may mean that you have to use certain computer instructions that may seem confusing at first.

In the early stages, avoid this by insisting on the supplier doing the setting up for you, or finding someone else in your organization who will help. The actual instructions are not hard to learn and eventually you will need to master them. (See Chapter 6 on training).

Because the disks themselves spin fast, like a record, the disk drive uses a motor which is capable of going the way of all machines just when you need it. The drive can be noisy, though you are more likely to find that the row which you quickly learn to love or hate, in fact stems from the computer's cooling fan.

You can manage perfectly well with a computer that only has one disk drive, though you will be constantly shuffling disks around. A business personal computer should have two drives. Sometimes one or both of these are housed in a separate box beside the computer. In theory there can be a dozen or more other disk drives all connected up to your computer but your likely need for such facilities is either far off in the distant future or non-existent.

Two terms which keep cropping up are *program disks* and *data disks*. The former are usually the ones which hold the software package, that is, the program(s). Data disks are the ones containing your own information. These must be constantly backed-up, or copied, to ensure that there is never any chance of losing laboriously-created files of valuable data.

The keyboard

Nowadays there are advertisements showing a manager chatting into a microphone to his computer. But the main way you will be talking to yours will be via the keyboard. Speech-responsive computers with a human-size vocabulary and at an economic price are far off. Much the same applies to computers that talk back at you with human-style speech. In fact, the best thing about a keyboard is that it is silent!

For many years to come the keyboard will be the main way that managers will interact with the computer. The keyboard itself usually looks similar to that of an electric typewriter but while the latter usually has around 50 keys, the computer has around 100.

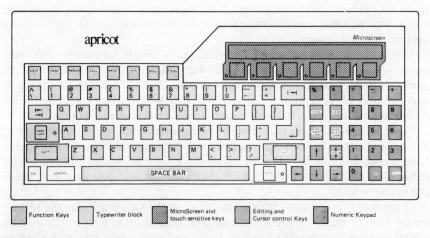

Figure 1.3 Keyboard from Apricot Personal Computer

The extra keys all perform a variety of different jobs, depending on which combinations are pressed. This is no place to explain what they do since there is simply no real substitute for getting your hands on them!

A recent development you will also be hearing about is a *mouse*, the gadget that allows you to interact with the computer by a small device that you can roll around on your desk. The movement of the mouse is shown on the screen, usually with an arrow and thus you can give instructions by 'pointing' to various words or symbols shown there.

Mice are fun but probably irrelevant. They are certainly useful to give you the initial feeling that the computer is easy to handle. But after a short while they can become a great irritant since you will find it inconvenient to keep taking your hands away from the keyboard.

The visual display unit (VDU)

The final part of the computer is the monitor, the television-like screen which allows you to see what is going on when you begin communicating with the machine.

The VDU is the equivalent of using a sheet of paper. Unlike paper though, you can correct what you've written, no matter where the errors are on the screen and no matter how widespread the mistakes might be.

Many VDUs have a special coating to stop light reflecting off the surface and thus making it easier to read. The characters are also made to appear more solid.

Just as there is a confusing choice of computers, with an army of experts and salesmen ready to blind you with science, so there is with VDUs. You can have screens with a slow fade and virtually no flicker, or screens with a definite flicker but brilliant colour. You can have screens of all shapes and sizes, in black and white, or a relaxing green, brown or some other delicate shade. Although it is desirable to have a choice about such an important piece of equipment in practice, you have to accept what comes with the machine or pay extra to change it.

The screen is important because you will be looking at it for many more hours than you ever expected when you decided to become computer literate. Without becoming too immersed in the arcane world of VDUs you may need to investigate aspects such as the amount of glare, flicker, adjustment in the angle of the screen, the extent to which what is on the screen is crisp and clear (*resolution*) and whether or not you need full colour.

The printer

If VDUs and computers themselves are a minefield for the unwary then printers are the boobytraps. A printer allows you to produce a hard copy of the work you have done on the computer. It can usually print out whatever is on the screen in varying degrees of quality, depending on the type of printer.

Even the professionals go into a state of gloom over printers because there are so many different ones available. Before your computer can talk to one it has to be told some basic technical facts about the specific machine which you intend to use. Have as little as possible to do with setting it up ready for first time use. Let your dealer or supplier handle this task.

What *you* need to know is how fast the printer will type, how clearly the letters or characters emerge on paper, and what method is used to print.

Numerous complicated ways are used by the multiplicity of printers on the market to produce the actual characters on the page and the machines vary greatly in their speed. Some work by tapping out anything up to 132 tiny dots to print characters, others spray thin jets of ink onto the page.

More familiar is the daisy wheel printer invented in the 1970s which produces the same quality print as a normal electric typewriter. The wheel rotates rapidly and contains spokes on which there is usually one, or sometimes two, characters which a hammer strikes to produce the mark on the page.

As a working manager, a critical facility that you need from your printer is speed and the ability to do any specialist jobs you require, such as producing graphics. At one time the choice was between a printer which worked slowly but produced high quality print and one which worked fast but with low quality results. Increasingly there are printers which offer the alternative of high speed for producing drafts or much slower output for what is called *near letter quality* (NLQ) printing. The standard of NLQ is nowadays increasingly high and much management work can probably be done on a machine which sacrifices top quality printing in favour of speed.

A printer may seem phenomenally fast when being demonstrated but you may soon find that it is agonisingly slow once you become used to it and are waiting for large documents to be run off or for complicated tables to be printed.

Finally, what do you not need? Almost certainly at this stage and for the next year or so, you can live without a whole set of additional gadgets to add onto your computer. You are going to have enough pressure on you to use the basic computer properly to improve your own work methods without increasing it by acquiring another set of expensive add-ons that will take time to master.

For instance, you can probably do without *modems*, the devices which will link your computer with others around the country, and indeed the world. When you're ready for this extra your own instinct will certainly tell you loud and clear. Right now such a device is a misplaced luxury.

The revolution in working methods that the personal computer has begun derives from the fact that it is indeed personal. It is your machine and it is meant to work for you, not a score of other people.

Even so, you will soon hear about multi-user systems that offer the same apparent facilities as a personal computer but with access by a whole lot of other people. It makes sense to check that any computer you are involved in buying has potentially such a facility for an additional add-on price later. But right now it is yet another technical triumph to avoid.

There is usually the opportunity to insert extra memory chips and other internal devices into the computer itself to enhance its capabilities. Again, steer clear of this area until you are much more confident that you can really make sense of the pros and cons.

SUMMARY

If you do not understand, it is they, not you who have the problem.

Be ruthless about asking for explanations and for help.

Remember, a computer is really a large filing system or more pro-saically, a vast array of minute switches.

Hardware are the things you can touch: the box, screen, keyboard, wires and those ubiquitous microchips.

Software consists of instructions to your computer as programs.

Do not believe what you are told about a computer or the software, say, 'Show me!'

The five main parts of your computer are: the central processing unit (CPU), one or more disk drives, the keyboard, the visual display unit (VDU) and the printer.

What distinguishes a business personal computer from the rest is mainly its size of internal memory.

You need around 256K of random access memory (RAM).

You must have a disk, not a cassette tape system, for storing and loading information into your computer.

Disks come blank or can be bought with programs on them.

Disks containing your information are called data disks; those with computer instruction software are termed program disks.

Choose your visual display unit (VDU) with care, as you will be looking at it for more hours than you expect.

Select a printer with the maximum speed that you can afford.

2 Software Basics

Takayoshi Shiina is a talkative, smartly dressed man who at the age of 27 started the Sord Computer Corporation with around £2000 and one employee. His mother still does some bookkeeping for the firm which in a recent nationwide survey now tops the national growth league out of 600,000 other booming Japanese businesses.

Sord has become the second largest maker of small computers in Japan. The average age of its employees is 26 and the company turnover in 1983 was over £80 million. The name Sord stems from SO for software and RD for hardware, explains Shiina. 'We make the software first, then build a machine to perform up to its requirements. That's exactly the opposite of what everyone else does.'

Shiina's insight is an important one for all practising managers who want to turn the computer into a personal tool of real power. Your fundamental concern needs to be focused unwaveringly on what instructions or programs will be used on your machine.

Ideally, like Shiina, you should begin with no computer at all and if you are currently in that situation be glad. You have a real chance of making the computer become the helpmate that the advertisements and your imagination keep promising.

'Software? It's multiplying like wire hangers in a dark closet' is the graphic way that Pennsylvania-based Alfred Glossbrenner, President of Fire Crystal Communications and a prolific writer, describes the present torrent of computer instructions for sale. When Caxton invented the printing press people must have reacted in much the same way.

The sheer quantity of computer software now becoming available is staggering. Even the giant IBM has long since apparently abandoned recording what products are available for its personal computers.

Within the next few years a deluge of entirely new software is expected to gush from the Orient as the Japanese once again target a US and European industry and attempt to drive it into second place. If the task of selecting the right software has always been a maze then it is rapidly becoming a labyrinth.

In many ways, *Understanding Management Software* really starts here. From the previous chapter you should have obtained enough of the basic hardware concepts to make sense of the software territory through which we are about to travel.

THREE TYPES

Your computer uses three types of instructions or software. These usually arrive not as written lines on paper but as coded messages prerecorded onto a floppy disk. The software consists of the following types.

Instructions to make your equipment operate and organize its memory, disk drives, keyboard and so on:
  • operating system software

Instructions that use a collection of words and rules to allow you to talk directly to the computer about practically anything you choose, in a language that you can both understand:
  • programming languages

Instructions that do specific, carefully defined and useful jobs for you as a manager, such as word processing, personal finance, handling your particular information in an organized database and so on:
  • applications software

These are three alternative names for what is essentially the same thing, namely instructions for your computer. Each may be written in a different computer language, most of which would be incomprehensible to the average person.

Although you will need to become involved with the operating system, as a manager you are unlikely to have much time to learn about and use programming languages. Your main attention will need to be devoted to applications software. This should be your first consideration.

Updating

A feature that all three types of software share is that they will usually be regularly revised and updated. Improvements are always being made and incorporated into a new edition. Thus if a disk label states that the program is version 1. 1, it probably means that some minor changes have been made to the original product. Version 2. 0 would usually mean that your software had been radically altered since the first edition was produced.

Depending on how much the software cost and the supplier's policy, you may be entitled to free upgradings of your purchase as improved versions are issued. More likely though, you will be required to pay a fee and return your old disk to obtain an upgrade.

The operating system

You have just flown in from New York. At the airport you are met by a rich friend in a chauffeur-driven car who is staying with you this weekend. Unfortunately neither he nor the driver has been to your home before. And the chauffeur only speaks a remote Bavarian dialect!

Luckily your friend can talk to the driver and give Bavarian directions on how to reach your home. In this admittedly unlikely situation you are the equivalent of someone using a computer. Your friend, who translates your directions into Bavarian, is performing like a computer program. The chauffeur is the operating system, taking instructions and then making the car perform so that eventually you do in fact arrive home. The car, of course, is equivalent to the computer.

The idea of an operating system at first seems confusing, though in fact it is a familiar concept. When you put a slice of bread into the toaster and expect it to pop up again shortly, you are using the gadget's purely mechanical operating system. This system is built into the toaster so that you do not even think about it. That is also how it should be with computers.

But computers seldom aspire to being toasters. Before they will work it is usually necessary to feed in some purely technical information (the operating system) about how to respond to all the other instructions that are going to follow.

Just what do these operating systems do? Amongst other things they control:

the keyboard, so that the machine knows when something has been typed

the display of characters on the screen

how the disk space is to be divided up, so that information can be stored, found again, and tidied up as with any other filing system

the other devices attached to the computer

the loading and running of programs

housekeeping jobs, such as copying disks, printing, deleting information and so on

If you have the impression that the operating system is important, you would be absolutely right. Without it, the computer would be impotent, which is why the operating system is regarded as the foundation for computer software.

For day-to-day purposes though, you will be using the operating system merely as a way of making your computer act like a computer should, namely able to use your application programs. In other words the operating system sits in between the computer and your software package.

The system comes on one or two disks, sometimes more. All you do is put the main one into the disk drive and the operating instructions are then automatically transferred into the computer's memory. After that it waits for more instructions from, for example, your word processing package or whatever.

Another way of thinking about the operating system is as an intermediary between your software package and your computer and any other equipment which you may use.

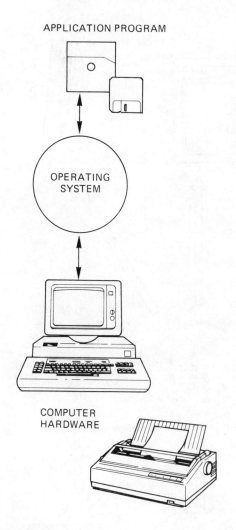

Figure 2.1 The operating system sits between the computer and the software package, controlling both

When you switch on the computer and insert a formatted disk with the operating system on it the latter goes straight to work, looking around for components like the keyboard or the screen and for software like your applications program which it ought to begin controlling.

This procedure of getting the computer running and ready to receive more instructions is given another piece of computer talk: to *boot* the system, or to *boot up*. You certainly do not need this ungainly term but as everyone who uses computers seems to love talking about booting up, you may as well be familiar with what it means!

Once the operating system is in charge, the computer is ready to begin using your software package. The next step would normally be to use the

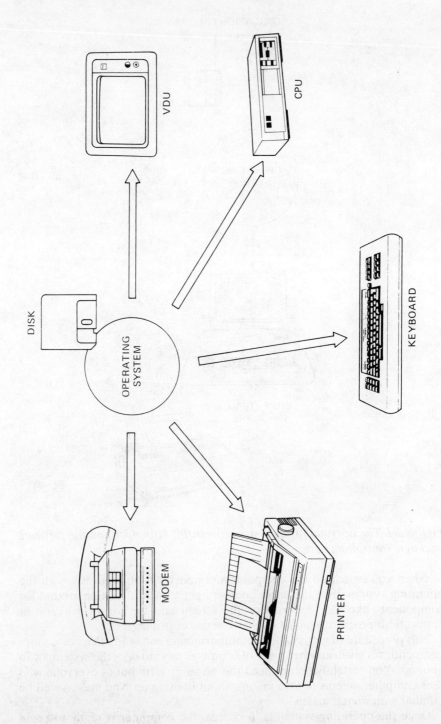

Figure 2.2 The operating system can control a whole range of equipment

keyboard to call up your particular software application program. Since this means a further delay, it is common practice to adapt the operating system slightly so that when the disk is originally inserted the whole process happens automatically. First the operating system takes over, then straight away it calls up your software package for immediate use.

Before about 1976 computers would only take notice of operating systems whose instructions were written just for their particular make. So each machine used to be sold with its own unique operating software to make it perform.

Lack of a common set of working instructions meant that other kinds of software designed to do useful jobs for managers were changed to suit each new make of computer. This time-consuming and costly requirement forced an urgent search for a system that could be used on many different computers.

The first commercially viable operating software designed to control a variety of computers became available in the late 1970s. From then on, operating software burgeoned. When IBM announced that it was adopting one particular type in 1982 even its rivals breathed a sigh of relief. At last there would be some common standards in an otherwise increasingly fragmented and indeed disorganized market.

There is still no general agreement on what precisely should be contained in the operating software. But as a manager you are not going to have to worry too much about this whole area, although the computer wizards might try to convince you otherwise!

The operating system provides the ground rules for your computer and makes the other types of more specialised software usable on a whole host of different computers from all over the world.

Like toasters or washing machines some computers, particularly those at the cheaper end of the market, have their operating system built into them as a preprogrammed microchip. The personal computer used by businesses and other organizations however, will normally require the operating software to be inserted by way of a floppy disk.

The combination of the operating software sent into the computer via a disk plus the wired-in computer chips constitutes the full meaning of the term *operating system*. You will not need to know much about the operating system, which will mainly be invisible to the user.

The amount that you will need to know depends on two factors. First, what kinds of tasks you want to undertake and secondly, how much thought has gone into making life easy for you by the maker of your particular computer.

For example, the Apricot personal computer provides its users with a specially designed, easy to follow set of linked steps on how to perform basic tasks. These include preparing a disk for use (formatting) copying the contents of one disk onto another, listing a table of contents from a disk, or transferring what is on the screen to the printer. There are no codes to learn, merely a series of choices presented in straightforward English. Other computers though, may require you to learn at least some of the coded instructions to conduct these routine chores.

You certainly have not the time to become involved in the complexities of operating systems unless you are planning to write your own computer programs. Doing that is a time-annihilating activity. Begin it and you will probably have ceased being an effective manager. What should concern you more is the answer to one crucial question:

> What application programs are available now for use with this operating system?

Should you become embroiled in a baffling technical discussion about the merits or otherwise of a particular operating system, respond with a simple:

> Look, let's talk instead about what application programs are currently available under this system.

Operating systems are thus merely a means to an end. They start your application programs running. It is probably useful to know that currently the most popular operating system is the one used by IBM called PC-DOS. Translated, this is merely short for Personal Computer Disk Operating System.

This is also available for many other computers under a slightly different brand name, MS-DOS. The MS incidentally, stands for Microsoft, the name of the company that makes the software. Similarly, another well known product is called CP/M, which stands for Control Program for Microcomputers.

Given its importance, it is hardly surprising that many computers are produced with the ability to use one or more types of operating software.

Even though your computer has the right central processing microchip, the right operating system and the right software that a particular application needs, there is still no guarantee that it will work on your machine. For example, some software requires you to have disk drives able to use both sides of the disks. Others will only run with single-sided disk drives.

Similarly your printer may not be able to perform all the wonderful graphics that the software can produce on the screen. Or the software may demand that you have an extra wide screen or special keys on the keyboard.

If you only have the MS-DOS operating system but the application uses CP/M 86 then you will not be able to run the program. Somewhere amongst all that mound of product literature which you have acquired about various software packages, there should be a small paragraph stating what are the exact system requirements. If such essential information on the operating system is missing, together with the other systems requirements, you may just have successfully avoided making a costly mistake. After all if the software company fails to tell you such vital sales information what else will they conveniently forget?

Much the same applies to the salesperson with whom you may deal. You should be told what are the precise system requirements of a piece of software. If you do not obtain straight answers that you can fully understand then perhaps you should try a different dealer.

When you are considering buying software you should always ask:

- What operating system does it require?

You follow this up by a second key question:

- What are the precise system requirements and will it work on my (name and model) computer?

Finally you nail it down once and for all by saying:

- Show me!

Installation

When you buy a software package it would make sense if you could just create a back-up copy and immediately start using it. But the computer world is seldom that simple.

Quite often a package must first be *installed* or *configured*. This usually means that before using it you must perform a number of quite complicated routines. These ensure that it will work properly with your printer, or they may enable the program to use features like highlighting text or underlining on the VDU.

Other installation procedures may be part of the copy protection system used to prevent software piracy. These packages may require the user to perform a whole routine of disk swopping and transferring of files before the programs will work at all.

If you pay full list price for a software package insist that it is fully installed by the dealer. Do not be fobbed off with promises that the procedure is simple and shown step by step on the screen.

The fact is that even the best software packages available occasionally arrive with a fault. There is nothing more disappointing than to unwrap your brand new package and get well into the manual, only to find that the actual disks are faulty. Usually the problem is a minor one, such as the new disks being wrongly labelled. But occasionally there may also be a faulty product.

Thus always ask the dealer:

> Will you fully install the program on my own equipment so that
> all the features of the product work properly?

Commands

'Help! I bought a computer and two software packages from you last week and I'm stuck. How do I format a disk?' Computer dealers report that soon after they have sold a new machine to someone the commonest requests for help, usually made over the telephone, are about how to perform certain elementary routines that are needed for everyday purposes.

Thus the differences between one operating system and another are of much less importance to you, the average manager, than being able to use whichever disk operating system you eventually acquire on your particular machine and with your chosen software.

Initially you will only need to learn enough to run your application programs. But you will quickly become more ambitious. After that the quality of the instructions on how to use the system will matter a great deal.

Most of the manuals on how to use the operating system which are supplied by computer manufacturers are as about as friendly to the user as a technician's top secret guide to nuclear fusion.

Luckily there are a growing number of books being published that carefully take the user through a graded series of steps to gain familiarity both with their particular machine and also a specific operating system.

Within the next three or four years though, even these publications may become obsolete as, through competitive pressures, the computer industry is forced to produce far more effective forms of user guidance.

For the moment though, you will almost certainly have to learn at least half a dozen simple commands to get the computer to perform basic routine tasks. These commands will rapidly become second nature to you.

Commands are usually codes such as ˆ P or sometimes in a more English style such as Copy. The ˆ sign means that the user presses a special control key while simultaneously pressing one or more other letters or symbols.

In most of the software which you will be using the commmand instructions appear consistently in a special place on the screen, such as along the top or highlighted along the bottom. There may also be a list of user instructions in what is called a *display area*. The remaining space which is left, usually in the middle, is called the *work area*.

There are six main tasks you will need to perform regularly, using the operating system.

1. Prepare (format) a blank disk for use with your software applications. You may also want to add part of the operating instructions to this disk so that it is readily available each time you start up the computer and insert this particular disk.

    To format you merely insert a blank disk into a drive and, using the operating system, give the formatting instruction. On some computers, like the Apricot for instance, this process has been reduced to a near foolproof series of steps. It is certainly necessary to minimise the chance of making a mistake since if you format a disk wrongly, at best it may not be usable with certain programs and at worst you could erase all the information on the other disk which may contain the operating system.

2. Change from using one disk drive to another. Naturally this only applies where you have more than one drive.

    The computer can normally only use one disk drive at a time, so usually it must be told which one you want it to work with. Since both drives can contain information, you will need to become familiar with swopping between using one drive as your working drive and the other temporarily playing a passive role.

    Your working drive has yet another jargon term attached to it, the *default* drive. Like booting the system, default is one more pretentious piece of computerese that you will nevertheless need to conquer. It causes more than its fair share of confusion.

When you drive a car the accelerator pedal needs to be depressed before the car will go forward. Thus the default position is up and nothing happens until, through moving it downwards, you effectively give instructions to the contrary.

Likewise a computer. When it uses the default drive it is merely saying, 'Until I have instructions to the contrary, I am going to assume this is the drive you want me to use'. This is therefore the default drive until you countermand the order.

Another example of using the word 'default' is when you are asked one or more questions while using a software package. If you simply ignore these questions and carry on then the package may use *default answers*, that is those which it assumes on your behalf.

Similarly, if you have a printer there may be a choice between printing, say 80 or 120 characters per line. However the default value may be 80, which it will use unless you give different instructions.

3. Copy a file to another part of the disk or to an entirely different one; or make another copy of a whole disk.

   These are simple commands to learn which you will be using often, since a basic principle of computing is always to make several copies of everything. A back-up is essential in case anything happens to the original.

   As with formatting you can easily make a disastrous mistake and copy material to the wrong place. Again, at best this may merely create confusion for yourself while at worst it can overwrite existing material and erase it!

4. Call for a directory. This lists out the contents of a disk. You can usually have just a summary or a detailed version which also states how much space is used for each file.

   When you generate files you will quickly reach the same situation as with a conventional filing cabinet: there comes a time when you want to find a particular file, right now.

   With computers you cannot just open a drawer and peer inside to survey physically the files stored there. Instead you must either keep a complete list on paper or ask to view such a list on the screen by asking to see the directory. You can then decide which files to weed out, copy or retitle (*rename*) or amalgamate with others to form a consolidated version.

   There is often little difference between a computer-based list of files and those of a real filing cabinet. The computer merely offers greater flexibility and speed in how you handle the contents.

5. List out the contents of file. This allows you to check quickly what exactly is held in the file. What appears on the screen may not be as neatly presented as it would be with a word processing program, but this command is merely for rapidly reviewing file contents.

6. Check how much free space there is on a disk. This is another facility that you will use regularly, particularly if you are moving files around frequently. When using an application program it is sensible to check that there is enough free storage space left on the disk holding your data. Otherwise in the middle of an important job you might inconveniently run out of space.

    Disk operating systems vary in how much information they provide when conducting a check. Some merely summarise the space available in bytes or the equivalent of roughly how many characters can still be stored. Others are more helpful and show the space left as a percentage of the whole disk.

Programming languages

Just as you do not need to learn the remote Bavarian dialect of your friend's chauffeur mentioned above, so you will certainly not have to learn a programming language. Instead you will be relying on software packages that other people have written in languages whose names you might recognise but whose rules and vocabulary are irrelevant.

You will therefore occasionally come across program language names such as BASIC, FORTRAN, COBOL and so on. Amongst the computer fraternity there are intense debates about the merits or otherwise of one particular language compared to another. One is easier to use, another is faster and takes up less computer memory, still another allows you to do more complicated routines. Similarly, some are more suited for scientific as opposed to business purposes.

The native tongue, as it were, of your central processing unit is called *machine language*. It consists of endless quantities of 0s and 1s and is called a code with some justification since it is virtually incomprehensible to everyone but programmers or engineers.

Various ways have been developed to help a wider audience write programs by translating machine code into easier to use English-like computer languages. The closer these languages come to pure English, the more they move from the original machine code and hence the slower they will tend to be when the actual program starts to work. Languages like BASIC, FORTRAN, COBOL and PASCAL are well removed from the original machine code but if you had the time you would probably be able to master them.

Languages that are just one step away from the original machine codes are called *assemblers*. Programs which are written in them work quickly. If speed is what really matters, then when you come to buy your application programs it might be worth enquiring if they are written in *assembly language*. However, the language in which the application program is written will generally make little practical difference to a busy manager.

You may decide to take a closer interest in the language used for your application package because:

● it might help assess two competing programs for speed and general performance

- one day you might wish to alter the application program, to suit your particular special needs

- it might reveal that you will need more than just the program itself to run your package

By concentrating on well known and tried packages though, you can avoid becoming involved in the complexities of which language works fastest and so on.

Applications software

Acquire a software catalogue from a large supplier and you will find it neatly divided into various kinds of software, for example:

> word processors and word processing aids
> financial modellers and spreadsheets
> database management systems
> personal productivity aids
> management decision tools
> training software
> accounting software
> communications software
> sorting programs
> programming languages and development aids
> operating systems
> code generators, utilities and menu systems

Each section of the catalogue will then describe the various products available, what each can do and its system requirements.

Like any other product you have to take the catalogue cameos with a pinch of salt, treating them merely as guidance about the kind of items that are available within your price range.

Of the list above the first seven types are what can be called application software. These are software packages which you apply to your particular set of problems. They are the ones in which you are mainly interested since they offer practical ways of making the computer useful.

After studying the software catalogue in more detail you may conclude that, for doing any job on the computer, you are spoilt for choice. Some of the differences though are a crucial indication of how useful the packages will be.

Menus and commands

To control any software application you will have to learn its unique set of instructions. These take two forms. The first is a set of multiple choice questions. The screen shows a set of choices in a *menu*, and you instruct the program by selecting one.

FRIDAY! MENUS

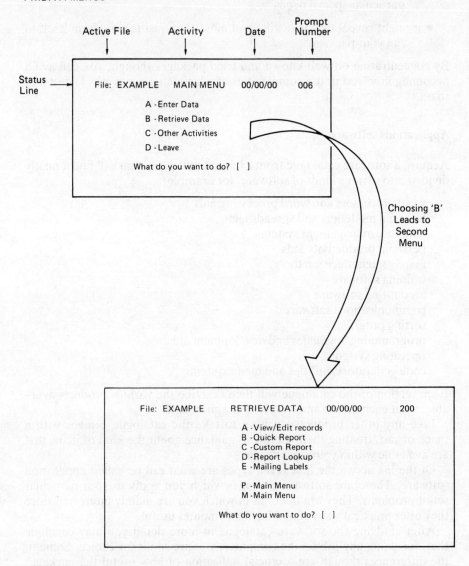

Figure 2.3 Typical menus. (Friday! is a registered trademark of Ashton-Tate)

The second way of controlling the program is by using a set of codes called *commands*. Again these commands are usually unique to that particular software application.

A package which is only menu-driven is usually easier to learn. But once you are familiar with it and know what commands to use, the repetitive menu can become a source of frustration. The better packages allow the user to chose either a menu or a command approach.

Files, records and fields

Want to retain your budget and sanity in a reasonably healthy state? Then you must be willing to acquire a working understanding of at least these three software terms. Without them you will be heading into a bewildering blizzard from which you, or at least your confidence, may never return.

There is much about computers that you will be able to avoid learning, but mastering the meaning of files, fields and records is virtually inescapable.

Your local telephone directory is the best way of explaining these terms. The directory itself is simply a large *file* of information with a reference title like London Area A – D, or Merton Area 1984, or Yellow Pages London South West. Packed tightly on each page are individual *records* of subscribers. Each record is in turn broken down into the person or company name, their address and finally a telephone number. The name, address and telephone number are three separate *fields*.

Similarly, when you write a cheque you are completing one field when you state the amount, another when you add the date and a third when you put the name of the payee. When you write the complete cheque you have created a record and a whole pile of these constitute a file.

The concept of a file usually appears in every computer program and most programs consist of dozens of separate files. Files can be big and cumbersome, like a complete list of all a firm's customers, or just one item, as when you decide to save your curriculum vitae on disk. When you need to make a job application, you call up the relevant file and there is your personal history ready to be amended.

Though the use of a file is common throughout the computer world, the other smaller sub-divisions of field and record may only arise in programs that handle specific jobs like mailing lists or sorting detailed records of sales or employees. (See Figure 2.4)

Information placed into any particular field and hence record will of course vary. Both fields and records are like a blank form that has to be completed, the layout itself stays constant while the contents vary.

When buying software you will need to investigate how many files, records and fields the package can handle. For instance, it could prove embarassing if you need to keep at least 50 records per file only to discover that the package is restricted to just half that number. A similar restriction may exist regarding the number of separate files that can be handled by the package without resorting to special procedures to avoid a bottleneck.

Amongst software packages there are often surprising variations in both the number of fields allowed (usually from about 10 to around 250) and the field size (ranging perhaps from around 25 characters to possibly up to 250).

The combination of numbers of fields and characters allowed in each field may not seem to matter at this stage but once you start using the package it can prove a fatal flaw to have chosen software without investigating this aspect.

What do you do, for instance, when the package that you have just bought only permits say 25 characters per field and you want to store a name like Caribbean International Investments Limited? You could compromise and

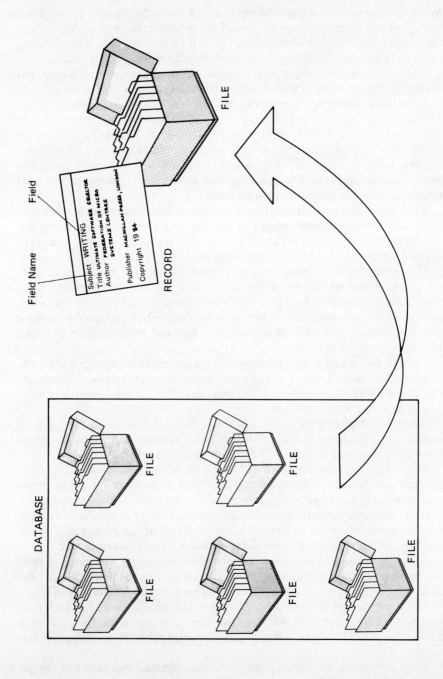

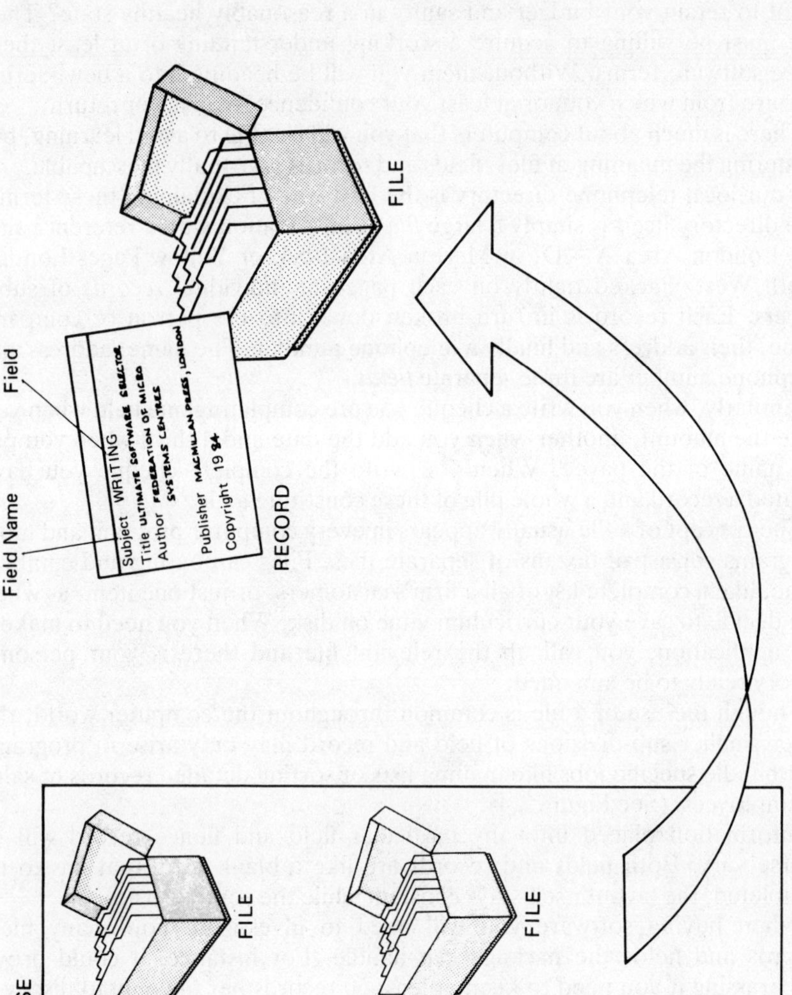
FILE
Field Name
Field
Subject WRITING
Title ULTIMATE SOFTWARE SELECTOR
Author FEDERATION OF MICRO SYSTEMS CENTRES
Publisher MACMILLAN PRESS, LONDON
Copyright 1984
RECORD
DATABASE
FILE
FILE
FILE
FILE
FILE

Figure 2.4 Files, records and fields

write Caribbean Internat. Inv. Ltd. But if this is used for a mailing shot it would hardly look elegant on the personalised letter to the managing director.

You also need to check how many fields there can be in any one record and above all, how many records can be added to a file. Some packages boast an ability to handle virtually an unlimited number of records. Others may have tight restrictions on the number of either files or records that can be handled as the price paid for making the package easy to handle. In practice most packages are limited by disk capacity, not by computer memory.

Help!

Increasingly applications packages are aimed at novices. Thus there are facilities for asking for on-line advice during the use of the package. By pressing the HELP key it is possible to call up advice when you become stuck.

On-line advice tends to be of two kinds. The first is fairly general, covering a number of points in a blunderbuss technique. For example, faced with an incomprehensible set of choices labelled just:

C D F G I M N R S X Z CR / LF TAB ESC ?

you may want to know what each letter will do if pressed. Using a general help facility will produce a complete explanation which may extend over one or more screens.

The second form of help tends to be highly specific. Faced with a number of choices such as:

VIEW QUICK CUSTOM LOOKUP MAILING MENU

it may be possible to highlight one of these choices by moving the cursor over it and then asking for help. This time the advice that arrives is solely confined to that item.

Some of the better applications programs have taken the help facility even further and will offer several layers of help. Thus if the first explanation does not clarify what to do next then you can press HELP again and get help about the help!

Integration

The popular idea around at the moment is that of an *integrated* applications package which combines a number of facilities such as a spreadsheet, word processor, database and so on. There are about 30 such packages on sale at present.

A number of general points are worth making at this stage. First, these usually cost considerably more than any other single package devoted to one task. But with good quality individual systems costing around £250, an integrated package with four modules could be worth £1000 and yet many are sold for about £500.

Figure 2.5 Typical software package

There are two types of these integrated systems. One keeps all of the program in the computer's RAM memory and only uses the disk for permanently storing the data. When it is working with data, that too must find space in the computer's memory.

The other type uses the disk for constantly referring to the program for instructions and can use the disk for storing the data, rather than holding it also in memory.

Both systems have their advantages and disadvantages. A system totally dependent on the size of the computer's memory will tend to limit the sophistication of the various facilities which the package can offer.

On the other hand, disk-based systems are much slower since the computer has to keep referring to the instructions held on disk. The need to load in programs can prevent a rapid shift between one facility of the package and another. Similarly it can limit the ability to display more than one application simultaneously on the screen.

Integrated systems are a consequence of greater computing power becoming available through the personal computer. There will be a minimum memory requirement before the integrated package will run properly on the computer.

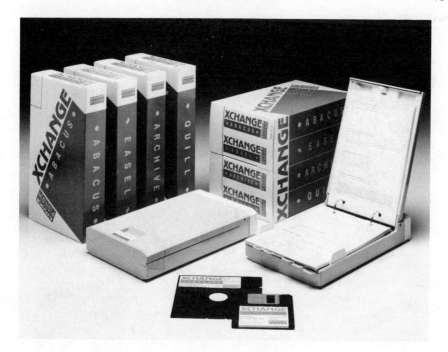

Figure 2.6 Typical software package

Windows

To managers the concept of a *window* is familiar. If you want to look at your diary, jot down some notes and check a telephone number, all these actions can happen in one smooth process of referring to close-at-hand sources.

The equivalent on the computer is the ability to open a window on an existing job and conduct another task, after which you return to where you left off.

A window is a portioned area of the display which acts like a miniature screen. Many windows may be displayed simultaneously and you can usually conduct work in each, moving rapidly from one to another.

Desktops

Because integrated packages are expensive, complex and virtually supplant software which has been painfully mastered already, a new breed of package has been appearing.

The desktop is a type of package which assumes that you see the computer as an electronic extension of your desk. Writing, filing, communicating and calculating tools are designed to be instantly to hand. Desktops are designed to let your computer do two things at once. (See also Chapter 10)

Figure 2.7 Typical software package

What's in the box?

Finally what does a package actually consist of? At the bare minimum it is a disk with brief instructions on how to use it. At the other extreme you may receive a hefty box sometimes made of rigid plastic, packed with manuals, a quick reference card, illustrated booklets, several disks, a template to place over the keyboard to help learn the commands, licence agreement and so on.

The hidden part of the product, apart from the actual way it works, is the support you can obtain once you have bought the product. (See Chapter 5)

SUMMARY

The main types of software are operating system software, programming languages and applications software.

Operating software is essential. Controlling a host of important computer functions, it sits between the hardware and your application program.

Always ask:
 For this operating system, what application programs are available now?
 What does this software require as an operating system?
 Tell me the precise system requirements for this software and will it work on my (name and model) computer?
 Can you show me?
 Will you fully install this software package so that all available features work properly on my equipment?

You will need to learn how to format a disk, change disk drives, copy a file or disk contents, call for a directory, list out the contents of a file and check how much free disk space is left.

Default means the value or answer that is assumed in the absence of other instructions.

If speed matters, check that a software package is written in assembly language.

Application programs or packages are applied to your computer to do useful jobs like word processing, financial analysis and so on.

Application programs are usually off-the-shelf products and described in product literature and dealer catalogues, which you should regard with caution.

Three terms commonly used in many computer programs are files, records and fields; before buying a package always check how many of these it will handle and what are the limits.

Applications programs work by allowing the user either to choose from menus in order to decide what to do next, or to issue commands by way of codes.

Applications programs usually have help facilities built into them which respond either with general or sometimes highly specific advice about what to do next.

Integrated packages offer a number of advantages but cost more and are more complex than single purpose products.

Windows are ways of making the computer screen show several jobs at once.

Desktops are special applications programs which treat the screen like an electronic desk.

3 Foundations

Charlie Chaplin might have been sorely tempted, had he still been alive, to make a film equivalent of his famous *Goldrush*, entitled *The Software Boom*.

All the ingredients are there. Enthusiastic amateurs, ruthless men on the make, countless suckers, a sprinkling of true professionals, and personal fortunes to be gained from a heady mixture of native skill and numerous lucky breaks.

Occasionally a news item appears such as: 'Ten year old makes a million from selling computer software' or 'Schoolboy starts own software house – employs fifty university graduates and owns a Rolls Royce'. Fortunes have indeed been made from writing computer programs and sometimes by near-adolescents. The classic fairy story of the software industry is how Dan Brinklin, a graduate student at the Harvard Business School in 1978, got bored adding up rows and columns of figures and making other cumbersome adjustments to a financial case study.

There had to be a better way and he devised the microcomputer spreadsheet. It was a simple concept: an electronic blackboard and chalk that constantly adjusted all the numbers in a grid of rows and columns. The computer did all the recalculations every time a user made changes to one or more items.

The resulting package was called *VisiCalc* and it has sold over 300,000 copies, more than any other package in the world, with probably as many again pirated. It made Brinklin and his two friends marvellously rich, helped launch Apple Computers into the financial stratosphere and is often credited with stimulating the microcomputer revolution.

It also underlined more forcibly than a thousand books or lectures that it pays to start with software and worry later about what computer to use. This view is sometimes dismissed as old fashioned but it still makes sense.

Today there are over 40,000 software packages for sale and more bombarding the market daily, almost hourly. To reduce this flood to a manageable stream one needs a workable strategy for reaching sensible and informed choices.

It is possible to hand the job of selection to someone else. But this may cause two more difficulties. First, it may be expensive, especially if you make a mistake about whom you pick. The average small firm or executive in a medium sized organization seldom has the resources to buy the best, most objective advice, even if this can found.

Secondly, you will not learn much, which may prove even more costly in the long run. The key to choosing useful software is to become involved in the selection, not to opt out.

SPECIALISMS

If you buy a chainsaw, a lawnmower and a cultivator all three may use a virtually identical power unit. In theory you should be able to purchase just one such unit, changing it from one gadget to another as required. But consumers have been successfully led to believe that it is better to have single purpose machines for chopping wood, cutting grass and digging over the vegetable patch.

Much the same applies in the computer software market. Constant advertising, subtle public relations and forceful sales techniques have made it seem that if you have a particular job that needs doing a specialist program is preferable.

Confronting this attitude is the relatively new breed of software which combines several different types of programs into one all-purpose, integrated package.

You can probably manage with just four or five, and initially probably only three kinds of software packages. By choosing the right ones you can apply these to a vast range of managerial problems. Also, you have to take account of the time/effort/payoff equation.

THE TIME/EFFORT/PAYOFF EQUATION

The advertisements or the salesmen seldom reveal what will be involved for you, the actual manager, in mastering a program in sufficient detail before it begins making a real difference to your personal efficiency.

At least one recent book has argued this point forcibly, with the author claiming that just about anything you might do on a personal computer can usually be done more quickly and simply on the back of an envelope!

It is naturally tempting to think that the computer will automatically make you more efficient, when the reverse may happen. For example, you can keep your daily appointments and schedule on a special computer program. But in practice an old fashioned desk diary is usually quicker and simpler. Have you ever investigated how long it will take to master say, the average database package?

One Cambridge-based specialist subcontractor, who writes manuals for software applications and therefore must master their full workings, estimates that it takes him two solid weeks, including weekends, pounding at the keyboard before he grasps the full complexities of a package.

As a working manager you are unlikely to gain real competence in using a reasonably sophisticated package in less than six months.Hence the time/effort/payoff equation which says:

> A personal payoff from a software package requires more time and
> effort than you would have committed if you had realised the full
> implications at the start.

As a busy manager with other staff to supervise, can you afford the time to learn how to use a software package and are you willing to make the necessary effort, even if you have the time?

The more power the software application provides, the more time and effort it will demand to deliver not merely an organizational payoff, but also any personal benefit.

Packages can be deceptively easy to use at first. It can be an intoxicating experience seeing one demonstrated or trying it out in your office for just an hour or so. Once it is permanently within reach, however, it may take days if not weeks before enough of the facilities are mastered really to achieve something genuinely useful.

A training course may cut some corners, giving a flying start with a particular package. It can also enhance your basic knowledge. But once again, can you afford one or more days on such a course? Generally, the amount you learn is never enough.

Another aspect of the time/effort/payoff equation is that often somebody has to feed in all the data before a system can be turned into a management aid. That person may have to be you if there is no-one to whom it can be delegated. A little input each day may be one way of overcoming this problem but will you sustain the momentum? Will the system flop because you cannot spare the time or it becomes just one more chore?

Will you even have time to use the package at all? Many managers find that because they have different software products to perform separate jobs – like write reports, draw graphs, create budgets and so on – the tedium of shuffling disks around, keeping track of what data is held where, and transferring information from one package to another demands more hours than they had ever anticipated.

START SIMPLE

Given the number of software packages potentially at your disposal, the successful approach to making management software useful is to consider the following foundation packages:

- training
- word processing
- filing and database systems
- spreadsheets

Of these, the first three probably offer rapid personal payoffs if the choice of package is a good one. The spreadsheet is a financial workhorse which, though easy to learn initially, is a specialist application. In fact many managers never need to sit down and personally draw up elaborate budget statements and 'what if' scenarios. However, the spreadsheet is certainly not just a financial tool. It is more akin to a programmable calculator, invaluable for endless types of figure work.

Two other categories of software could also possibly qualify as foundation packages:

- management aids
- communications

The order in which you should acquire these is highly debatable but there is a strong case for buying them in the above sequence. In this way you will gradually build up the necessary skills to turn the computer into more than just an executive toy.

The speed with which software prices are changing suggests that it would be tempting fate to put an exact price tag on the cost of a complete set of the foundation packages. Excluding training software, which can usually be shared across many other managers in the same organization, the other three types can currently be bought for a total of around £500 – 700. You may even find that all come 'free' when you buy your computer.

After investigation, you may well decide that the best initial investment is a really powerful database system along with a cheap and cheerful word processing package. The latter, for example, are available at ever decreasing prices and the simplest sells at below £50, though it would be extremely limited in scope.

The extent to which these packages mesh together is important.Their flexibility may permit a multiplicity of jobs to be performed, thus avoiding the need for more specialist types of software.

For example, a good word processing package may offer a facility for bulk mailings, while a good spreadsheet package can eliminate the need to buy different kinds of programs for doing a wide range of numerical and accounting tasks.

Management aids and communications software are two other types which you may decide to explore either earlier or later in your approach to the computer. For instance, some management address-keeping systems are simple to use but may prove no more convenient or quick than the traditional small black notebook.

Similarly, communications software, which allows your computer to 'talk' to other machines anywhere in the world, is again a specialist application. Leave this type of activity until you have acquired more solid computer experience. After all, there is little point in trying to dial the world before you even know how make local calls!

By concentrating on just three or four programs you can learn them thoroughly and thus begin to achieve real gains from each.Familiarity generates ideas about new applications that would previously never have occurred to you.

Training programs help you start learning in a more systematic way and at a pace that remains under your control. Simple programs that teach keyboard skills or some of the essential operating commands like moving or copying files can convey more in a few hours than could struggling on your own for several days. Training is discussed more fully in Chapter Six.

Software extras

There are frequently hidden extras in buying all types of software, that the dealers may conveniently forget to mention.Though seldom enough to deter you from buying any particular package, these add-on costs need to be allowed for when budgeting how much to spend.

Disks

The need to make several back-up copies of your master disks was discussed in Chapter One. Though the costs of extra disks and facilities like fireproof safes are minimal compared to the outlay on the computer and the software, the bill will steadily mount.

Not all software packages are designed to let you make copies of the master disks, which can leave you vulnerable to expensive disasters. Usually though, some arrangement for replacements at an economic price is negotiable with the suppliers.

Disks wear out and occasionally develop faults. This could also mean losing some painstakingly accumulated data. Somehow, the latter has to be rescued.

There are now several specialist software programs which act as disk 'doctors', extracting the precious information and allowing it to be transferred to a fresh, uncorrupted floppy disk.Compared to the cost of replacing the original data these programs are cheap. It may be false economy to wait until disaster strikes before acquiring one as a contingency measure.

Blank disks are usually supplied in multiples of 10 or 12 and come in neat cardboard boxes which are perfectly usable for daily purposes but which, with heavy use, can quickly become grubby and weakened.

As the number of back-up disks and data disks multiply, you will need some of the specialist plastic containers designed to hold disks in units of 10, 20 or 50, which separate them with neat dividers like an index card box.

These attractive, highly functional aids are cheaper than the traditional metal filing cabinet which they replace, but they still add to the overall cost.

More hardware or software?

Buy the wrong piece of software and you could find yourself with an extra bill for more hardware. Incredible though it may seem, there are people who will sell you software and not explain that to make it work properly you need to adapt your computer in some way.

The worst situation is when you actually buy the software and only then discover that it needs more computer memory than you thought. For example, to run the integrated package *Symphony* you need 300 – 512Kbytes of computer memory.

You may discover that the software cannot operate your printer properly or that it will not talk to another program without an extra piece of equipment.

Similarly another additional costly item that you may need to get the best from some packages with a graphics facility is a high resolution monitor, or a special card to insert so that the system will handle colour and so on.

If you discover these needs after you have bought your new software it may be difficult to obtain redress from the supplier who may justifiably claim that he thought you were aware of the essential hardware requirements. The only solution at this stage is usually to pay up.

After you have been using your new purchase for a while, you become aware that it is either too slow, does not hold all the information that you want, or simply cannot perform well enough. A good example of this is when managers discover how much faster their software works when transferred to a hard, as opposed to an ordinary, floppy disk.

While the answer may well be more hardware, it may could also be still more software. For example, some of the more expensive multi-use packages like *Lotus 1-2-3* let you swop backwards and forwards between one type of job and another. One second you are word processing and the next you are doing some fancy figure work on a spreadsheet.

Single-use software does not allow these switches so some enterprising software suppliers have introduced add-on packages that permit this kind of swopping, though in a slightly more cumbersome way.

Similarly, you may find that besides a word processing package you need an application that checks your spelling or grammar. Likewise, it may become clear that it would be helpful to create your own menus which offer a choice of calling up a whole range of programs in a systematic way.

The software that you originally buy may be missing these valuable features, hence you have to purchase them as separate programs. This resultant upgrading leads to a growing awareness of a program's limitations and you start hankering after better things. You begin scanning software advertisements again or pester colleagues who use different packages, or contact dealers for demonstrations of possible alternatives. Anyone who has bought hi-fi knows this syndrome only too well.

Upgrades

A variation on the above theme happens when the software producer introduces an improved version of the package which you have bought. Sometimes the new developments are free, you just mail your old disk and receive the new one.

Usually though, the new version costs extra. Perhaps not much, but occasionally the change is so dramatic that virtually a new product is created. When this happens you are tempted by an attractive trade-in price to gain the benefits of the new product.

Hotlines

Most reputable suppliers, whether dealers or publishers, will help you to extract the best from your software. But, like lunch, advice seldom comes free. One way or another you pay for help, either in the initial cost of your purchase or later through buying the assistance of a hotline service.

Hotlines may well be offered by your dealer or publisher but how easy is it to make contact? Are the lines constantly engaged? Will the person at the other end talk you through your difficulty or merely give you general advice, leaving you to try it out?

Access to a hotline can vary from around 10 per cent upwards of the original price of the software. Psion Systems Ltd, for instance, charge 15 per cent of the price of their integrated package *Xchange* for a hotline service and promise to 'maintain' the product.

Sometimes a software house will waive the cost of the first year's subscription and a fee is payable after that, when presumably you do not need much help anyway.

Adjustments

Another hidden extra may arise when you decide that your software needs modifying in some way. This may be because it does not meet your organization's specific requirements. But it could also stem from a bad mistake in choosing that particular package.

If you hire a programmer for making adjustments to your package or resort to consultancy help, the eventual bill could outstrip the cost of the original investment, which is why selection of the right package is so crucial. Generally though, if you stick to the foundation packages and combine this with careful selection of highly relevant programs there should be no need to hire programming skills.

Publications

Tour the average computer exhibition and what will be the most crowded stands? Almost certainly the bookstalls! Despite the microchip and floppy disk age, traditional paper publications are burgeoning.

Thousands of computer users need advice and information in a highly accessible form. So far, the book remains more economic than, for example, selling the same material on disk. This may well change radically in the next five years as microcomputers continue to proliferate and the problems of compatibility are overcome.

Popular software packages like *dBase II* or *VisiCalc* may have several books written about them from different angles. Once you've invested in a package it may quickly become apparent that the manuals do not offer sufficiently clear help. However, book publishers charge what the market will bear; in the computer field it can be joltingly high.

Other hidden costs

As you become more familiar with your software and identify an increasing number of useful applications, you may reach an input bottle neck. For example, it may be necessary to feed in large amounts of raw information to create a database. Or to take advantage of the capabilities of a spreadsheet you may first have to input a large quantity of detailed budget information.

It may be a totally uneconomic to do this yourself, since it may take hours or even days.

While the obvious solution is to delegate this task to someone else, you may first have to teach them what to do and be prepared to check their work carefully. Add up the hours invested, including your own and the hidden cost may prove unacceptably high.

Finally, there is an undoubted hidden cost in respect of training which is discussed in Chapter Six.

Guidelines to choosing

Evaluating and selecting computer software is rapidly becoming a human field of discipline in its own right. It is not merely that there are so many packages from which to choose. But to conduct proper tests to decide which is the best from even a narrowed down selection can be extremely demanding.

As a working manager looking for effective software, aim to use existing knowledge, not to conduct original research.

The main difference between an effective personal computer system and computer assisted disaster is a careful blend of these ingredients:

- training

- a prove-and-proceed approach

- careful preparation

- adequate back-up

- personal commitment

It is worth emphasising that in the early stages you need the chance to learn more about computers and what software can do than is contained in a book like this. What you require most is *hands-on* practical experience of trying out different software packages in a non-stressful environment.

Secondly, you should adopt a slow but steady approach that moves through various stages in selecting software. This demands a measure of self discipline, particularly if you do not yet have a computer permanently at your disposal. The allure of the actual hardware tends to detract from focusing first on software needs.

The various steps of a prove-and-proceed approach are described in the next two chapters. The main point though, is to avoid rushing. The aim is to reduce the inevitable pressure to make early decisions until you are sufficiently sure of your ground. Training can help to give this degree of confidence.

Careful preparation implies that you narrow down to manageable proportions a list of possible software applications. This will involve a mixture of adequate reading, discussions with other users, talks with one or more dealers and the possible use of several independent or semi-independent sources of information. Also, seeing packages in action and trying them out yourself under conditions discussed later.

Adequate back-up is usually defined as a reliable dealer or software supplier who accepts your need to go slowly and learn on the way. It is also someone who can talk to you without resorting to jargon, explaining what they mean when jargon does arise. This aspect is also dealt with in more detail later.

Finally, how committed are you really to going any farther? By now you have an appreciation of the extent to which you will need to become involved in obtaining a personal payoff from the computer.

If you have a significant number of staff to manage, an appreciable amount of your effort is probably committed to meeting and talking with them, encouraging and motivating. Might the computer become an expensive distraction, engrossing and thus destroying your personal availability?

To absorb the computer into your personal work style means finding a new balance between your current contacts with people and time spent at a machine. In the early period of learning this means perhaps hours a week just getting to know your software and machine. Hands-on training courses can speed up this process and one view is that they are absolutely essential if you are to save valuable time in breaking into the computer world.

However, another view is that there is no substitute for having the time to make mistakes in private. Hands-on training can only give you limited help in the earliest stages and is likely to be more in the way of familiarisation that a direct transfer of practical skills.

Because your workplace inevitably creates pressures, finding several hours a week for maybe three to six months could prove a real strain. Depending on the portabililty of your computer you may decide that the best place for learning is at home. What will this do to your private life? Like most jokes, the one about a new generation of computer widows has a ring of truth.

When the initial enthusiasm wears thin, your personal commitment to using the computer must take you beyond the stage of merely possessing more knowledge of, and confidence in, its potential as a management tool. You will need an adjusted work style, continually trying out new ideas in a spirit of permanent experimentation and exploration.

If you have definitely decided to proceed, then now is the time to consider the main steps in choosing and implementing a series of software applications. These steps are described in the next two chapters.

SUMMARY

To achieve a personal payoff from a software package you will spend more time and effort than you would have agreed to invest, had you realised the full implications before you started.

Foundation packages are: training, word processing, filing and database systems, and spreadsheets.

Software extras may imply: more hardware, additional software to enhance the basic package, product upgrades, publications, training and back-up.

An effective personal computer system involves: training, a prove-and-proceed approach, careful preparation, adequate back-up support and personal commitment.

4   The Seven Steps to Choosing Software

There is a Catch 22 about choosing management software. You will know for sure what package you really want, some time after you have bought an entirely different one! Only when you become familiar with how a particular application works, will you appreciate its snags and the lack of facilities which would be most helpful.

Following several discrete steps for purchasing management software develops critical awareness of potential snags and benefits. Choosing films, books or records involves assessing the worth of someone else's creative efforts. Similarly, selecting software is based on judgement and knowledge.

The main steps are given below.

1. Preparation and investigation
2. Clarifying musts and wants
3. Finding a dealer/supplier
4. Assessing documentation
5. Demonstrations and personal trial
6. Defining back-up support
7. Implementation

The first four of these are dealt with next and the remainder in the following chapter.

STEP ONE: PREPARATION AND INVESTIGATION

As indicated, basic preparation requires some simple 'hands-on' training to gain familiarity with the computer and selected software applications. Initial reading is also desirable and the references in Part Two plus the bibliography at the end of this book provide some additional material which may be helpful.

Sources for identifying potential software applications include:

software catalogues
computer magazines
software directories and guidebooks
visits to computer exhibitions
discussions with dealers
user groups
consultants and independent advisory services
colleagues in the same organisation or profession

Tapping these sources may produce possible applications that might be worth investigating in more detail. As a busy manager though, your scope for doing a thorough survey is limited, which is one reason at this stage for sticking to well tried products. Scanning magazines, checking directories and so on, will highlight certain packages as well known and perhaps worth short-listing.

What does it mean if a package is well advertised and promoted? Probably that the producers have used a considerable amount of resources getting their product to the market. The cost of producing effective software is escalating rapidly. The days when someone could produce an instant winner with a few weeks' programming plus the minimum of packaging and advertising have virtually gone.

Now is also the time to make brief visits to dealers and places like exhibitions where you can begin to see programs working and gain a clearer idea of what is available in your price range.

Explain to everyone that you are not ready to buy but are conducting a careful review of potential products. Collect product literature but resist sales pressure by declining offers of a detailed product demonstration solely for your benefit.

Exhibitions

At exhibitions demonstrations are increasingly being made using a large screen for mass viewing. You can watch these in quiet anonymity, acquiring a feel for the way different programs work. If there are no such presentations join a group around a computer, watch and listen.

Computer exhibitions can be overwhelming, particularly if you do not know what you are seeking. But thcy do provide a useful overview and a chance to make contacts for subsequent follow-up. Chat to other potential buyers, they may by now have discovered aspects about a package that you should consider.

Exhibitions are too crowded for serious investigation but at this stage you are not seeking prolonged discussion and trial, merely a chance to gain a feel for what is available.

If you search diligently you will find that there is a computer exhibition somewhere in Britain on almost every day of the year. The six main ones are:

January	**Which Computer? Show** A huge Birmingham-based bonanza sponsored by the magazine of the same name
February	**Info** Business and home computers, usually held in London
May	**Midland Computer Fair** Business and home computers, usually held in Manchester

September/October   **Personal Computer World Show**
Has a large section devoted to small
business systems; home computers
and games are much in evidence.
Usually held in London

November   **Northern Computer Fair** Business
and home computers, usually held
in Manchester

November   **Compec** Said to be Britain's biggest
computer show, lasts four days in
London

There are also specialist exhibitions such as **Computers in Personnel** and
ones aimed at particular types of businesses.

Although exhibitions are informative, do not expect much emphasis on
software. Software houses are usually too small to afford regular attendances at these jamborees but distributors may well be there in force.

Small specialist shows on software do occur occasionally and the dates of
these can be found in the computer magazines under forthcoming events.
Most business-to-business and equipment exhibitions have stands for
software firms but again, do not expect a wide market coverage.

User groups

User groups and local computer clubs are another pressure-free way to learn
more about potential programs. Locate these groups through local libraries,
computer companies and magazines.

Do not yet contact user clubs devoted exclusively to one particular
software product. Such members are committed enthusiasts. Having made
their investment of time and money, they are seldom sufficiently objective to
help you keep the options open.

Reviews

A basic source of valuable information at this stage is the software review.
Reviews appear regularly in computer magazines but vary considerably in
quality and depth of investigation.

At one end of the spectrum you will find a review that almost takes
a software product apart, providing detailed technical measurements
(*benchmarks*) by which it can be judged against comparable products. At
the other end are reviews just a few paragraphs long, giving a brief outline of
the product and perhaps some kind of star rating for performance, value for
money, documentation and so on.

As a manager you are probably used to scanning a wide variety of
literature to extract information. You will soon learn to do the same with the
computer reviews once you have surmounted the initial jargon barrier.

Most computer reviews are clearly written but a significant proportion stem from what can only be called computer boffins. Their knowledge of machines and software is formidable but their ability to communicate in lay terms is negligible. One prolific writer for example, produces interminable and detailed reviews but the material seems mainly aimed at other reviewers!

You can trace reviews through several sources. Your local library may stock a copy of *Microcomputer Alert*. This is an index to literature on microcomputers for home and business. It covers around two dozen computer and other relevant publications, such as *New Scientist* and *The Financial Times*. The index is published quarterly and identifies which subjects have been covered, cross-referencing them in alphabetical order. Computer magazines too usually produce a summary index of software applications that they have reviewed in the last couple of years.

You can also contact some of the Microsystems Centres run by the National Computing Centre (NCC). These independent advisory centres will often keep a list of software reviews or be able to direct you to where a particular review can be found. They also produce a regularly updated publication on software packages.

Always read more than one review as opinions, contents and coverage vary widely. Since the products themselves are often regularly improved, an article published say two years ago could be outdated, many of the earlier problems having since been eliminated.

A package consists of several elements and a good review should normally deal with each of these in turn. There is the program itself, its various features and performance; how it handles when you make mistakes; ease of use; quality of the accompanying documentation; and finally support, either from the original producer or via a credited supplier.

Retain a critical view of what is said, few if any of the reviewers are actual practising managers. Articles are seldom reports on using the product in a practical management environment.

Nor are such reports definitive statements of software capabilities since authors may take the basic capabilities for granted. To make the article more interesting the writer may concentrate on some new but irrelevant feature.

Also, a reviewer can test the program itself more easily than the quality of the back-up service. Software producers will usually respond promptly to a reviewer's enquiries and request for help since doing so is in their interests. When *you* ring asking for help, the response may well be different. Thus if a review comments on the poor back-up treat this as a significant warning.

STEP TWO: CLARIFYING MUSTS AND WANTS

Because software applications vary so much, a sound approach is to try to list both the features that you must have and without which the purchase would not make sense and the wants which can be sacrificed if the budget will not stretch that far.

For instance, you may not feel that a spelling checker is essential for a word processing package while perhaps a mailing list facility would be. Or the ability to vary the field length in a database might be considered vital while a special query language to conduct complex sorting of information could be low down on your shopping list of features, although neverthless something to be acquired if possible.

Many simple ways exist to firm up on your musts and wants. First, check in a software selector to see what various packages have on offer. For example, the *Microcomputer Software Directory* (Computer Publications Ltd) gives summary details of thousands of software applications and classifies them in various helpful ways. This publication is being replaced in 1985 by the *Software User's Year Book*.

If you want more detail,you could try *The Ultimate Software Selector for Business Micros*, compiled by the Federation of Microsystems (1984) which gives a detailed breakdown of various kinds of software facilities.

Around 50 database packages are listed in the *Selector* which answers such questions as: can data be sorted, is it possible to make back-up copies, how is data updated, may field and record lengths be varied and so on.

Secondly, you can seek direct help from consultants and others like the National Computing Centre in Manchester or its offshoots the Microsystems Centres. The latter offer low cost help and are willing to see you for as little as half an hour to point you in the right direction if this is what you require. Consultancy though, is generally not really an economic proposition for a single manager.

It may also be helpful to use a simple form of personal checklist setting out musts and wants and clarifying priorities. This can help you to focus on what you are really seeking from a software package and not lose sight of these needs in the confusion of advertisements, reviews, discussions, demonstrations, trials and and sales presentations. A musts and wants form is shown in Figure 4.1.

Consultants

There are broadly two kinds of consultants: independent and dealer- or manufacturer-linked.

Independent consultants are seldom as independent as they seem. Many sell consultancy as part of a much larger range of services, including the sale of software, hardware and the design, installation and even maintenance of complete systems.

Though they may not have a direct link with any particular supplier, they may nevertheless do regular business with a selected number. Thus they may not offer such an unbiased view as you might wish, though they are unlikely deliberately to distort their advice. They will nevertheless have certain preferences and you may ultimately pay dearly for someone else's enthusiasm.

These consultants usually charge on the basis of time expended or sometimes for a specifically defined, completed job. Since they cost hundreds of pounds per day you need to do plenty of homework in specifying

CRITERIA LIST FOR ASSESSING SOFTWARE NEEDS

Name of Package:................   Type:........

Memory Size needed:.....   No. of Disk Drives:.....

Operating System :.....   Cost   :.....

USER REQUIREMENTS

	Seen	Not seen	Comments

MUSTS

1 ....

2 ....

3 ....

4 ....

5 ....

6 ....

7 ....

8 ....

Wants

1 ....

2 ....

3 ....

4 ....

5 ....

Notes

....

....

....

....

....

....

Understanding Management Software

Macmillan & IPM, 1985

Figure 4.1

your wants and musts before seeking their rarefied help.

Dealer-linked consultants seldom charge for their initial services. But there are no giveaways here either. The hidden cost is that you will usually be advised to place your purchase with a supplier from whom the consultant will claim a commission. While the package which you buy this way may be adequate, your choice of applications and dealers will be limited to those with whom the consultant is linked.

Some dealers employ their own full-time consultants, though cynics might prefer to call these people salesmen in disguise. However, genuine dealer - consultants may only offer their particular services after you have made your purchase, hence they provide simply technical support.

Certain consultancies also offer a special two or three day seminar on evaluating, selecting and using software packages. These can cost at least £500 and are aimed more at specialists concerned with system design and those who advise large organisations.

Professional bodies

There are several professional bodies to whom you could turn for help in firming up your musts and wants. If you are in a particular profession such as personnel or accountancy then your own institute will probably have informed advisers able to point to relevant literature, experienced users and well-tried products.

Within the computer field itself there are several agencies offering help and these are shown in the appendix on Useful Addresses.

Conceptualise

The final way of firming up on musts and wants is a conceptual one. You begin to define what the output from the computer might look like if you were using the software. If that proves too difficult it might mean that you should not be buying the software at all.

You have to imagine yourself using the program and answering the apparently naive question:

What do I want my software to do?

The process of answering this question involves trying to clarify a list of the detailed tasks that you have in mind for the software. Define the kind of reports which you would require and how often; identify jobs that are standard (such as VAT and income tax calculations) and ones that are not, like stock order levels. How will the program handle these activities?

In other words, what will you need to do to produce results? Will you need to learn a complicated set of codes or will the program merely ask some multiple choice questions?

When you can identify a specific task to perform it is a great help in deciding not only the musts and wants, but also the merits or otherwise of a program. By trying to clarify the precise steps that will be necessary to generate a specific result, you can identify the strong and weak points of a program. For example, how does a database cope when you have a sudden change of mind and decide that there should be more fields than you originally planned, after information has begun to be recorded?

Or suppose that you want to list all employees. What are the exact items you must record and in what order? Will there be enough room for them and when you need to make changes to all employees' records for salary adjustments, how difficult or time consuming will this task be?

Defining the output is not easy but start by trying to answer the above question in a fair amount of detail. Alternatively, try this idea:

> At the press of just one key, I'd like the following layout to appear on the screen.

Draw an imaginary screen on a piece of paper and start to block out what information would ideally appear there if you had no worries about making the actual software package work. Begin working backwards from here to what information would need to go into the computer to achieve this result.

For example, suppose that you were in charge of a large organisation's job evaluation service, placing employees on various pay scales. You might begin by defining the output as:

> I want to know what all these decisions are costing us each year.

To find the answer would require keeping track of each award and its annual cost, then accumulating these into a grand total. So the first requirement would be the monthly awards expressed as an annual cost.

Next you might ask yourself what else you want to know. The answer might be:

> Show me the awards by department and group them by size.

Once again this helps to identify what further information would be needed before this could appear on the screen. This is a demanding exercise but it nevertheless concentrates effort on teasing out some of the musts and wants.

STEP THREE: FINDING A DEALER OR SUPPLIER

It is essential to distinguish between a software producer, a publisher and a distributor. The software producer may well be a firm of just three or four people, selling only one product. However this approach is becoming increasingly less viable.

Distributors are the retailers who may sell not only software but hardware as well. Software is not necessarily their main line and indeed some firms merely stock programs on a sale-or-return basis. Their knowledge of a particular product may be minimal.

There are currently a few firms that can be called software publishing companies. They commission other organisations to produce packages to a specific brief, taking on responsibility for marketing and distribution. Again the problem in dealing with such firms concerns their knowledge of the product and their degree of commitment to it.

In considering the issue of a suitable supplier, assume this immutable law:

> no matter how talented you may be or how much time you invest in computing, you are definitely going to need help after you have purchased a software package.

The only exceptions to this are a few training and human relations packages or some really elementary programs that offer limited facilities. Always act on the assumption that back-up is mandatory.

Because there are so many software packages available it is unreasonable to expect every supplier to know in detail how they work. This may not matter for a £50 program, but if you are considering spending several hundred pounds or more, you are entitled to talk to someone who knows their stuff. The problem is finding this rarity.

If you have managed to produce a shortlist of software products in which you are interested, seek a supplier who actually specialises in each package. One way of doing this is to contact the software house that produced it and ask for the name of a knowledgeable dealer in whom they have confidence. They may even suggest a specific person to contact.

Stability

A supplier's stability as an ongoing business is of prime importance. There are several reasons. First, because there is never certainty that a particular package is free of errors (*bugs*). Even well-established products, that have been in use for several years, can behave erratically under certain conditions. For example, *Cardbox Plus*, a remarkably good filing system which has been around for some time, developed problems when run on the Apricot personal computer. After some good detective work the errors turned out to be with the operational software not the package itself. Nevertheless the producers of *Cardbox Plus* took the trouble to warn customers of the problem and to suggest ways of dealing with it. A supplier with no eye on the future might not have bothered.

Also, a surprising number of packages arrive at the customer's with minor problems such as an incorrect or faulty disk, a section of the manual missing, an outdated version of the software, damaged packaging and so on. Of the 30 packages used for this book at least a fifth arrived with such problems. If that happens to review copies what about the average customer?

Secondly, good software is constantly being improved and updated versions issued by the producers. This is less likely to occur if the supplier is financially unsound.

Thirdly, as emphasised, you are going to need backup support on a variety of topics. Some help might relate to the software package itself, or to expanding your system to include new forms of software. If the supplier has helped establish the system, you are more likely to obtain an informed response than starting afresh with a new firm.

Assessing the stability of potential software suppliers is no different to evaluating any other type of business. For example, how long has the company been operating? Five years in the computer industry is respectable and three is about average. Are they doing sufficient business with adequate margins to grow profitably?

How generous do they seem with discounts? If they are cutting the prices significantly this usually means you will not receive adequate back-up. In the computer world you get what you pay for. The dealer who sells at a reasonable price but also has commitment to maintenance and support is likely to survive with profits stemming from repeat business.

Is the firm responsive in the early stages and does it have a professional approach? Are they capable of explaining what the software can do in a language which you can understand? Make contact by telephone with some of the firm's customers and try to discover their opinion of the organisation, its products and its service.

Look closely into whether the potential supplier carries a wide stock of software or only offers the juicy, expensive items. You may be surprised at how few packages a supplier actually holds in stock. If they do not carry the one in which you are interested, their working knowledge of it may be limited.

Consider how familiar the supplier is with your particular type of work and whether there is a real attempt to discover what particular problems you are facing. Is just one product recommended or several in the same price range? What are the detailed arrangements for maintenance and support and how much will this cost? Do you seem to receive honest answers or do you sense that the replies are vague and somewhat elusive?

A point worth checking at this stage, which will become much more important later, is whether the dealer is willing to loan you the system, perhaps a demonstration version with more limited facilities. Or will he lend it to your local Microsystems Centre or perhaps local technical college, under their supervision on equipment that matches your own? Dealer margins are not high enough for you to expect the supplier to lend you hardware as well.

Ask whether the supplier has facilities for training you or your staff and roughly what such support costs. How local is the potential supplier? The telephone may reduce some of the need for proximity but assistance may be less attractive if, to take real advantage of it, you have to spend a whole day out of the office.

Ask to see the terms of sale and consider whether these seem reasonable and fair to both sides. Do not take much notice of product guarantees and warrantees as they are seldom any protection.

Sometimes you will be faced with two sets of purchasing conditions, one imposed by the originators of the software and one by the distributors. As part of this process another key question always to ask is:

Can I make back-up copies of this software system?

The importance of this has been stressed before, but now is the time to look at this issue in more depth.

Copying

Foiling computer pirates is now big business. It has to be, since it is estimated that in the UK alone software piracy is costing a minimum of £150 million a year in lost revenue. Micro-Pro, the makers of the popular *WordStar* package, believe that for every one that they sell three more are pirated, at a loss of £2 million a year.

Managers and businessmen who would never dream of cheating on the tube fare or feel uneasy about fiddling their income tax return, often have no conscience about acquiring or even selling stolen intellectual property. Ultimately it's the honest users who suffer.

Software prices have to be set to reflect this counterfeiting epidemic. In fact it may come as a surprise, but when you acquire a software package you are rarely buying it at all. Somewhere amongst all that mound of documentation there is usually a sentence such as that found on the envelope containing the disks for *Lotus 1-2-3*, the best-selling spreadsheet package:

> Each Lotus product sold is licenced by Lotus Development (UK)
> to the original purchaser of the product for use only on the terms
> set forth below.

This licence is thus for a specific user; copying the disk and giving it to anyone else is stealing.

New ways are being constantly introduced to combat software piracy. The simplest is to produce the manual on paper which cannot be photocopied. Other packages require a special device (dongle) to plugged into the computer before the program will work, though this method is rapidly becoming obsolete. Similarly, some packages use a master disk that cannot be copied.

The Vault Corporation, one of many firms now offering software protection, sells a system which, should you rashly load a pirated disk into your computer, warns:

> This is an illegal duplicate. You have 30 seconds to turn off your
> machine or risk damage to your data or your computer.

If the rogue disk is nevertheless used, a 'worm' in the program apparently causes erratic data, erasure of certain information and other storage problems.

Microsoft's *Project Manager* is equally ruthless. One file contains the words:

> ****Internal Security Violation****
> The tree of evil bears bitter fruit, crime does not pay
> THE SHADOW KNOWS

This is followed by the alarming message:

> Trashing program disk

Copying *Project Manager* illegally could mean saying goodbye to £200 worth of software which is apparently programmed to self-destruct. Ever more elaborate methods are being developed to prevent illegal copying.

Given the cost of producing software and the ease with which much of it can be duplicated, an obsession by producers to seek protection is understandable. Yet making back-up copies is essential for a genuine user's own protection. One bite from the cat, a sudden slop from a carelessly handled cup of coffee or inadvertently touching the surface can ruin a disk forever.

Similarly, erasing data is only too easy as you may discover if you mistakenly leave a disk under the telephone or if the wrong keys are pressed without proper thought.

Piracy, combined with disk frailty, has important implications for selecting a software supplier. The most obvious concerns the integrity of the dealer. Most are doubtless hard working and honest. But there are unscrupulous ones around and you could be sold, or even lent, an illegal copy by such a dealer. The latter may be in financial difficulties and hoping to persuade you to buy hardware by offering cheap or free software as an inducement.

Another implication concerns the need occasionally to replace your master disks if you cannot copy them. Buy from a less than totally reliable dealer and you could face difficulties when the time comes to obtain a replacement for perfectly legitimate reasons. You may be asked to pay an excessive replacement cost, or the dealer may have ceased handling that particular program or even stopped trading.

The final implication relates to the majority of programs that currently have no physical protection against illegal copying. The ease with which both disks and supporting documentation can be reproduced means that once you have purchased a software package it is usually non-returnable.

Non-returnable products are by now familiar, for example, hi-fi records, prerecorded videos and other items that are easily shop soiled. As indicated, a mistaken software purchase can lead to more costs in trying to make it usable. A reputable and understanding dealer may be more helpful in these circumstances than one who has sold you the program through the post or at a cut rate.

The better products are now increasingly designed to warn you that they are non-returnable, even if the dealer does omit to mention it. For example, if you buy *DataMaster*, an American database system it arrives with the disks in sealed containers with a clear consumer warning:

SAPPHIRE SYSTEMS SOFTWARE
Important notice

In this envelope are magnetic disks upon which are embedded
SAPPHIRE SYSTEMS computer programs. The copyright in
the computer programs is owned by Sapphire Systems Limited.

DO NOT OPEN THIS ENVELOPE
until you have read the Software Licence agreement which is
enclosed in the front of the manual. If you do not find the terms
of the licence agreement acceptable, then return the entire pack-

age with this disk envelope UNOPENED within 10 working days of purchase to the company which supplied it to you and the company will refund or credit the full price.

IF YOU OPEN THIS ENVELOPE
then by doing so you accept the terms of the licence agreement and forfeit the right to a refund or credit of the purchase price as mentioned above. In order to become a registered user and so benefit from the opportunities to acquire product updates, customer service, free product reference guides and newsletters you must complete and return the enclosed acknowledgement card.

Buying by mail

The final decision about selecting a supplier concerns whether you should buy through the post. Although mail order produces substantial savings usually it also means minimal back-up.

Mail order firms reduce the retail price of a software package by anything from 15 to 45 per cent. The difference may justify a gamble that you can manage without dealer support. If help is needed later, then you might have made sufficient saving to afford it.

If your organisation owns a copy of a program and merely wants an additional one for you, then it can make sense to buy via mail order. But software houses will usually offer generous discounts to buyers of multiple copies so that a mail order deal may be less attractive.

Because you are a manager with many other responsibilities, the importance of adequate product back-up cannot be overestimated. Buying through the post is usually only justified for cheap programs costing around £40–80.

STEP FOUR: ASSESSING DOCUMENTATION

Send for an inexpensive British database system and all you might receive is one disk. The disk is used to print the 26-page manual at your own expense. At the other extreme is the package which has so much documentation that about the only item missing is instruction on how to find time to read it.

Documentation is the Achilles' heel of the software industry. Perfectly sound packages are marketed with the most appalling documentation and a contempt for the user which is breathtaking. The cause lies in the complexity and cost of producing good software.

It is a creative business which takes brains and know-how. To make money you have to market the product just at the right time. Pressure to put the package on the market and start recouping the large investment in programming is considerable, particularly with a small organisation. Documentation tends to be left till late in the day and to be written by the equivalent of the office boy.

Even when a software house decides to try hard and make the documentation effective it still may not have the skills to do so, being composed of computer people who know all about programming but not much about users.

Increasingly, software producers are recognising this weakness and are commissioning specialist sub-contractors to handle their documentation. But after creating a dozen or more manuals for different packages, even these specialists begin losing their original sensitivity to what it is like to start completely cold with a new product. They start assuming a certain level of knowledge by the new user that is unjustified.

Because there is no industry-agreed standard for documentation and many perfectly effective packages have poor documentation, you may have to accept second, or even third best in this area of product selection. There are few packages with documentation that impresses with its completeness, its usefulness and its clarity.

What therefore can you expect in the way of documentation? You should be able to identify:

- a statement of which documents are supposed to accompany the package

- clear instructions on how to tailor the package to work on your particular computer and possibly on your printer

- a manual on how to use the program, including a list of the special keys on your particular machine that produce various commands

- a list of error messages and what to do when they occur (an *error recovery procedure*)

- the computer language used by the software house (the *source listing*), or an indication that this is held by a third party such as a bank or an independent organisation like the National Computing Centre, in case the supplier goes into liquidation

- the terms under which the software is being supplied; usually this is a licence to use the package and make back-up copies but not the right to offer it to other users. A large firm, for example, may have to negotiate special terms so that a package can be used by many of its employees

- an indication of what arrangements are made for upgrading disks and replacing ones that cannot be copied

- the name and address of the original software producers, though these may be in any part of the world

- a statement concerning customer support

The above are the minimum items of information and documentation that should come with a software application. However several additional items that you might hope to find include:

a written tutorial, either within the main manual or preferably as a separate document an interactive instruction disk; preferably in addition to the tutorial manual or alternatively as a substitute for a written tutorial

an audio cassette training programme to be run with the package. Usually these are sold as optional extras

training arrangements at reasonable cost from reliable, competent sources. Usually optional extras

sample files on disk that, together with the tutorial, show how the program operates and save you dreaming up imaginary data as you are learning the ropes

a quick reference card summarising the main commands of a program

a customer registration card or agreement, which may entitle you to various benefits, including telephone advice, access to free publications produced by the firm or other organisations, replacement copies of your master disks if disaster strikes

an indication that faulty disks will be replaced free of charge if returned within a reasonable period

a maintenance agreement which indicates that the supplier will remove any program errors (bugs) at no expense to the user and agreement on reasonable charges for user modifications and those occasioned by changes in the law

a list of well-known organisations that have purchased the software application

a customer user club which entitles you to various benefits including additional support, discounts on new products, specialist literature and so on. These facilities are usually treated as optional extras

the address of an independent users' club, sanctioned but usually not run by the software house itself. The users' club may charge to join but you should be able to obtain free help through it from informed and enthusiastic users, many of whom will have wrestled with the same problems as you are about to face. As an example, the declared aims of the *DataMaster* User's Group include:
- interchange of *DataMaster* techniques
- central error reporting to the company and members
- added pressure upon the authors to fix any errors
- user group software file
- assistance in software development at reduced prices.

Inside the documentation

Given that so much documentation for software is dreadful, it might seem pointless to dissect it in more detail. But the variation in standards justifies a review of what you might look for in buying a package. You will almost certainly not find any package with all the characteristics described below. If you do, it will probably conform to another minor law of the computer world:

The ideal package is the one that you can hardly afford.

You should not expect to make much sense of the documentation without quietly studying it in a relaxed environment. Many dealers and software suppliers will consider sympathetically the request to borrow the manual for a few days, if they think that you are seriously considering a purchase. Alternatively they may sell it for a few pounds to be credited against an eventual sale of the whole package.

Quality of production

When computers were at the equivalent of the toddler stage, instruction manuals usually came in large ring binders so that constant corrections to the manual could be issued! The material was often copied by the cheapest method of reproduction. The legacy of that age is that manuals often still arrive in cumbersome ring binders and for economy are taken direct from typewritten text and litho printed, not typeset.

While you cannot 'judge a book by its cover', a rule in the software world is that a well produced, sumptuous manual usually means that the suppliers have gone to a great deal of trouble and expense over their product. Their support may still be awful but the chances are somewhat reduced.

The best manuals are usually typeset, in at least one other colour than black for highlighting and emphasis. A good example is Ashton Tate's *Friday!* manual. Apart from high quality printing, instructions for using the computer and copies of screen layouts are reproduced in green, which contrasts with bold black headings to help the reader through the text.

Spiral bindings are particularly helpful. Not all ring binders perform well, for example, the monster manual for *Open Access* hardly matches its name since it is exceptionally difficult to turn the pages in bulk. While this may seem a minor issue it can add up to a long term irritant when constantly using the material over a prolonged period.

Well-produced manuals will have the different sections visibly separated by protruding tab dividers for easy access and there may be other aids such as colour-coded dividers. Within the text itself, the equivalent of tabs would be bold headings and other typographic devices to help you find your way around the material.

A manual with a strong tutorial approach may come in a binder that folds into an easel, propping up on your desk like a music stand. Other features include a fold-out or separate card that gives an overview of all the commands and how to find your way around the package. These can be in a flow chart or linked boxes or other visual devices that act as a route map. The one for the *Friday!* package is shown overleaf.

A debatable point about manual quality is whether it should show pictures of what the screen looks like (*screen images*) after you have entered various types of commands. This can be helpful and reassuring but also demanding

Friday!

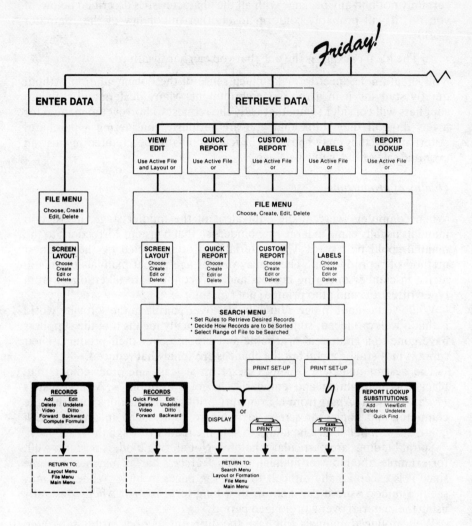

ENTER DATA	RETRIEVE DATA

	VIEW/ EDIT	QUICK REPORT	CUSTOM REPORT	LABELS	REPORT LOOKUP
	Use Active File and Layout or	Use Active File or	Use Active File or	Use Active File or	Use Active File or

FILE MENU
Choose, Create
Edit, Delete

FILE MENU
Choose, Create, Edit, Delete

SCREEN LAYOUT	SCREEN LAYOUT	QUICK REPORT	CUSTOM REPORT	LABELS
Choose Create Edit or Delete	Choose Create Edit or Delete	Choose Create Edit or Delete	Choose Create Edit or Delete	Choose Create Edit or Delete

SEARCH MENU
* Set Rules to Retrieve Desired Records
* Decide How Records are to be Sorted
* Select Range of File to be Searched

PRINT SET-UP   PRINT SET-UP

RECORDS	**RECORDS**			**REPORT LOOKUP SUBSTITUTIONS**
Add Edit Delete Undelete Video Ditto Forward Backward Compute Formula	Quick Find Edit Delete Undelete Video Ditto Forward Backward	or		Add View/Edit Delete Undelete Quick Find

DISPLAY   PRINT   PRINT

RETURN TO:
Layout Menu
File Menu
Main Menu

RETURN TO:
Search Menu
Layout or Formation
File Menu
Main Menu

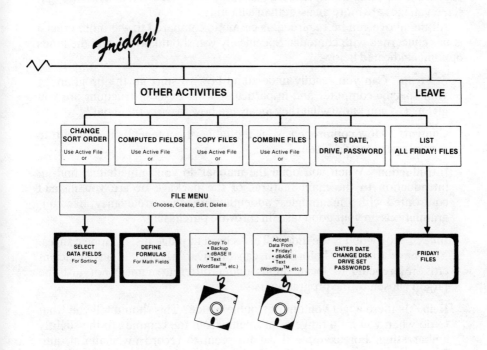

Figure 4.2 To help the user navigate around a package, some products provide a flowchart, like this one from Ashton-Tate's Friday! (Friday! is a registered trade mark of Ashton-Tate.)

of space and presentation, leading to a bulky document. On balance though, screen images are more an asset than a liability.

All the above can be regarded as cosmetic compared to the more crucial issues concerned with contents. Specifically you should investigate the kinds of points indicated below.

Start up   Can you readily understand how to start up the program on your specific computer and in particular what exact instructions are you given? Do you know what they mean and how to carry them out?

Contents   How comprehensive is the table of contents; is it a substitute for a proper, detailed index?

Introduction   When you open the manual do you immediately find an introduction to the main features of the package or are you instead confronted with a meaningless addendum or other irrelevancy, like congratulations on your good taste in software purchasing?

Index   How good is the index? This is hard to judge just by appearances. You have to use it before you can discover whether it has sufficient cross-referencing to locate items under different names, not just the jargon chosen by the programmers.

Help   Is there a 'get you out of trouble' guide? This should tell you what to do when you hit a range of problems from the complex to the slightly embarassing. For example 'I cannot seem to record my material onto disk.' To which the reply might be 'Please check that you have inserted the disk properly and that it is formatted'.

Style   How readable is the writing style? Do you feel that the writer is patient or wants to cram information into you in large indigestible chunks, such as complicated statements plus half a dozen codes that you are supposed to enter?

Are there reassuring, conversational-style comments? For instance *Files and Folders*, produced by the Starcom Computer Corporation, has plenty of these:

You made a mistake? One of your boxes is not the same as the illustration. That's easy to fix.
Recheck your screen. It's OK? Good. Press EXIT to make the next set of function keys available.
By now you are saying, 'I would like to see this Database work. '
But we haven't illustrated all of *Files and Folders*' bells and whistles yet. OK, we'll illustrate more features in our later illustrations.

Complexity   How complex is the writing and hence possibly the program itself? Test this by opening the manual at random and read a page or two. If you have to struggle to follow what is being said and many terms are unknown codes or sequences of instructions, assume that the manual is not going to be a tower of strength.

Size   Do not assume that because a manual is dauntingly bulky it is necessarily hard to master, or even that it will take an exceptionally long time to complete. Firstly, manuals are seldom read from cover to cover. Secondly, to explain instructions absolutely clearly can sometimes take a surprising amount of space. A chunky manual may merely mean that the producers have painstakingly broken down instructions into easily under-stood stages.

Examples   Are there plenty of examples in the text? Look for signs that the author really wants to explain to you how the program works. Several worked examples in each section is an indication that help is available not merely in using the program, but for learning how to use it.

Error messages   Look for a list of the error messages that can arise while using the package and whether these are understandable. Is there a technical section in case you get ambitious and want to discover or even alter some detailed aspect of the package? Is there a brief glossary of terms used in the manual?

Musts and wants   Finally, use the list of musts and wants devised earlier, to check through the manual and decide if the package matches your requirements.

SUMMARY

Please see the end of the next chapter.

5   Seven Steps Continued

STEP FIVE: DEMONSTRATIONS AND PERSONAL TRIAL

With computers there is no substitute for personal, hands-on experience. In choosing management software this crucial step decides whether you waste days, weeks or even months. Miss this step or conduct it badly and you may never turn the computer into a viable personal tool.

You are seeking to achieve two main aims:

- a detailed personal presentation by an informed user of the package so that you gain an understanding of the strengths and possible weaknesses of the software

- an opportunity to try out the software yourself under certain predetermined conditions

The only time when you might consider dispensing with these two requirements is with software costing perhaps under £50 where an informed risk might be justified. For any other package these two steps are mandatory if you are to buy with confidence.

Ideally both the demonstration and your own trial of the software should occur on equipment identical to that which you either own or intend to use regularly. Software on a different make of computer, or even a different model of the same machine, may not work properly and its performance could vary drastically from how it looked during the demonstration.

The best example of this happening is when the software is demonstrated on a computer using a hard, instead of a floppy disk. On the hard disk a program may perform like lightning, while with a floppy it slows to a positively pedestrian pace. Also, what appears fast during a demonstration may soon come to seem irritatingly slow once you are totally familiar with what is supposed to happen.

Demonstrations

A serious demonstration lasts perhaps an hour or more. Less than that, for a program costing say £350, is inadequate. You should see the program used by an informed user, not someone who blunders around wasting your time with faulty knowledge.

If the person demonstrating the package is not particularly familiar with it, although they can find their way around it you may gain a misleading impression. They will almost certainly avoid tackling difficult tasks and by sticking to simple routines make the package appear too easy. The reverse can also occur. Their fumblings and errors can make the package seem needlessly complex.

To provide a comprehensive demonstration of a package is an expensive investment by a dealer or software supplier. Only request one if you have:

- narrowed down your choice of possible packages to a short list of three or four

- short-listed three or four potential software suppliers

- a serious intention of buying at least one of these programs

- done your homework on defining your musts and wants and studied the manual or supporting material

- set aside enough time to see the demonstration

- given the dealer or supplier adequate notice that you require a comprehensive demonstration and an indication of the particular musts and wants that you are seeking

During a well-managed demonstration it is easy to become lulled into watching the other person's fingers flying over the keys. Combined with trying to follow what is happening this leaves little time for thinking critically. Use the lists of musts and wants to force yourself to discover clear answers to whether and how the program does what you want.

Take along some real life examples of work that you would be doing on the computer. Ask the demonstrator to use them and watch carefully the routines that are required. The package may have sample files and tasks that have been devised to make the demonstration look impressive, so how does it perform when it has to process *your* data?

It helps a great deal if you are looking for a specific result from a particular piece of software. For example, one manager wanted to produce a set of data as two single-line statements, followed by lengthy additional data. He also wanted to sort this in different ways.

Numerous demonstrations appeared to show that certain packages could do this job in different ways. But by insisting on seeing his own 'live' data used and then displayed in its final form on the screen, eventually he identified only two packages that could do the job properly and, above all, simply.

Always remember that there are tricks to every trade, including selling software. If you watch a database being demonstrated, for example, it is perfectly legitimate to use only 50 records, or 500 records with only a few fields on them. The results may give a spurious impression of speed and power, the truth only being revealed when there are say 1000 records each with a substantial amount of data recorded on them.

Similarly a word processor presentation can appear slick and appealing but cumbersome procedures or missing features may never be mentioned.

Personal trial

Various methods exist to enable you to gain this essential experience. If you work for a large organisation which owns a package in which you are interested you may be able to borrow it for a few days or even weeks. Even if you do not have this advantage aim for something similar.

One way of achieving this is where the dealer or supplier offers a demonstration disk. This may be available either free or at a low price, the cost to be credited against the eventual purchase of the package.

Demonstration packs are usually crippled disks. That is, they are usually the real package but without certain key facilities, such as the ability to print, or to handle more than say 20 records. Alternatively, the demonstration disk may contain all the package, but you are locked out of using some of it without a special secret code which may be unique to that particular disk.

Another way that you may be able to organise a personal trial is through a local computer club, though usually the members are not there for that purpose and might not be the best people to ask for help at this stage.

A different form of club that might assist is a user club associated with the particular package. The members are all users of the system and may only be too glad to share their knowledge about a package, warts and all.

Another possibility is to contact one of the NCC Microsystems Centres around the country. These centres possess a large stock of the more popular programs and for a small fee you can book time to try the packages of your choice. There is usually an informed member of staff to answer your queries and you may well be able to use the package on an identical make and model of machine to your own.

Even if the centre does not own the program ask if the supplier is prepared to lend it, to be used under their supervision. In practice this means the centre promises that it will ensure that you will not pirate the software by making an illegal copy.

Once you have finally got your hands on the software package, perhaps only for an hour or so, what do you look for? Firstly, you will be checking on your list of musts and wants, finding out by personal experience what is involved in achieving these particular results.

Secondly you establish how easy the program is to use and a useful technique is the flying blind test. The latter is a software supplier's nightmare since, to be fair, few programs emerge with full marks.

Flying blind

Use the program without any reference to the written instructions. See how far you travel with just your own ability and help from the program itself. If you have previously reviewed the manual you will gain an even better idea of ease of use by adopting this approach.

On this test, for instance, one bestselling database package is a resounding flop. Right at the start all you see is a single dot on the screen and it is equally hard going after that. Despite its phenomenal commercial success that particular package is totally unsuitable for the average manager and the flying blind test demonstrates it with brutal clarity.

There are two kinds of software users. Those who like to study the manual and work systematically through from beginning to end and those who enjoy thrashing around the package testing different features until they get the hang of the whole thing.

If you have plenty of time then you can afford to be the second type. But if you have only limited access before buying it, then it makes sense to use the time efficiently, discovering answers to certain basic questions of which many are simple to pursue. They include the ones that follow below.

Menus or commands Is the package menu-driven? That is, does it display multiple choices regularly so that you won't need to keep referring to the manual? The alternative, in which you use coded instructions (*command-driven* programs), demands far more from the user in terms of looking up and learning codes. But once learned, these programs are usually much quicker to use. Can menus be abandoned as you become confident or are they always there and unavoidable?

Help Does the program offer plenty of help screens? That is, when you get stuck in the middle of trying to make something happen can you press a key to obtain instant help? How clear is this advice and is it really problem-orientated (related to the activity in which you are currently engaged) or so general that it is useless?

A good quality indicator of on-line advice is whether you can demand help at several levels. You are saying 'Help! I don't understand what your help means. Tell me more'. If you are impressed with the amount of help offered, check a follow-up point. Such help facilities absorb large quantities of disk space. Eventually you are likely not to need such assistance. Can you then remove the help files from the ones you intend to use regularly or is it built in permanently?

Prompts When the program offers specific prompts for you to take some action (*program prompts*), where do these appear on the screen? Are they always in one consistent place, or do they keep popping up all over the place? How are these prompts presented? For instance, are they mainly codes which then need translating via a help screen or a manual, or are they in straightforward English? In particular are the prompts presented in instantly readable form or a confusing mess of highlights and different text sizes? You will be seeing these many times over and you could soon come to love or hate them!

Commands How many regularly-used sets of instructions are there and how easy are these going to be to learn?

Function keys Does the program use your computer's special purpose (*function*) keys so that, for example, by pressing them you can avoid using a more complicated routine to achieve the same result?

Blank screen When using the program does the screen suddenly go virtually blank for any reason; if so, is it clear what to do next?

Deliberate mistakes   What happens when you play dirty and deliberately make a mistake or defy warnings not to do something? For example, on some packages you may get a message that threatens 'You must return to the main menu after completing this task or you may risk not recording all the data'. Since this is precisely what you may do in a hurry, discover what such a warning means.

Hang up   Does the program grind to a halt (*hang up*) for any reason, leaving you with a screen on which absolutely nothing can be made to happen? While the simple answer may be to start up (*reboot*) the program again, this could cause a major problem in a real working situation.

Frozen screen   A variation on the hang up theme is the frozen screen effect. Because you do not remember what key to press next, absolutely nothing will move. Or you keep getting an error message that implies 'Do it again correctly!' If pressing keys like escape, control, finish, home or menu still produces no result, this could be a real weakness. When later it is revealed that you should have pressed the UNDO key your view of that particular program may be less than enthusastic.

Foolproofing   What happens when you hit illegal keys or, while the package is performing some important job like sorting a set of records, you do stupid things such as remove the disk temporarily and insert a different one and try to continue, or hit all the keys at once by putting a whole hand on the board? A good program will cope with all these events.

File/field names   If you try to use a file or field name which is longer than the amount permitted does the package refuse to proceed or simply shorten the name without asking if this is acceptable?

Printer   If you don't have a printer connected, will the program seize up and refuse to work?

There are many techniques that can be used but you are not evaluating this package for a multiplicity of users and producing a sophisticated analysis of program weaknesses. As a practising manager you merely want to discover whether the software works well coping with the main problem areas that the above questions cover.

Two concerns that you may not be able to check easily are:

Data transfer   Can you transfer data between this program and another that you may own or be thinking of buying? For example can the two packages share the same information, such as between a word processing system and a spreadsheet?

Full disk   What happens if you fill a floppy with information and are in the middle of working with some important data? Does the package enable you to store the work in the computer memory on the last remaining disk space or, as second best, can you insert a new, ready to use, disk and record the information on it?

It is possible to test both these situations if you have time and know-how. It is probably better though, to ensure that you find out the answers by directly questioning the dealer.

For one package to use the files created by another, the information has to be stored in a universally recognised language. The most widely accepted one is the American Standard Code for Information Interchange (ASCII, pronounced 'az-key'). The dealer or manual will quickly reveal if the package can use the ASCII code for accepting (*importing*) and sending (*exporting*) data, not only to other programs but to other machines.

Check form

The above points are guidelines, do not expect to be able to cover them all during one visit to a dealer. It may take several trips. The important task is to prepare carefully so that you systematically check musts and wants over whatever period you have allowed for evaluating the packages. It may also be helpful when visiting a dealer to use the simple assessment form shown in the previous chapter. The careful preparation that precedes demonstrations plus personal trial should help you to reach a sensible decision about which software to buy.

To reduce the whole task to its simplest you are trying to answer just three evaluative questions:

- How helpful will this package be to me as a practising manager?

- How easy will it be to use?

- Does the package do what the suppliers claim it can do?

For specific types of programs like word processors or spread sheets there are also a variety of other points to bear in mind and these are discussed later in the appropriate chapters.

STEP SIX: DEFINING BACK-UP SUPPORT

When you need help in using a package the engaged signal on your telephone acquires a whole new meaning. There you are, puzzling over how to make something happen with your software application and you want the answer *now*.

The ability to lift the telephone and obtain immediate help is a vital, often neglected, aspect of purchasing software. There are few comparable products where sales follow up is so essential. No matter how clever you are, support is likely to be needed occasionally. It is probably more crucial to you as a busy manager than to many other types of users.

The need for support explains why you should avoid buying software on the cheap. Initially the saving may be a few pounds; later, when urgent support is wanted, it may turn out to be a false economy. You could spend more than the original saving, either in cash terms or using your own time.

For example, inadequate support may cause you to run a program so inefficiently that it demands more effort than is necessary. This waste could extend over months, even years.

You can legitimately expect to receive support from two different sources. There is the original software house that created the program, though this may be located halfway round the world with no local agent in this country. Then there is the dealer or supplier, who may not be a sole distributor.

Because most of the programs that you will be buying should be the more popular ones, it is unlikely that the software house will not provide a telephone number. But check all the same. Being able to contact a software producer and ask about user problems is a normal feature of this kind of business. Be extremely cautious about buying any package where the producers cannot be contacted by telephone.

Support means:

- the supplier ensures that you receive a fault-free package with all relevant contents and readily provides replacements if the product is defective in any way. Errors in the program are dealt with free of charge

- the program comes ready to run on your particular computer without requiring any adjustments; you should not therefore have to 'install' the application

- you receive enough basic instruction to get you well underway in using the package. On a package costing say £350 you can reasonably ask for between half to one hour of personal instruction, though this may be partly contained in the full demonstration which is provided for you

- you are sold the latest version of the product. If a new one is issued shortly after purchasing you should be entitled to a free upgrade, if much later (say a year) then expect to pay a fee to upgrade your package

- the right to call the supplier for help. Different dealers offer varying arrangements and it pays to ask explicitly what help you can expect from them during the first year.

Advice is not free

Time is money to the dealer, as it is to you. Do not expect the software supplier to act as a consultant by turning the software package into a fully working system, unless you are prepared to pay for this service separately.

You can reasonably expect the supplier to answer questions about the package and its various features. Do not expect much help in applying the package to your particular problems, which is consultancy, not support.

Many dealers operate a consultancy service. In trying to sell a particular package they will stress their desire to help you achieve a successful working system. Look carefully at the true costs and benefits of this add-on support.

Abusing your support is a fast way to lose it. The supplier will quickly realise if, for example, you are not even bothering to check through the manual properly or you are being unduly slapdash in entering commands.

Good support is usually provided by a technical expert who spends most of his or her time answering new customer queries on the telephone, guiding them out of trouble spots.

Be sure to discover who deals with telephone support, checking these questions:

- Do they concentrate on one or perhaps two packages, or cover a dozen or more?

- How many people are normally on duty?

- Are they available on a special telephone line for enquiries or will you first have to queue up through the supplier's normal switchboard?

- Do they have more than one telephone line for support? How busy is it during the day and what is the average time that it takes to make contact at different times of the day? Check this point with one or two users if you can.

- Are they available during normal working hours or restricted, for example, to just afternoons?

Finally, ask how long you can expect to receive support. There may be a charge for it, either immediately or from the second year onwards.

Be clear about the distinction between a supplier who offers to answer your queries and a specifically-created hotline service that deals only with customer problems. The latter may require you to pay an annual charge and issue a special licence number that must be quoted each time that you call for help. Sometimes the service may have a free telephone number.

STEP SEVEN: IMPLEMENTATION

Having chosen and bought your software, you now have to get it working and paying you back for all the trouble taken to select it. If you are like most users, you will feel at least some thrill as you unwrap the product from its protective covering and settle down to explore its potential.

Since every person differs in how they use software, there can be no strict rules to follow. But because time is particularly precious to you as a busy manager, there are some important lessons to draw on. Some of these you will find helpful and adopt, others you may consider irrelevant.

The first suggestion in starting to use a new software package is to pace yourself. Do not expect to have it up and running in a day, producing real benefits. Allow a lead-in time of at least a month during which you can consider yourself to be learning, not using. This can be shorter with simple applications.

The fastest way to learn is by immediately applying the package to some practical problem which currently you are facing. By now, you almost certainly have several of these lined up.

Try not to commit too much real data to the new system until you are sure of what you are doing. For instance, do not start a major database containing dozens of lengthy files until you have tried out a small scale version.

Secondly, complete any tutorial that comes with the package, working your way through it systematically. Some people hate this approach, preferring to dip into the manual and gradually acquiring a feel for the product. That is fine, but it can lead to neglecting the basics which can stand you in good stead when the going gets tougher.

Experiment with as many of the features of the package as you can, even if you do not immediately master them. The idea is to gain a feel for what is possible, not to grasp fully how to make everything work.

Do not worry if some of the features seem esoteric or even useless, stick to the main ones and become familiar with these. Tackle others only as you gain confidence. For example, in learning how to use a word processing package you may not immediately need an automatic page numbering facility. Later, though, you will find yourself ready to locate this feature in the manual and try it. Once mastered, it will be added to your repertoire and you will move to new conquests.

In starting your new software application, use a small notebook in which to write reminders to yourself on how you achieved certain actions on the computer. These may merely be shorthand versions of what is in the manual. But this information will prove particularly useful if you are the kind of manager who must often leave the office to visit staff and buildings elsewhere. It may be a day or so before you return to the computer. Instead of ploughing through the manual again, the essential computer commands that you need are more easily accessible in the notebook.

If you have bought several software packages, resist the temptation to try mastering them all simultaneously. Even experts get confused with dozens of codes and it is worth remembering that in some ways you are learning a new language. Few people try to master French and Russian at the same time!

Stuck?

Never suffer in silence. Always ask! If you become seriously stuck or confused, seek help. Never spend hours trying to unravel the problem in the mistaken view that this is how you will learn.

Take all the right actions like reading the manual extra carefully, re-check the instructions that you are giving the computer, and experiment to see if the difficulty is really just a minor misunderstanding.

Also, are you tired? Would it better to stop for a while, making a fresh start tomorrow? Most people find that once they become involved in using a personal computer it is so absorbing that the hours fly by and they hardly notice their efficiency is dropping sharply.

Given the generally low quality of documentation, be ruthless about seeking help if you are starting to spend more than thirty or forty minutes on any particular problem. This might be unreasonable for a person more involved with computers but as a manager you are trying to turn the machine into a personal tool not become an expert.

These two examples suggest how essential it is to seek help once you seem to be going round in circles. Most experienced users could describe similar experiences.

One busy manager was using a new, and well-respected database system. He was well on the way to mastering many of the functions. But no matter what he did, he could not make it produce reports on the printer.

Eventually, after an hour or so, he rang the hotline service.The adviser explained patiently that there was a standard set of instructions contained in the program under the code TTY. 'But I can't find that anywhere in the manual', complained the executive. Apologetically, the hotline adviser agreed. 'I'm afraid that the manual was printed before this facility was developed and apparently no-one has yet inserted an addendum.'

The second case concerns a manager who was happily working his way through the tutorial section of the manual when the program came up with the message *File terminated unexpectedly*. He tried going back several steps but each time the same thing happened. Exasperated, he rang the suppliers. Their reply was reassuring to his dented confidence, 'Sorry! You've got a faulty set of disks, send them back and we'll replace them immediately.'

If you have a particular job for your software package that may have been tackled by other managers, it is worth spending time seeing their system in action. You may be able to track down these people through the various routes already mentioned such as user clubs, the supplier, trade and professional organisations and specialist information or advisory services.

As you familiarise yourself with your software, it should become clear that an important requirement is to prepare carefully before trying to implement any major new application.

With databases, where, for example, the wrong choice of field size may prove embarassing, invest adequate time planning the record card. It may be difficult or virtually impossible to remedy mistakes after installing the system.

The importance of careful preparation is also shown, for instance, in creating a computerised diary-keeping system. This may eventually prove a better way of controlling your appointments and personal schedule. But first gain a clear idea about what information is really needed and how you are going to use it alongside your secretarial or clerical support. Avoid plunging in immediately, attempting to put a whole year's activities on disk. Instead, try using it for just one or two weeks and then review.

Define how often and how much information will be needed to maintain any system before fully implementing it. Some packages, like *Everyman*, make the user go through phases of creating a working model:

defining the model
testing it with limited, but live data – any changes destroy the live data
full implementation

As a manager you will have a limited capacity to input data personally and if you have to rely on someone else the system may soon be out of your immediate control. If you come to rely on a particular system that you have created and the person putting in the data is sick or away, will you be left with this chore?

Floppy disks may be a great invention but they can be a source of total confusion if you fail to document what you are doing, for example by labelling them properly. As you expand your use of the software the number of files will escalate and so probably will the number of disks.

Keep everything carefully labelled. Retain one set of disks for your experiments and learning, and another for storing important data.

Avoid the temptation to squeeze too much information on one disk. This may merely give you an unnecessary headache analysing which files to delete and which to retain.

SUMMARY

The seven steps in selecting software are: preparation and investigation, clarifying musts and wants, finding a dealer/supplier, assessing documention, demonstrations and personal trial, defining support and implementation.

Read reviews of software for help in assessing a product.

Check in published software selectors what various packages offer.

Use published guides on software features, consider if it is worth using consultants, approach professional bodies and think through what kind of output you need by asking yourself what you want the software to do.

Distinguish between a software producer, a publisher and a distributor.

No matter how talented you may be or how much time you invest in computing, you are going to need help after you have bought a software package.

Preferably use a supplier who specialises in the package you want to buy.

Assess a supplier's stability as a commercial concern.

Review the supplier using criteria listed above, such as how much stock is carried, the amount of effort put into your particular problem, whether you can borrow the system and so on.

Always ask 'Can I make back-up copies of this software?'

Remember that software is normally non-returnable.

Only purchase by mail if it is a cheap program or you have an existing copy.

There are no industry standards for software documentation and most of it is terrible.

Review the documentation using the kind of criteria given above, such as readability, whether there is a guide on handling trouble, whether you can understand the installation instructions and so on.

Use your lists of musts and wants to check through the manual to assess if the package will do what you require.

Check carefully the type and amount of follow up support you can expect.

Begin applying your package to small, experimental problems; do not commit yourself to putting in too much live data till you are confident and properly prepared.

Never suffer in silence, *ask!*

6   *Training*

'It takes a lot of time to learn a personal computer package, which means a lot of money, and the training that people get is generally appalling.' This damning view of what you can expect if you make the wrong training decision comes from David Ferris, the managing Director of Ferris Corporation, a training firm with offices in both Britain and America.

For many managers computer training is a dismal prospect. It is why they have not yet made the important switch from general computer awareness to practical computer know-how. The situation is caused by the failure of so many computer courses to send their students away able to use a software package and build it into their daily work routines.

If you are a successful manager you may have many subordinates, some of whom have been trained to use the computer or have learned to use one in their own time.

If you are involved in supervising and policy issues you may have little time for either training in computers or for learning-by-doing during the working day. Thus you may well have to rely on junior staff to perform the kind of data manipulation and word processing that computers do so well.

It is thus easy to conclude that the computer is not for you but for other people, particularly subordinates. Tackling this problem has been a matter of concern for a number of major employers around the world.

HANDS-ON FOR MANAGERS

In a windowless room deep in a Hartford, Connecticut office block, 15 executives are coming to terms with the computer and using software. Two instructors prod them to thumb reluctantly through the loose-leaf training manuals to locate the exact mixture of numbers and letters that will make the programs work. One frustrated novice complains, 'I run a $300 million division on a daily basis and I can't find the A on the keyboard.'

At United Technologies, the giant conglomerate that makes Otis elevators, Carrier air-conditioners and Sikorsky helicopters, about 1,100 of the executives in the firm, who earn $50,000 a year and upwards are taking three-day courses on personal computing.

United Technologies (UT) discovered that to many managers computers meant just another expensive status symbol. They decided to find a remedy. A principle aim of the project was to acquaint executives with the possibilities of the personal computer.

John Bennett, head of corporate processing at UT, has predicted that 'only 20 per cent will become day-to-day users, another 40 per cent will use theirs occasionally and I suspect the remainder of the computers will drift towards users' homes.'

A controller at UT, Robert J. Bertini, took his machine home 'so I could make mistakes in private' and after three weeks of self-training felt that his productivity had increased by 10 per cent. Another top manager, Stephen Melvin, who heads an aircraft manufacturing division in the same firm found the training sessions 'humbling, like golf.'

From the UT experience, the significant fact emerges that despite many executives passing through the training, early estimates have suggested that less than one in five managers employs his personal computer daily on the job and about the same proportion switch it on occasionally.

Rethink

The recognition that computers have not reached thousands of otherwise perfectly competent managers, has prompted a rethink by the computer industry about minimising the need for training. New forms of easy to use software and simpler machines have followed.

But the need for effective training remains if managers are to make the computer a personal tool, rather than an aid used around the office. There is so often a lack of clarity about what kind of training is needed for managers that it is worth emphasising that you should be judging any proposed training not by whether you become better informed, but by whether you acquire actual skills in using the machine. With computers, understanding must be linked inextricably with doing.

As a manager primarily concerned with mastering enough of the software to make it useful, training is not an area that you can afford to delve into too deeply. It would not make much sense, for instance, attending a three-day training seminar on evaluating, selecting and using computer software packages. These are mainly aimed at people concerned with specialist roles such as system design and data processing.

The three main training issues for the average working manager to establish are:

- the nature and quality of the training
- the specific training objectives of a course
- the cost in money and time

NATURE AND QUALITY OF TRAINING

When computers were sold a few years ago software and training were included in the price. Because training seemed somehow free, the quality and content were seldom the subject of much scrutiny. Nowadays training costs are often equal to the combined price of the hardware and software.

The 'training comes free' inducement has thus now almost ended. Recently in Britain, the first training course was offered in which part of the advertised attraction was a 'free' personal computer.

The training that you should be seeking as a practising manager must be 'hands-on' experience. In other words, if a large part of the course is not spent actually sitting at a computer and gaining practical experience under an experienced instructor, then you will almost certainly be wasting your time and money.

In some ways a hands-on course is a contradiction in terms. By definition, if the real learning stems from doing it yourself how can a course sitting at a computer help? The main benefit is that part of the course will provide a rapid overview of the field, whether that's a particular software package or a whole area of software, such as spreadsheets. Also, you will not be forced to wrestle with certain simple problems that are only solved at the price of acquiring keyboard-phobia and a tension headache.

A hands-on course provides a flying start. It gives your confidence a boost, leaving you ready to explore the software package in more depth.

Courses seem to be aimed at either absolute beginners or those who are advanced users. So check carefully the level at which the training is pitched and do not assume that you are a complete beginner. If you have read this far without skipping, you have a useful grasp of the main areas that many courses are going to cover. It's the hands-on working at a computer with informed guidance that you need most.

For beginner courses you can expect to spend between one and two days learning the basics and having the experience of trying out computer commands, and perhaps experimenting with certain easy to use facilities of a few software packages.

The Microsystems Centres, for instance, offer three introductory hands-on courses:

Micro Computer Appreciation. Two-day hands-on trot.
Financial Modelling on Micros. One-day 'how to choose'.
Databases for Micros. One-day 'how to choose'.

These are highly practical sessions supervised by experienced computer staff. There will usually be six or more other students but everyone has a significant period personally experimenting at one of several machines.

Most basic training consists of how to switch the machine on and do some of the basic housekeeping tasks like copying disks and making back-up copies and so on. Software courses concentrate on getting you started with the package, installing it on the machine, if that is necessary and not completed by the supplier, and doing some simple tasks using your own data if that is available.

Where can you go for basic training? There are variety of sources, these include:

the company that produced the original software
software and hardware, distributors

specialist computer training agencies
consultants
general training agencies
technical colleges and other bodies such as the Microsystems Centres
user's own organisation

Although training for a particular software package may sometimes be described as 'free', you pay for it as part of the original purchase price.

A package may be less of a bargain than it appears once you discover that there is either no training supplied, or that what passes for training is a cursory two hour canter over the main functions, in company with several other recent purchasers.

Many buyers ask their dealer for training because they believe in retaining a single source for all their computing needs. But in practice, dealers often sub-contract such training to specialist firms or individuals.

It is therefore worth discovering from the seller exactly who is going to provide the training and whether they are on the supplier's full-time payroll. If not, it may be cheaper and better to go direct to the training company.

Since quality of training is what matters, you need to consider whether it would be better to have training at your place of work instead of the seminar approach where several people are taught in the classroom, usually at a special training company.

Opinion is evenly split amongst computer experts about the need for one-to-one training conducted at the customer's own site. It is usually more expensive but often far more effective.

SPECIFIC TRAINING OBJECTIVES

The vague aims of many management training courses are probably all too familiar. Computer training is no different. There are no clearly recognised standards, although increasingly attempts are being made to define them. Circuit UK, for example, a specialist training firm, has worked with the Royal Society of Arts to produce computer courses with a recognised content and level of achievement.

Try to nail down exactly what a course is trying to teach. Apart from the general statement that it is an 'introductory hands-on course' for a package or whatever, a good training programme will also have some clearly stated end results.

These results should be expressed as what the trainee will be able to do by the end of the course. The prospectus for a course on using the MS-DOS operating system might state that after completion trainees will be able to:

copy a disk
format a disk
create a file
rename a file
copy a file

display the contents of a file
delete a file
change the current disk drive
display the amount of RAM memory
examine the free space on a disk
create a directory and display the current directory

There might be some more intangible aims, such as a general understanding of operating systems and how they work. But if you cannot identify some definite skills that will be acquired, look elsewhere for training.

Dealers and software houses offer different levels of training for software. Pre-sales courses give a guide to what a particular package can do and might, for instance, include a comparison of more than one type of spreadsheet program. User courses are designed to teach purchasers how to make the best use of their investment.

A good example is the training run by Compsoft Ltd, to support its best selling database package, called *Delta*. One-day training sessions are run regularly at the company's beautiful manor house, set in its own grounds near Guildford. Trainees are brought up to a level of confidence that should allow them to go 'live' without more assistance. Anyone who has not used a computer before is given extra help during the practical session.

The morning is devoted to working through a training routine covering file creation, entering records, sorting and searching files, printing reports, writing letters and so on. The afternoon is spent on interpretation of particular applications and learning how to mould the software to a student's unique needs. A more advanced one-day course takes one deeper into the mysteries of *Delta*.

One-day or two-day training courses, like those for *Delta* which teach you about a particular package, are now common. Look closely at what they intend to cover and in how much depth. There is widespread evidence that students return from product introduction courses feeling that the time available was simply not long enough. If you are going to be in a classroom situation with ten other people you may not receive the attention that you need.

In choosing a training course you are also selecting the training agency; it is worth asking some basic questions such as the ones below.

Qualifications How qualified are the trainers? Someone who knows a package inside out is not necessarily the best person to teach the absolute beginner. A well-trained instructor, as well as a merely knowledgeable one, suggests that the firm is committed to trying to do the job properly.

Reputation How much of the training activity represents repeat business? A company that has a record of regularly providing introductory and advanced courses to larger organisations is probably a sounder choice than a small firm that offers a cheap deal.

Hands-on How much of the course will be spent actually at the computer? That is, how much hands-on experience backed up with trained guidance, can you expect?

Hardware   How much hardware is available on which to learn? Will there be enough to go around? Finding that there are twice as many students as machines may mean a queue and unwelcome pressures once it is your turn.

Systems   What kind of equipment is available? How closely does it match yours? There may only be minor differences between learning to use a software package on one machine compared with another, but sometimes there are significant changes that may make the training less valuable.

Documentation   What kind of supporting documentation is provided as part of the course?

Testimonials   What do people who have been on the course think of it? Has it helped them, for instance, learn to use their software or merely reduced their anxiety levels?

For specific software applications basic training should offer a painless introduction and advanced courses a consolidation of knowledge. Since learning about a package usually stems from the often unavoidable sweat of sitting at a computer keyboard, it really is worth carefully assessing the extent to which any proposed training is likely to be effective.

COSTS

Training is normally charged on a daily basis. The prices quoted by specialist firms are usually slightly lower than those of dealers, since the latter's overheads are spread less thinly.

At the beginning of 1985, the rate was between £125 and £150 a day. Most of the successful computer dealers offer some kind of course at these kinds of rates. However, firms that run the same courses frequently, in support of a particularly successful software package, often charge much less.

As indicated above, the price of training will tend to be less when it is provided in bulk to a group of perhaps ten students. But a more personalised form of tuition may be far more effective, particularly when orientated around your own particular work problems.

The cost may also be more justified if you have done some preparation in advance, either by reading or perhaps by trying out a particular package and beginning to identify areas where you feel help would be needed.

The big users of computer training are the large corporations. They have recognised the benefits and also have the resources to pay for managers to take time off to train. Smaller firms find the costs a deterrent, yet may spend more money buying additional help to rescue their stranded computer systems.

The cost of computer training is rising rapidly. For the average manager wanting to use the computer as a personal tool the investment should almost certainly not exceed more than around half the price of the hardware in the first year.

Although it would be unwise to expect training bargains, there may some that are worth pursuing. For example, during one year one specialist firm offered an exceptional deal in which for an overall investment of around £250, customers could attend as many courses run by the company as they wanted. The firm stopped the deal after a year but another offered a similar arrangement at the start of the next year, this time charging £500 a person. The only drawback was that busy managers could not afford the time to go on more than one or two training events. But the arrangement was certainly good value for money.

SELF-TUITION

Desmond will teach you about microcomputers and never get impatient or tired. If you want to examine the uses of microprocessors in the home and work environments Desmond will spend hours giving you friendly, personal tuition. His name stands for Digital Electronic System Made Of Nifty Devices, which is part of an Open University education pack originally developed for teachers. Desmond is now available to managers and anyone else who is willing to spend just over £100 and dedicate about 40 hours of study to the subject. It is a teaching machine based on a micro chip.

Increasingly computer training is relying on using the computer itself. Thus many software packages now come equipped with a self-instruction disk and a specially prepared manual. A software package with a self-tuition disk may prove far more effective than a one-day training course. People learn in different ways, a combination of disk-based tuition and a training course may be sensible.

Some software producers go to great expense to create really powerful disk-based training in support of their software products. An effective training disk, for example, is the *DataMaster* tutorial, which is almost like a film. It develops a definite pace to keep the student's attention, and even uses graphics to help liven up the learning process. Working your way through the disk and the written practice examples would probably be a better investment of time than a one-day presentation by a consultant.

Many training packages based on the floppy disk are sold in their own right, that is, separately from any software application. Most are cheap, often £50 or less, and teach generalised subjects like an introduction to computers, the MS-DOS operating system or how to use the keyboard. Others, like MicroCal's *Hands on dBase II*, or Microguide's tutorial on *WordStar*, are interactive training programs aimed at purchasers of the applications software.

The best time to buy a tutorial disk is before or at the same time as obtaining your main software package. If you have to send for the tutorial it may arrive long after you have made sufficient progress on your own using the manual.

Some software producers have adopted audio cassettes as a way of training. Cassettes are now well established for word processing programs. Other subjects are also being produced by suppliers as a key element in their training strategy.

ICL, for example, is one major corporation now applying the principle of self-training to the company environment. Its Traderpoint retail outlets are selling a series of training packs based around audio cassettes and book courses. These cover learning to use the more popular operating systems, *WordStar* word processing, a course on simple programming and so on.

With cassette-based learning the danger is that one might be merely buying a boring series of lectures that are not particularly demanding of the student. The presentation is therefore important. One critic reported that the tutor on the ICL tapes sounded 'almost as if the chap's giving a lecture in front of a seething crowd of drunken students. In short, he sounds nervous.'

As with the disk-based tutorials, the problem is finding the time to plough through the training program in an undisturbed environment. It demands considerable discipline to complete 20 or more hours of automated tuition.

However, learning in the privacy of your own mistakes is an attraction which, combined with the cost advantages, will probably make this method of training increasingly common.

Since a well-produced tutorial will definitely save wasted hours at the keyboard and may also reduce or eliminate the need to attend a software training course, investigate the merits or otherwise of a package's tutorial.

If the tutorial does not use a disk with an interactive program (that is, where you the student take part and practise different tasks) then it is no different to a text book and should be judged by that criterion.

In evaluating tutorial disks as a possible source of personal training you are trying to decide whether they might be a substitute for a more expensive and time consuming course.

The issues to investigate include the following.

Time   How long will it take to work through the tutorial? In other words, how much training is being provided? You could find that most of the disk is filled with dummy information to show worked examples, without student involvement.

Objectives   What exactly is the program supposed to teach you to do by the end of it? You are trying to gain a picture of the learning experience that is being offered.

Manual   Is the disk tutorial linked to a written manual? Is this relegated to the back of the main manual or a completely separate item? If the written part is placed at the start of the main manual at least the authors have recognised how important it is to teach you to use the product.

Documentation   Do you have to complete any documentation as you progress or is the tutorial solely confined to the screen interaction? Making the student keep a record of progress can indicate that the authors have a sound grasp of learning theory.

Structure   How is the program structured? Are there a series of discrete modules or does the program run straight through from beginning to end? A modular approach is more flexible.

Level   Is the tutorial written at one level or is there a beginner's section followed by a more advanced one?

Continuation   If you do not complete the tutorial in one session will the program remember where you have reached? Some tutorials demand that you start at the beginning each time, others permit you to continue where you left off.

Unfortunately, many perfectly good software packages are sold without any tutorial, other than perhaps a written version at the back of the manual.

Because a software application is without a proper tutorial does not mean the package is no good or that training is not available. Similarly because a package does include a tutorial disk, do not assume that it will avoid the need to go on a proper training course.

SUMMARY

Training is an important aspect of learning how to use management software.

Check the nature and quality of any training facility, the specific training objectives, time and money implications.

Hands-on courses are essential.

Introductory courses usually last about one or two days.

Courses may be general or based around a particular package.

Check such matters as qualification of trainers, time spent at the computer under supervision, type of equipment available, supporting documentation and the opinions of previous students.

Identify specific skills that will be taught on a training course.

Do not expect training bargains; the average cost at the start of 1985 was £125–150 per day of training.

A self-tutorial disk-based training program may be more effective than a seminar style course.

A tutorial that is not interactive, making the student respond to the computer, is no different to a lecture, and probably no more effective.

Check how long it takes to complete a tutorial and what the program teaches. Also whether it is linked to a written tutorial, has different levels of difficulty and remembers where you leave off each time.

Do not be over-impressed just because a software package offers a tutorial, investigate what is really involved. A training course may still be a sensible, worthwhile decision.

7 Word Processing

'They're selling word processors like soap powders these days', the director of a small software firm complained recently, 'We've decided not to promote our WP package any more, we can't afford the advertising costs.'

Word processing, or WP, is now commonplace. Publicity and a continuous flurry of new products mean that few managers are unaware of its existence. It uses the computer to handle typing and editing jobs that once took forever on a traditional typewriter.

Busy managers develop a love-hate relationship with WP. On the one hand, fast results of incredible quality can be obtained. On the other, more flexibility and increased capacity to edit text encourages ever more finely tuned drafts. These can create more, not less pressure, on the available typing resources. The total time to complete a finished document can actually increase, not diminish.

PERSONAL GAINS

Once, few managers would be seen dead tapping at a keyboard. Personal computers have made working at a keyboard respectable. Executives are increasingly prepared to seek the substantial gains from using word processing as a personal tool.

What are these gains? Do they really offer benefits that match those of having a personal secretary doing the donkey work or an efficient typing pool?

For most busy managers the time when WP will really become a spectacular tool is some years off. When you can dictate direct to a computer which understands all the words spoken and types them out just like a secretary, then a new age will indeed have arrived. This era remains distant. Meanwhile, practising managers need to look carefully at what WP can do for them personally, and whether it is worth weening themselves from total dependence on secretarial support.

Amongst the benefits of personally using word processing are:

- putting thoughts down on paper and getting the finished product to the recipient(s) faster

- reports can evolve naturally as successive drafts are refined

- less reliance on typing staff and the delays which occur just when an urgent job arrives

- creation of reports, memos, letters and other documents that can be sent instantly across the country or around the world in seconds using ordinary telephone lines

- the ability to send and receive telex messages without reliance on an intermediary

- an easier time preparing elaborate reports that demand a variety of different functions such as incorporating financial tables, creating graphics, analysing data held on a database and so on

- greater confidentiality for documents

Finally a hidden benefit that cannot be over-valued is the educational spinoff. Word processing is an important route to gaining greater confidence in learning to use a personal computer.

For example, while using WP you perform all the common tasks associated with computers: creating and deleting files, examining and amending directories, making copies of disks, transferring data from one location to another, conducting searches for specific material and so on.

Confidence gained in this way leads in a natural progression to more sophisticated applications. For instance, it may stimulate you to investigate and then adopt the use of a communications package. The latter will almost certainly demand that you, the manager, type material instead of always handing this job to other people.

WP PRODUCTS

Word processing is a facility provided by not one but many products:

specialist software, like *Wordcraft* or *Superwriter*, designed for personal computer use

integrated software, such as *Open Access* or *Xchange*, which offers not merely WP but other facilities such as a spreadsheet program, three-dimensional graphics, communications, time and information management and so on. You can thus swop between these different facilities which are all mutually compatible

a multi-user computer, sometimes totally dedicated just to WP applications

hardware that only performs word processing, sometimes called stand-alones

upgradable typewriters that perform many of the WP tasks and can be developed into full scale word processors

The first two of these are of immediate interest to the average manager as personal tools, and are considered here. Stand-alones in particular are too limiting in their long term potential.

Most WP software applications are sold as a single disk, not linked to any other software. Features like a spelling or grammar checker, or the ability to produce mailing lists and standard letters, may be included or sometimes sold separately.

You can often save money by purchasing packages as a suite, instead of individually. For example, *WordStar Professional*, based on a best selling WP package, contains the basic program for word processing plus a spelling checker, index and mailing list systems. The total cost of each of these is over £700 compared to buying the suite at just under £500.

At the economy end of the market a £50 package may be sufficient if your typing needs are limited. One useful tool is a package which turns the clock back and makes your printer revert to being typewriter! It allows the user to address an envelope, type a couple of labels or jot down a few points without going through more elaborate procedures. A line of text is typed on the screen and after checking for mistakes a carriage return makes the printer produce the words immediately.

WP FEATURES

A good, standard WP package offers a large range of facilities. Some of these may be immediately available on call from a simple menu, without first requiring a specific set of commands. This arrangement allows you to start with an easy to use approach, without worrying about all the choices that the package contains.

Since packages now vary in price from under £40 to over £450 it can be worth exploring what exactly they deliver for the money. Because few managers are likely to be typing their own lengthy reports on a regular basis, the need for elaborate WP facilities will normally be limited. But if you share your WP package with a secretary it may be sensible to have a more advanced product.

Amongst the more important features which a WP package should offer are those following.

Screen Rapid display of text on the screen with no perceptible delay under most conditions. Do not take this feature for granted as some well-known packages have an irritating delay if you return to alter text while still in the normal typing mode.

Simple formatting The ability to define how you want the margins, tabulation and line space arrangements to work at the beginning of each new document.

Cursor commands Fast navigational commands to move the cursor any-where on the screen and to locate instantly the top, bottom or a specified page of a document. Similarly, commands to move the cursor forwards or backwards in jumps of a single word, line and paragraph.

Wordwrap The facility to choose how many words there should be per line, after that you should not need to worry about performing carriage returns at the end of a line. In practice this means that you just type continuously as if your material were all one long line and the computer works out the spacing.

Headers and footers   The automatic repetition of standard titles and footnotes on each page of the document. This facility is a boon when producing long, complicated documents.

Pagination   Automatic page numbering.

Insert/delete   The rapid correction of letters and words merely by moving the cursor over an unwanted item and either overtyping or issuing a simple command such as delete. If an entire sentence or paragraph or more has been omitted, the computer automatically reorganises all the material to expand or close up the text.

Search and replace   The capacity to search and find a particular word or phrase throughout a document and if necessary replace this wherever it occurs with a desired alternative (global search and replace). In lengthy documents this helps locate material quickly if corrections need to be made.

Function keys   One or two key strokes on a special function key to call up commonly used words or phrases, such as your own name, job title, and telephone extension.

Cut and paste   Fast block and column movement for swopping in and out different paragraphs, drawn from either the current text or a bank of such material, to produce an infinite variety of documents.

Saving files   The saving of text onto disk for recall later, once the computer is switched off. Some WP packages insist that after entering a certain amount of text it must be saved onto disk before proceeding. While this can be a good discipline it can also be extremely irritating.

WYSIWYG   Text on the screen appears exactly as it would on the printed page (what you see is what you get.This is often abbreviated to WYSIWYG and pronounced wizzywig!). A disconcerting aspect of WP is that often a package will permit actions like underlining, emboldening a word, using double spacing, and right hand justifying but only when the text is produced on a printer. None of these features may appear on the screen and the instructions to make them happen may even be hidden from sight unless you ask to see them.

Packages vary in the extent to which what you see really is what you get (*visual integrity*). For example, few go as far as Psion System's WP application called *Quill*, which shows on the screen, italics and other more esoteric devices such as subscripts and superscripts.

Indent   Automatic indenting feature so that a whole paragraph or more can be rearranged as indented text by just one or two key strokes.

Calculation   The facility to allow you to add, multiply, divide or subtract a column of figures on screen. This avoids breaking off to use a hand calculator.

Pause print Printing can be suspended while additional text is entered before restarting printing.

Multiple copies Automatic multiple printing can be particularly helpful to a manager who wants to give a top copy to each recipient of a vitally important document.

Multi-tasking The computer can continue to be used for tasks like typing and editing while simultaneously printing out finished text.

Macros A facility for recording complete words or phrases and retrieving these at the press of one or two keys.

Advanced formatting Presentation features such as:
    justification on the right and left sides of the text
    proportional spacing to give variable gaps between words and letters to
    improve the overall appearance of text; usually also requires a printer
    with this facility
    added emphasis by underlining or emboldening letters to make selec-
    ted material stand out from the rest
    centering of words and text on a page, for example a title, using just
    one simple command

Fonts The use of different typefaces (*fonts*) to alter the style of text produced; this is governed by the printer's facilities.

Print formatting The ability to use the available facilities of the printer by incorporating any special instructions into the text, or 'piping' them direct to the printer.

It may not matter if a package lacks some of these techniques if the user has no intention of becoming their own typist. But it is surprising how, after a period using a package, one begins to want increasingly elaborate features.

For example, only some applications offer the ability to number para- graphs and sections of a report automatically so that when new ones are entered all the numbers are rearranged. This may be essential if you occa- sionally decide to type documents several pages long.

When preparing a report a manager will often work with several docu- ments at once, creating and editing one, reading another, extracting text from a third and using it in the first and so on. Some WP applications create the equivalent of this by splitting the screen into two or more sections (*windows*) each of which can be altered and handled separately from the rest.

SOME BASIC MUSTS

Any of the well known WP packages will probably be more than adequate for the average manager. Indeed, some of the low cost products now becoming available may prove better value for money. However, since WP is a building block for using the personal computer it is important to ensure that you do not choose one which you will outgrow quickly.

Because a package is popular this does not necessarily make it ideal for managerial purposes. It may have some extremely irritating features that were originally designed to assist the typist or secretary instead of being a simple, easy to use management tool. For instance, the application may indeed move blocks of text around easily, but only half a dozen lines at a time.

Ease of use with WP is obviously essential but you will only be able to assess this by using the program for a while. The manual may look inviting and well presented, but once at the keyboard you may feel differently about the program itself. Test at least two WP packages, spending a minimum of half an hour on each.

Speed

How fast is the application? There are several points of concern.

> How fast can you move the cursor over a full screen of text and then within the whole document? Try seeing what happens when you have a document of say, five pages and want to jump to the top or bottom. It should be almost instantaneous without the text having to scroll up or down.

> If you are not using a hard disk the program may take a perceptible time to perform certain basic tasks, like inserting text from one document to another or finding and replacing a word or phrase.

> How fast is a whole screen of text adjusted by the program to reform the layout, once you have initiated changes? Check whether it happens automatically each time, or whether you have to issue a special re-formatting command each time. Do not merely ask a dealer for the answer, test it yourself by changing several paragraphs in various different ways.

> Try filling the screen with text and then erasing a block and seeing how long the program takes to reorganise all the material; more than about three seconds is too long.

> As you type, is the appearance of text on the screen instantaneous? You should never be able to 'beat' the computer in typing faster than the letters appear on the screen. The one exception is when you give the computer two jobs to do at once, such as printing out text while you continue typing and editing.

Page and block handling

An important difference between packages when editing is their handling of pages, that is, information appearing on the same page when printed.

Some packages are page-based so that editing takes place one page at a time. When you complete the page the cursor is moved to a fresh page and the previous one is automatically saved on disk. This ensures that if the system fails for some reason all the changes apart from the previous page will have been recorded.

A preferable approach is the package which edits a copy of the document and only when you are satisfied with the changes are these then confirmed and the copy becomes the current version.

Check the size of document that the application can handle. Some programs require you to start a fresh document after say 10 pages. Others will only allow you to type so many lines of text before automatically starting the equivalent of a fresh page and clearing the screen.

Does the program start a new page by suddenly clearing the whole screen of text, without leaving some of the previous text as a point of reference? This can prove extremely disconcerting and occasionally inconvenient.

Can you enter the middle of a piece of text and temporarily remove all the remaining material from view, thus leaving a blank screen for new text? After adding the extra material the program should then close up the space below so that the text is now continuous again. Some programs will not clear away the space needed but insert blank lines which can be filled up indefinitely. The total clearing facility, not the line by line approach, is better.

The number of pages handled by a package is usually expressed in numbers of lines of text. A superficial look at a package may suggest that this facility is adequate. But there may in fact be a definite limit on the number of pages that can be handled. Since this effectively limits your total work space for any particular job it can sometimes be a serious limitation.

The ability to move blocks of text around is fundamental to WP, no package is likely to be missing this feature. But restrictions may exist on the size of block that can be moved; for instance it may be limited to half a dozen lines. Check on how easy it is to move blocks around.

Limitations on how many lines can be moved in one block depend on the available computer memory. Since this should not normally be a constraint with a business personal computer used for WP, you should therefore be able to move blocks of virtually any length from one part of a document to another.

Though most packages can move blocks of text around they may not handle columns of text in tables. If you prepare many tables this is a feature to check carefully before buying a WP system.

Most managers will probably not personally type documents longer than half a dozen pages, or be involved in complex block handling tasks. But if you think that you might, then check the block handling facilities and either test or enquire about the program's page handling restrictions.

Appearance on screen

When you are using a word processor what appears on the screen may be different to the final results on the printed page. If you want the screen to be a close replica of the final results then you will need a WYSIWYG package.

WYSIWYG is only important for longer documents where left and right margins, tab positions, bold print, underlinings and other layout aspects need to be seen on the screen if you are to avoid an excessive number of trial printings.

Disk full!

Imagine that you are preparing a vital report on how to reorganise your division. You decide to type it yourself, partly for security reasons but also to gain more flexibility in improving and amending it, shortly before sending it to the board of directors. In the midst of final preparations the computer announces: *Disk Full*.

With some programs a full disk can be disastrous. If it does not allow you either to insert a new disk and carry on, or to make space on the existing disk, you could reach an impasse. Text remains in the computer memory but there is no way to persuade the program to record it. If you try to insert a new disk and the system fails to record the data because, for instance, that disk is full too or faulty, then you may lose the entire material.

Ideally, the program should say what to do when a disk is full and permit one of several remedial actions that preserve recently typed text.

Compatibility

Another critical area to investigate is whether the package is compatible with other software that you might own. For example, can you extract data from a database and transfer it to your WP program for more editing? Will the WP package use a file from a spreadsheet? Similarly, if you later buy a spelling checker it will need to be compatible with the WP package.

The need to transfer files between the WP program and other applications has been one reason software producers have created integrated programs that perform a whole range of different tasks, apart from WP. In these software applications files are interchangeable.

Integrated packages are really several applications rolled into one and are consequently more expensive than single use products. One way to cope with this is to buy a program like Psion System's *Xchange*, which is produced in modular form. Each application (word processing, graphics, spreadsheet and database) is sold separately or as a combined product.

Compatibility may prove a problem with your printer too. Check that the package can be made to work (configured) with your printer and that the application can use all the print facilities which the machine provides, such as proportional spacing or varying type size.

Spelling and grammar checks

Managers presenting a report are often putting their personal credibility on the line. A perfectly sensible document can be marred and made to seem unreliable if it contains presentational errors such as spelling mistakes and ill-chosen grammar.

Although a package that checks spelling can be purchased separately from a WP application, this makes little sense for a manager who is not likely to be doing a vast amount of typing. Nowadays, many WP applications pro-grams contain their own spelling check facility. Be wary of buying or becoming too committed to using a package which does not offer this facility.

Checkers compare the words of your text against a dictionary held on file. This is usually around 20,000 words but some, like Palantir's *Speller*, have nearly 60,000 words while others are still larger.

The checker queries words that it does not recognise and either offers to change them immediately or to mark them in the text with a symbol such as a query (?). Beware of checkers that require you to go back to the text to find the error and change it there. This is time wasting. It is far better if once the mistake has been identified you are able to alter it immediately in the document itself.

Similarly a good checker will do more than just throw up a suspect word. It will show this word in a brief extract of the context in which it appears in the document.It will also make suggestions about what the appropriate word might be.

For example, with Palantir's *Speller,* if the checker finds the dubious word: suspcet, it will show the context and then respond:

> I guess:
> 1.suspect
> 2.suspects
> 3.suspected

By choosing one of the numbers you can automatically have the word inserted into the correct place in the text. Alternatively you can ask the speller to make more guesses from which to choose.

More limited checkers may merely list the dubious words or present them one at a time for a decision to be made about their accuracy. *Superwriter*, for instance, which was used for this book, offers these choices when reviewing suspect words:

> mark the word in the document
> add the word to the dictionary of 20,000 words
> ignore the word
> review decision about the previous word
> conduct a quick review in which all mismatched words are added to
> the dictionary, ignored or listed on screen or printer.

A large dictionary facility will probably only be helpful to managers if they can also use this to look up a word to check its possible spelling. If you type as much of the word as you can remember and insert blank characters such as ? or * the dictionary will suggest the proper one.

More important than a large dictionary though, is the capacity to add words to it. This is particularly useful if you are in a field where technical or jargon words abound. Over time you can build a dictionary that reflects your special words so that the checker becomes an integral tool for ensuring that complex reports are free of spelling errors.

Establish whether there is any limitation on adding words to the dictionary. Can you add words without first conducting a spelling check? Can you list words added to the dictionary and the whole dictionary or just selected parts of it? The dictionary facility should be flexible enough to allow the deletion of words and the creation of bespoke dictionaries to handle special jobs.

If a spelling checker is to be useful to a manager it must be fast to use, no matter how long the document being processed. Assess the speed by giving the program 200 words to check. More than about thirty seconds is slow.

Other features may include a word count, a thesaurus, which offers alternatives to particular words being used, and a word profile analysis. The latter can sometimes be a useful facility in a particularly long document for not only seeing whether there is excessive repetition but also for deciding how to structure raw material before it is ready to be put into report form. If certain key words or ideas keep recurring this may indicate the need for a special section on this aspect of the work.

It is also possible to buy a program which checks your grammar. This is seldom included within a conventional word processor. Many managers will conclude that this particular WP application is of limited personal value. But it can be helpful to be warned about wrong punctuation, missing parentheses, vague words like 'very', 'quite' and 'rather' or to have the chance to weed out redundant phrases like 'in order to'. Such packages will also highlight potentially misused words like 'advice' instead of 'advise' or 'accept' instead of 'except'. If you happen to be in an organisation particularly sensitive to women's rights some grammar checks will pinpoint sexist words and phrases.

Mail merge

Look at the advertisements for a WP packages and you will often see mailing list facilities offered and the ability to produce personalised letters in bulk (*mail merge*). This means that the program will usually do two separate activities.

First, it performs some of the functions of a database, allowing you to sort the data by some criteria, such as everyone who lives in Glasgow who has bought two of the firm's products, and then it creates a special mailing list, along with address labels.

Secondly, the package may allow you to use the word processor to create personalised letters by drawing on information from a master file of names and addresses. This is the mail merge facility. It may be restricted to say, 200 names or it may have a larger capacity plus extensive other facilities.

Few managers need either mail merge or mailing list facilities as a personal computer tool. For example, sending a personalised letter to all staff is a job to be delegated to a typist or a secretary.

COMPARISONS

Comparing one WP package with another is not easy since potentially many factors can be examined. These include documentation, file control, scrolling and cursor movement, insertion, block commands, searching, screen format, layout, page control, text control, document design and output control. These in turn can be broken down into over 120 different criteria.

Reviews in computer magazines often publish surveys making direct comparisons between several products and perhaps giving a star rating for items such as documentation, ease of use, amount of functions, use of the computer's facilities and value for money.

There is no universal standard for assessing WP packages and the reviews are seldom comprehensive in their coverage either of products or facilities. One of the most extensive comparisons of WP packages is Phillip Good's *The Critic's Guide to Word Processing with the IBM-PC* (Chilton Book Company 1984). This ranked 20 packages against dozens of criteria which produced a maximum attainable score of 119 points. The results of the top ten rankings were:

Spellbinder 104
Wordperfect 99
Leading Edge 84
Palantir 83
Samna 78
Superwriter 78
WordStar 77
Benchmark 76
Final Word 74
Easy Writer II 74

Another useful reference source is *The Ultimate Software Selector for Business Micros*, produced by the Federation of Microsystems Centres and published by Macmillan Press. This publication has a section devoted to WP and compares over 70 packages by 31 different criteria such as price, menu versus command-driven, display as printed, move word block, find and so on. While these are useful forms of checking a WP package, they are no substitute for using it yourself.

SUMMARY

Managers can obtain several benefits from personally using word processing, particularly as a route to gaining more familiarity with computers.

Check the main features which a WP package offers such as rapid display of text, fast navigational commands, wordwrap, automatic pagination, search and find, function keys, visual integrity, calculation facility, disk full response, compatibility with other programs and your printer.

Spelling checkers are a normal feature of the better WP applications and a useful management tool

Evaluate a package's features by reading reviews and reference books but above all, try it for yourself.

8   Databases

Just four letters spell widespread confusion in the software world: DBMS. They appear in advertisements, catalogues, articles and reviews. They usually stand for DataBase Management System(s), though you can never be absolutely sure. Often the Management (M) is omitted entirely.

DBMS means different things to different people. It is a grand term for a method of controlling a collection of information, anything from the telephone directory to a stack of customer files, from a grocery list to a complete set of employee records.

In the personal computer world the constant use of the word database has devalued it to mean practically anything that involves records held on the computer. It is important to distinguish between the concept of a database which contains information; and some method or system which then organises and controls that data.

If you kept on disk all the memoranda which you wrote using a word processor, this would be a form of database. The trouble is, analysing and controlling the material would not be particularly easy using just the WP program.

To manage the database therefore, a special program is needed which specialises in tasks such as sorting, selecting, analysing, comparing and so on. Hence the term Database Management System.

Databases are the computer equivalent of a manual card index. They are designed to handle records with a regular structure. Typically databases might be a record of staff mailing lists, stock files, telephone numbers, product lists and so on.

Once, the word database meant that information was organised so that a set of records or files were linked. Altering one key record affected all other relevant ones. One could demand certain information and the computer would find it, even if it was scattered widely over thousands of records or dozens of files.

This original ideal, of a system in which all records and files could be easily linked together, has proved hard to translate into practice without enormous computer capacity and complex programs that few people really understand.

Nevertheless, sophisticated database management systems have been developed and their impressive capabilities have led software suppliers in particular to encourage the unwary to believe that DBMS on a personal business computer means goodbye to filing cabinets. 'Buy our super-simple database system', they imply, 'and you will enter a new, paperless era.'

The reality is more prosaic. Though many database management systems are indeed powerful, few such products can completely eliminate the ubiquitous steel filing cabinet.

POWER

More important than the database itself is the ability to manipulate it, so that useful facts and information can be extracted on demand. A DBMS means being able to store, sort, locate, print and generally mess about with data.

Thus DBMS is about power. Or more accurately, control over data by you, the person who knows about the job in hand, not by some computer science graduate who writes programs but is out of touch with your particular work or set of problems.

Even today, most database management systems on a personal computer are unsophisticated. When reduced to their essentials they are often merely a form of electronic card index.

The majority of database systems store data in the equivalent of a brown folder, namely a file. The file is given a name and holds records, sometimes running into thousands. Each record is then broken down into various items or fields (see Chapter 2). These systems are sometimes called a *flat file system* because they work essentially with one record or file at a time.

When looking at advertisements, therefore, remember that although virtually every system for managing a database is called a DBMS, in fact few really have the true power implied by such a term. Acknowledging this, many packages simply call their product a database.

DATABASE CREATION

To create a database the first step is to design the way that information will be stored. In practice this means defining a blank form to complete or the equivalent of a record card that would be used in a traditional card index system.

It is usually best to design the form or record card on paper first, later transferring it to the screen. But sometimes the system you want may be so simple that it is merely a case of defining the main items (fields) as you go along. With many systems you literally start with a blank screen and type in the various field names where and how you want them. This process is often called 'painting a screen'.

Because of the power of computers it is possible to relate items of information on the record card with each other. So, for example, filling in someone's date of birth could automatically produce another item showing their current age, once today's date has been added.

Since these links between one field and another can become quite elaborate, the design stage of creating a database is often complicated. Careful planning is needed if the system is to be both efficient and also really useful. Once large amounts of data have been fed into the computer redesigning the database may prove time consuming, costly and occasionally impossible.

Only after sufficient information has been placed in the database is it worth using the various DBMS facilities. The need to input large amounts of data before a system becomes useful to a manager is often a major limitation and leads to a basic management question:

Why do I want a DBMS?

NEED FOR A DBMS

There is little point in computerising an existing system if it works fast and well. But most manual systems are capable of considerable improvement with the careful application of a database management system.

If you keep a list of personal contacts on file and would like to have the telephone number of everyone who drives a Ford car and who has not given an order recently, then a DBMS may be what you need. Can your file locate all the names that seem roughly similar, like Steven, Stevans, Stevenson or Stephenson? Would you like to know which of your staff last had a training course and the average length of time spent on it? Have you a need to mail a selected group of people from a large list of possible targets? All these applications may indicate that you could gain from using a database management system.

The majority of DBMS that are created though, are designed not as personal tools for a busy manager but as an improved office system. There may be important spinoffs for managers but this is not the same as having your own personal database and making it an aid in your daily work.

A useful database is usually part of a larger system and may also be linked to a word processor, a communications package or a spreadsheet.

You may discover that you have a limited need for using a DBMS as a personal management tool unless it is part of a much larger system, probably available to many other people too. Because you can keep all your telephone contacts on a database does not always mean that doing so makes sense. It may be simpler and quicker to stick with that small ring binder in your left hand drawer.

Most managers are busy doing a full day's work consisting of a series of tasks that they perform reasonably well. Unless the database improves the productivity of such tasks it may simply be an electronic frill.

As a practising manager, therefore, you must avoid becoming involved with a complex system which will demand large amounts of your personal time to learn, create and operate. Most personal databases used by active, energetic managers are designed to help them keep track of certain information, to control their job of achieving change or to improve their ability to communicate with other managers.

Too many first class managers are turning into second rate programmers by trying to use database systems either unnecessarily or at too high a level of complexity.

OPTIONS

Database management systems come in all shapes and sizes, with prices and learning problems to match. Managers wanting to use the personal computer for controlling information are faced with three main kinds of DBMS: specialist packages, custom built packages and general packages.

Specialist software packages

Nowadays you can buy applications that tackle an impressive range of chores. Depending on what you are managing, for instance, you can buy: *Supercow* for dairy control, *Computehair* for running hairdressing salons, *Newsboy* for a wholesale newsagency or *Pot Green* for snooker clubs. *Hired Hand* is for keeping track of plant tool on hire, *Staff* for employment agencies, *Housebox* for law business and *Police* for public houses.

There are other packages by the hundred aimed at managers in catering, construction, contracting, engineering, credit, finance, fleet insurance, retail, jewellery, scrap metal, quarrying, printing, squash clubs, taxis, travel, warehousing, wine and so on. Often these products have been developed for a particular type of business by an industry leader and then made available to smaller organisations on a commercial basis.

Custom built packages

These are usually commissioned from consultants and are written in one of two ways. The consultant may use a conventional programming language like COBOL or, increasingly, an existing software package is adapted to fit the particular needs of the customer.

The best-known package used for this purpose is Ashton Tate's *dBase II*. There are many professional programmers who earn their living by using it to develop specialist applications for business and industry.

Many of these so-called 'adaptations' involve little more than setting up the database management system so that the customer and his staff can use it without having to learn anything about the way that the software package itself works or its true potential.

Custom built programs can be expensive and both client and supplier need to be clear about the problem that is to be solved by computerisation.

General packages

These manage a wide range of information on the personal computer. They are a compromise between a computerised card index and the more elaborate database management systems available on the mainframe computer.

Along with dozens of different new types of personal computers has come an even greater flood of general packages concerned with controlling data.

The Microcomputer Software Directory, for instance, listed, over 100 database software applications for sale in 1984.

This chapter is concerned with general packages – software applications that can be applied to a wide variety of problems under the umbrella of data management.

If you have decided that you do in fact need some kind of DBMS how do you choose from the plethora of products ranging widely not only in price but also in ease of use and complexity? An important step is understanding the different types of packages under the general package heading that are now available. These are: free form, filing systems and full database management systems.

Free form

These types of packages will accept information in a completely free form, unstructured in any way. There is usually no need to define more than perhaps one or two fields. Instead you can type in large amounts of words or numbers, in any sort of layout and without worrying about how you will later retrieve the material or analyse it.

Notebook, distributed by Raven Computers Ltd, is an example of a free form package. It handles text as if the latter were already organised in some systematic way. The user defines which words, phrases or cards shall be subsequently called up on command.

Such products do not have the same flexibility as the more complex products. *Notebook*, for instance, is popular amongst managers in a major clearing bank because text can be called up without complicated instructions; just type in the word or phrase you are seeking and up comes the selection of cards. Thus the package can be used for jotting down rough notes and miscellaneous, unconnected material. Sometimes this facility is called a *scratch pad*.

The problem with this type of package is that it seldom handles more than one file of information at a time and is usually limited in its ability to sort data. It may even be unable to sort the information at all, merely retrieving it.

Free form packages however, are easy to use, which may compensate for their limited capacity to manipulate data. It is their flexibility in accepting input that is compelling. You can choose to file just one sentence or a complete page. All the records are still part of a single file.

Filing systems

These are electronic versions of the card index. A well known one is *Cardbox Plus* which has many features akin to a full data management system. But again there are usually limitations on how many files can be consulted at any one time and the way that data is sorted may be cumbersome.

Many of the simpler filing databases handle an impressive number of records, such as 65,000, but are severely limited to perhaps 25 items (fields) on each record.

The filing system package normally demands that you first define the fields that you are going to use for data storage. Thus for example, you may decide to keep information on your staff on a simplified personnel record card as shown in Figure 8. 1.

```
         Personnel Record Card No: NNNNNNNNNN

    Surname            AAAAAAAAAA
    First Name         AAAAAAAAAAAAAAAA
    Employee Number    NNNNNNNNN

    National
    Insurance No       AAAAAAAAAAAAAAAAAAA

    Date of joining    DD/MM/YYYY
    Age  on joining    NN
    Post on joining    AAAAAAAAAAAAAAAAAAAAAAAAAAA
    Current post       AAAAAAAAAAAAAAAAAAAAAAAAAAA
    Current salary     NNNNNNN

    Qualifications     AAAAAAAAAAAAAAAAAAAAAAAAAAAAAAAAAAAA
                       AAAAAAAAAAAAAAAAAAAAAAAAAAAAAAAAAAAA
                       AAAAAAAAAAAAAAAAAAAAAAAAAAAAAAAAAAAA
                       AAAAAAAAAAAAAAAAAAAAAAAAAAAAAAAAAAAA
```

Figure 8.1 Outline for simplified personnel record card. Shows field lengths and letters to indicate the type of fields: N for Numeric, A for letters and numbers (Alphanumeric), DD for Day Date, etc.

The As, Ns and other letters show how much space is being set aside for alphabetical, numerical and date type information against each field. Thus for example, some 16 characters are being reserved for the first name of the employee and just two for their age. When the card design is complete it will appear on the screen without the letters so that the spaces can be completed with the necessary data.

Why careful planning is needed when designing a database becomes clearer when considering this personnel record.

Suppose that later, after you have filled all the records, you decide to include information about the person's attendance on training courses or which projects they have completed while working in your particular section of the organisation? There are usually severe restrictions on what changes can be made once you have designed the record card and entered all the data.

In the example above, if you acquire an employee with more than ten letters in their last name and want to lengthen the field to 14 characters this may prove impossible. To lengthen an existing field would eat into space used for other parts of the form, erasing some previously recorded information.

Similarly, if you have failed to anticipate all the categories of information (fields) that you require, it may prove awkward and at worst impossible to do anything about this once all the data has been entered.

Searches

Filing database systems require a clear structure and tightly defined fields to enable rapid search and retrieval. Each piece of information on a record has its own unique field. There is one set aside for name, another for address and so on. Every field can therefore be used as a basis for searching the records. The field acts as a pigeon hole for bits of information that be need to be found again.

By contrast, in the free form database you may have to keep defining the keywords as you enter data, marking them in some way so that the computer can locate them later.

Imagine that somehow you had created a database with 15,000 staff records, each with a dozen fields. Now you want to find all the people with the surname Jones. One way would be for the computer to be told to search all 15,000 records and all 12 fields one by one. This would certainly take a long time, maybe hours.

Alternatively, a more efficient way is to create an index. This saves the computer from searching through the record cards, allowing it to go straight to the field for surname and decide whether the surname is Jones or not.

The index tells the computer where to look. In a free form filing system you create an index by marking each item as it is recorded. By contrast, a filing database allows a particular field to be designated in advance as a basis for an index. The index is compiled automatically and once ready, the speed of search is fast, usually seconds.

The simple filing systems may also limit how many fields may be searched at any one time. Thus if you want to find all the employees who speak French, have two children and a good attendance record, you may be required first to create a list of employees who speak French, then using this selection of cards, exclude all those who do not have two children and finally locate everyone with a satisfactory attendance record.

Also, when creating the file, the system may demand to know in advance which fields should be capable of being searched. Once you have made your decision there may be no turning back other than creating the file again, including re-entering all the data.

The filing database normally requires the record card to be divided up into various blocks of information so that for instance, we could add to the above personnel record card another section that showed a history of the employee's absences.

Eventually though, the space on the card would be filled up. While there are ways of linking and merging second and third cards this may prove cumbersome when it comes to manipulating the data rapidly.

Another hidden problem that can occur is that the system requires all the records in the file to be of exactly the same length. For example, a lengthy personnel card may be appropriate for some employees but wastefully long for others.

Attractive though filing systems may be, their inability to handle several files at the same time and their often limited capacity to sort and manipulate data has led to the evolution of the full database management systems.

Full DBMS

A full DBMS is different from flat file systems such as the above two types in several ways. First, the package does far more. Generally it has more features offering wider choices at all stages of creating and managing a database.

Secondly, the DBMS can usually operate with several files or records at the same time. In some systems, for example, if you had 50 records you could look at record number 2, hold your place there, examine record number 30 and hold that open, then check record number 40, before returning to the still available number 2.

A simple filing system will normally only let you access one record at a time. Similarly, if you want to examine the contents of several files you must close one before opening another.

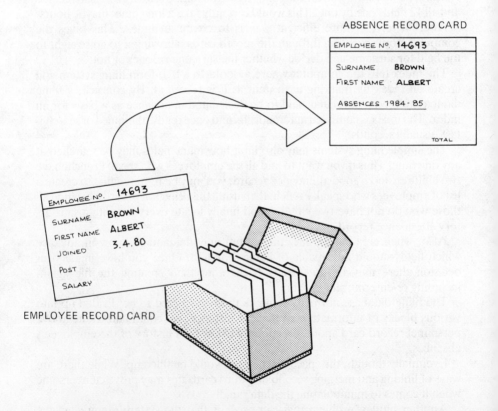

Figure 8.2 A simpler form of relationship is where one record card is only related to one other card, as with an employee's record card and the person's absence record card.

The personnel card mentioned earlier, for instance, is limited and does not contain a variety of other information which might be useful to a manager. It might prove sensible to create a second record of the employee's attendance on training courses, a third that monitored absences and a fourth that summarised the results of the annual appraisal. There might even be a fifth record linked to the appraisal card that showed potential career moves.

Each of the five sets of records on the employee would be held in separate files. What the full DBMS does is to link each of the files so that the information in all five can be related. Hence the term *relational database*. This is the third important difference between a full DBMS and a simple filing system.

Relational databases

If the letters DBMS are open to considerable misuse then 'relational database' must qualify as the single, most misused phrase in the personal computer world.

The point about the relational database is that information should normally only be entered once. Thus one set of records usually depends, in some way on another. In our personnel example, while we could have a record for an employee without necessarily creating an absence record, the reverse would not make sense.

It would be unnecessary to develop an absence record without there first being an employee card in existence to generate some base information for the secondary record.

Similarly, creating a record to show potential career moves depends first on having generated an appraisal card. One set of cards would tend to draw some of its information from the other.

Orders from customers and their invoices illustrate another important aspect of relationships. One customer would generate not one but perhaps many invoices. Thus we would expect to find one customer card linked to many invoice cards, as illustrated in Figure 8.3.

This is a one-to-many relationship and only some database management systems cope well with it. With a relational database you should be able to work with more than one file of information at a time.

It should be possible for example, to draw information from both a customer record card and the related invoice cards. Some database systems are less effective once you begin investigating their handling of this type of relationship. For instance, they may allow you to create a one-to-many relationship but not permit you to view data simultaneously across both sets of files.

Or they may let you view a master card and a series of linked cards or files as long as these are in a strict hierarchical relationship. You can look at and work with the master card and its descendants but not necessarily other files.

All this may sound increasingly complicated, but when you come to use the system, the handling of relationships can prove crucial. A full DBMS ensures that all the related records are properly joined together. Internally the system behaves as if there were just one, all-purpose record card for each employee, customer or whatever.

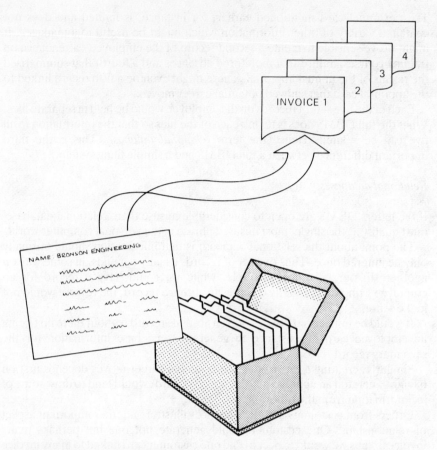

Figure 8.3 Relationships between records can differ. This shows a one-to-many relationship in which one customer record card is related to several invoice cards or records

Likewise it acts as if all the separate files were joined together into one enormous file. In the ideal system all files or records can be related to each other as shown in Figure 8.4. Hence the underlying principle of the full DBMS is that any piece of information should only be physically recorded once. Because relational databases are so hideously complex in how they work it is easier merely to study the end results.

Suppose in our personnel record system there is an employee called Miss Sandra Johnson. Although her name seems to appear on five different record cards this is an illusion. In fact, the name is only held in one place by the DBMS and placed on the screen in the right place when you need it.

Miss Johnson decides to get married and become Mrs Phillips. When her surname is altered in the database though, it is only done once. In one single action the results of the change are automatically reflected across all five records in the five separate files. In this way, a relational database saves entering repetitive information.

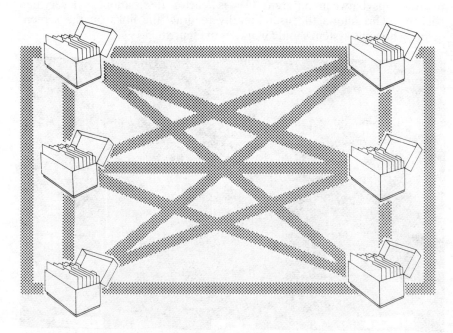

Figure 8.4 In a fully related database every file can be linked to every other file

Let us follow the example of a firm with, say, 1000 customers. Every time one sends in an order it would wasteful to type in the whole name and address. Instead, there is one set of customer files with all the main details that are unlikely to change over a period of time, like name, address, telephone number, type of business, credit rating and so on. Then there is another set of files for orders, on which the customer's name is entered.

When the DBMS goes into action it looks at the order, recognises the customer name and promptly begins rummaging around the name and address cards. It produces the rest of the information and thus completes the invoice to show both the buyer's name and address. Thus one set of files has been related to another.

Ease of use

Another difference between a full DBMS and the simpler filing systems is ease of use. Many DBMS involving the building of relationships between files and records are extremely hard to master. It can take months to gain proficiency and often a degree in computer science would not come amiss.

Power and complexity are wedded firmly together as far as database management systems are concerned. Valiant efforts have nevertheless been exerted by software houses to make their systems seem friendly. They have tried everything from chatty, well presented documentation to fast moving and occasionally entertaining tutorial disks.

One of the more innovative approaches to helping the user create a set of relationships between different files is Vector International's Everyman package. This allows the user literally to draw the links on the screen, defining how the system should work, as in Figure 8. 5.

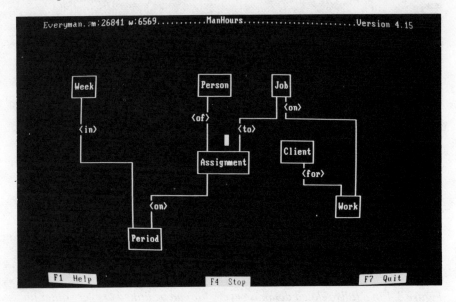

Figure 8.5 This unusual way of helping users to define the relationship between files is by Vector International's Everyman

Once the boxes have been created they become a menu and choosing a box leads to the correct file. (See also the review of *Everyman* in Part Two.)

Do not be misled. To use a full DBMS you will be at it for weeks and probably months before feeling that you can make it dance to your tune. However, it may not take until then before the package begins to be useful. With some of the better systems you can start putting simple databases together and conducting routine searches and reports in a matter of days. But the danger is that through lack of knowledge you will create systems which in the longer term have to be scrapped.

Like many software systems, database packages vary in how they are controlled by the user. Some, like *DataMaster* for example, expect you to manage them by answering carefully posed, multiple choice questions. These are menu-driven packages.

Others, like *dBase II* or the *Archive* system of Psion's *Xchange* suite, are strictly controlled by the precise instructions that you must devise using the manual. These products are called command-driven, and to use them you learn a highly simplified form of computer language.

The best database systems will offer a choice of either a menu- or a command-driven approach. Once you acquire enough confidence and knowledge, *Condor* and *DataMaster* for example, allow you to dispense with the menu and instead use the system's own special query language.

Another unavoidable fact of life about the database system which busy managers should consider, is that not much will emerge from the creature until it has gorged itself on a substantial amount of information.

Who will input all this data? Have you the staff to do it, how much training will they need, how will you keep the monster fed with the latest data, who will be responsible for checking the accuracy of what is entered?

Data management systems are also demanding of computer resources. It is essential to check that you have adequate memory and disk storage. Without these you may end up with a package that either won't work at all or runs too slowly.

Price

The final major difference between the full DBMS and other less sophisticated products is price. Free form and filing systems were selling for around £150–300 at the start of 1985. By contrast full database systems were offered by retailers at between £350–450, depending on the operating system used.

Whether the price difference is justified for a manager using the computer as a personal tool needs to be carefully assessed in each case. It is more likely to be justified if you are using data which is also part of a larger office system.

INTEGRATION

Another important aspect to investigate is whether you will want to use your database with other software applications, such as a word processor, a graphics package or a financial spreadsheet. Not only must the packages be able to exchange information but you will be learning several different products, each with its unique ways of working.

This is why integrated packages have been developed. At one time the individual modules that constituted the packages were much less powerful than the stand-alone products that they were meant to replace.

That is no longer true. Thus, for instance, Psion's *Xchange* is an integrated product whose four separate modules are roughly, though not totally, equivalent to the competitive stand-alones. Similarly *Symphony*, another integrated package, has a spreadsheet which is one of the best on the market.

Both *Xchange* and *Symphony* and other products like them not only share data between the various components but all the various modules resemble each other in how they present themselves to the user. Familiarity with one leads to familiarity with the rest.

COMMITMENT

Apart from the fact that a DBMS is more powerful and complex than the other type of systems and costs more, it will also demand a major commitment from the user.

You are unlikely to have time to master more than one DBMS thoroughly and having done so, there will be a natural tendency to stick with what has become familiar.

Therefore when a manager chooses a database system as a personal tool it is like getting married. There is sense in carefully investigating alternatives before taking the plunge. Having plighted one's troth, the commitment must, if possible, be made to work.

Data Protection Act

The ease with which databases can be created on the computer makes them an attractive management tool. Once you become used to using perhaps a simple, free form filing system, you may quickly start wanting to develop more elaborate systems.

Many of the systems which you create will be strictly your own concern. Just as when you decide to start a small card index system to help you function more effectively, so you may devise all kinds of helpful aids using the personal computer. After all, that is precisely what it is for.

But once you record information about people on your computer database you are no longer on private territory. There is now public legislation to ensure that computer systems are monitored and properly regulated to ensure that the privacy of individuals is protected.

You are not immune to this legislation. The 1984 Data Protection Act has implications for anyone who keeps information recorded on a computer. The Act says that anyone who holds or controls computerised data must register details of any personal data held by them.

It will become an offence to hold personal data without registering it or to obtain, process or disclose data in any way other than that allowed by the rules of registration.

While there are exemptions to these requirements you can work on the principle that no matter how small your database, if it contains personal facts relating to a living individual who can be identified from the information, and it is not for domestic, family or recreational purposes, then the data must be registered.

This includes opinions. So if you were to use a free form filing system, for example, to record some notes about what you thought about your subordinates, this would have to be registered under the Act. Maybe you'd prefer to stick to the old black notebook or the card index! Neither of these is affected by the Act.

Intentions are however not registrable. Nor can anyone claim the right to see such data. Intentions would include:

a specific plan to promote or transfer an employee

any other specific intentions in relation to the employee's future with the company, such as redundancy or early retirement

a planned salary increase

People who have information about them recorded on a computer are called by the Act *data subjects*. The latter have the right to obtain details of personal data held about them.

Data subjects can also apply to the courts for the correction or erasure of inaccurate data. If necessary they can also claim compensation in the courts for damage suffered as a result of data which is inaccurate, lost, destroyed or disclosed.

With thousands of personal computers emerging everywhere, you are not alone in wondering whether the Act can be made to work. How, for instance, would anyone even know that you keep information on your own private disk?

Underpinning the law though, is a Data Protection Registrar, who is likely to have a staff of around 20, all dedicated to making the Act bite. One reason for this determination is a purely commercial one. International concern over data protection could soon lead to a ban on allowing computerised data being sent to countries without adequate legislation.

If you work in a large organisation there is likely to be pressure to reveal and register any databases that you devise if they involve people. Failure to do so could leave your employer vulnerable to court action.

You can also be held liable for compensation due to inaccurate data generated during an individual's employment. Thus it may be sensible to clarify on your records whether the data has been provided by the data subjects themselves. In these cases you are not liable for their inaccuracies.

The Act is still untested and new; it will take several years before its effectiveness becomes clear. Meanwhile it is sensible to be aware of its main principles. In particular, personal data must:

- be obtained and processed fairly and lawfully

- be held only for one or more specified lawful purposes

- not be used or disclosed in any manner incompatible with those purposes

- be adequate, relevant, and not excessive in relation to the purpose(s) for which it is held

- be accurate and, where necessary, kept up to date

- not be kept longer than is necessary

In addition, two more requirements exist:

- a data subject is entitled to access, at reasonable intervals and without undue delay or expense, to personal data where he is the subject and where appropriate to have such data corrected or erased

- appropriate security measures must be taken against unauthorised access to, or alteration, disclosure or destruction of personal data and against accidental loss or destruction of personal data.

SUMMARY

DBMS means database management system(s).

Most DBMS on the personal computer are unsophisticated compared to their counterparts on mainframe computers.

Most manual systems are capable of considerable improvement by using a computer database system but there are plenty of exceptions to this.

Managers may have only a limited need for a database system as a personal tool; the real gain stems from using an existing data system.

Databases can be created by specialist software, custom built packages, or general database applications that will tackle a wide variety of jobs.

Database applications can be free form, filing systems, or full-blooded DBMS

A full DBMS differs from simpler systems in these ways:
    scope and facilities
    handling of several records or files simultaneously
    often relational: can relate one set of records to another and create
    information involving dependent relationships
    ease of use: tends to be more complex and hard to master
    price

Check if the DBMS is controlled by multiple choice questions (menu-driven) or by a special query language (command-driven); the better applications offer a choice.

To be effective a DBMS needs large amounts of information.

DBMS are demanding of computer power and disk storage.

If the DBMS is to be used with other applications such as word processing it may be cheaper and better to buy an integrated application.

The effort required to master a DBMS makes selection important. Once learned there is little incentive to change to perhaps even better applications.

The 1984 Data Protection Act applies to your databases if they contain records on individuals.

Personal data must be registered under the Act, this includes opinions kept on a computer, but not intentions.

If you keep information about anyone on your personal computer at work, they have a right of access to that information and to insist that it be accurate.

9   Spreadsheets

The idea of the spreadsheet was introduced in Chapter Three. The electronic blackboard or balance sheet is now a familiar tool in a vast number of organisations, particularly among accountants.

VisiCalc, the original spreadsheet, was launched in 1979 and has been followed by hundreds of copycat products that have removed the grind from countless numerical chores. If you have never used a spreadsheet before then you are in for a pleasant surprise.

Spreadsheets are conventionally used for creating balance sheets, planning budgets and conducting financial modelling. But they are infinitely variable in application.

They have been used for creating manpower plans, producing monthly statistical reports to management, geological analysis, and even simple word processing applications.

At their simplest they help avoid all kinds of minor tedious tasks such as checking figures, calculating percentages, altering subtotals and seeing the effects, ensuring that figures are all properly laid out and so on.

Spreadsheets project current information which you provide so that you can then ask 'what if' questions. In that sense they are an invaluable business decision-making tool for allowing managers to consider a variety of alternatives before making a final choice. Watching the results appear instantly is why managers and accountants are inescapably hooked on spreadsheets.

A spreadsheet is like a large piece of paper divided into a grid, laying out everything for you in rows and columns. Costs, taxes, interest rates, budgets and statistics can all be examined and rapidly changed when making a decision.

Each figure goes into a unique cell on the grid. Each cell is initially labelled numerically down the side and alphabetically along the top. Later you can add your own labels and captions.

Spreadsheets provide hundreds of rows and columns so that – in theory at least – you would be unlikely ever to run out of space. You cannot see much more than around 20 columns and rows at any one time, but by moving the cursor to the right or downwards the screen will scroll so that more of the spreadsheet can be viewed. Thus from starting at cell A1 you can end up thousands of cells away at, say, Hh 3000.

Inserting data into the cells allows the user to build up a complex matrix of facts which the spreadsheet can manipulate. Various techniques are used to allow you to look simultaneously at more than one portion of the entire spreadsheet. This usually involves splitting the screen into two or more segments, each of which can be worked independently of the other.

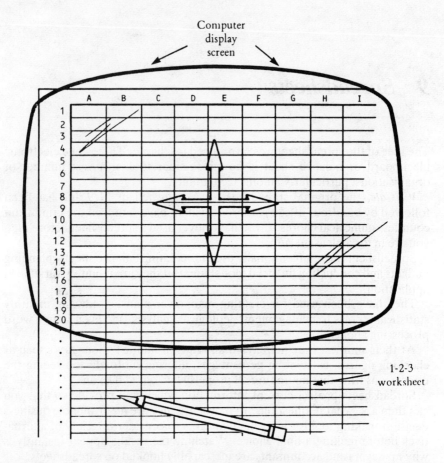

Figure 9.1 The spreadsheet is an enormous grid with uniquely numbered cells. Only part of the grid can be seen on the screen at any one time

But it is the bottom line or occasionally the far righthand column, that is usually the most important part of the spread sheet. These are the outcome figures that the manager seeks in arriving at a decision.

Adding a single column of figures on an ordinary hand calculator may be fine. But if there are dozens of such columns and each must also be expressed as a percentage of its respective total, with a grand total at the end, then using a calculator is tiresome. A spreadsheet does the job instantly, adjusting the results every time a figure is amended. The spreadsheet is a form of programmable calculator. Once you have used one for even minor numerical chores you will never want to give it up.

Spreadsheets permit managers to pose that classic decision question 'What if?' Detailed figures in a spreadsheet can be constantly altered to see what results different assumptions produce. A typical layout is shown in Figure 9.2.

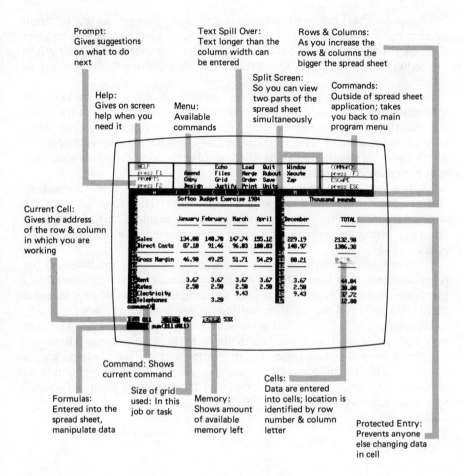

Prompt:
Gives suggestions
on what to do
next

Text Spill Over:
Text longer than the
column width can
be entered

Rows & Columns:
As you increase the
rows & columns the
bigger the spread sheet

Split Screen:
So you can view
two parts of the
spread sheet
simultaneously

Commands:
Outside of spread sheet
application; takes
you back to main
program menu

Help:
Gives on screen
help when you
need it

Menu:
Available
commands

Current Cell:
Gives the address
of the row & column
in which you are
working

Command: Shows
current command

Size of grid
used: In this
job or task

Memory:
Shows amount
of available
memory left

Cells:
Data are entered
into cells; location is
identified by row
number & column
letter

Formulas:
Entered into the
spread sheet,
manipulate data

Protected Entry:
Prevents anyone
else changing data
in cell

Figure 9.2 Typical spreadsheet layout. Abacus spreadsheet from the Psion Business Application suite of programs

FORMULAE

The core concept behind the spreadsheet is the use of formulae. Suppose that you were a sales manager and wanted to devise a bonus scheme for your team of 50 salespeople. You might produce a formula such as: the bonus will be three per cent of the value of extra sales achieved this month, compared to the previous month.

This might be summarised as:

$$\{(\text{Sales this month})-(\text{Sales last month})\} \times 3/100 = \text{Bonus}$$

If you had a record of sales over the last year or so, you could try this formula, discovering how much the company would have paid out and what different salespeople would have earned.

The spreadsheet can use this formula and then allow you to test different percentage payments. Instead of three per cent, what happens at two per cent, or at three and a half per cent? Each time you change the assumption, the figures in the body of the spreadsheet alter automatically – a joy to watch!

Not all spreadsheet packages will let you use actual words to build up the formulae. For instance some will insist that instead of the words for 'Sales this month', 'Sales last month' and 'Bonus', the user adopts the cell reference numbers instead. This is irritating and when buying a spreadsheet it is worth checking whether it can handle formulae by using the labels which the user has created to refer to the cells.

Using a formula is fine if you have a simple one and can devise it yourself. But often one may need a complex spreadsheet layout, using formulae which are needed for common problems. For example, calculating sales bonuses, insurance actuarial rates, or preparing annual tax returns and balance sheets.

To save bothering with devising the spreadsheet layout and inserting the relevant formulae it is possible to use *templates* which have the layouts and formulae inserted. All you do is load the template into your program and there is the required presentation waiting for you to add in the live figures.

Templates can be purchased separately but some of the better packages may include several of these, particularly to help new users. However, templates are still not that common in Europe and you may have to search out a package that includes this feature. For example, the UK version (1A) of *Lotus 1-2-3* does not include templates, though it has plenty of special formulae. Later versions are likely to have this facility.

EASE OF USE

Most spreadsheets are easy to understand and use. It will take longer though, before you can expect to do really elaborate tasks. But then, being a manager with a range of duties involving subordinates, you may not need to use a spreadsheet often or at a high level of sophistication. Alternatively you may be able to have the spreadsheet devised by a technical member of staff and then use it yourself in privacy.

Around 20–40 hours may be required by a newcomer to become familiar with a spreadsheet's full capabilities. Even some of the best packages are poor when it comes to teaching the new user. This is one area where it may be particularly sensible to consider attending a one or two day course run by a supplier. There are also separately sold tutorial disks (see Chapter 7) available for some systems.

One of the best tutorial spreadsheet disks is that included with *Lotus 1-2-3*. This is a fully interactive series of lessons. You learn about the facilities of the package, are shown how to create different types of spreadsheets and the lessons simulate a live session with actual commands being given. But you cannot go wrong since the tutorial is always in charge of events.

Alternatively, for the some of the very well-known products, like *Visi-Calc*, there are now several well-produced books that take you gently through the learning process in a less brisk fashion than a conventional manual tends to.

WHAT TO BUY

Most managers will have only limited time to assess a spreadsheet package before making the buying decision. Since there are dozens of these programs from which to choose and a considerable variety of facilities offered, it makes sense to stick to the well-known brands.

To evaluate a spreadsheet is also a complex, time-consuming task. For example here are some of the features that may be worth considering.

- Editing: will it copy formulae, alter cell contents without retyping, insert new rows and columns and move them?

- Recalculation: if you make changes are the corrections instantaneous? If you have to wait several seconds after each change it could seem to take forever when using a large model.

- Displays: are there good display facilities so that, for example, you can look at different parts of the spreadsheet at the same time?

- Functions: apart from simple arithmetic are there special functions such as net present value and facilities to handle awkward situations such as automatically checking whether a figure has reached a certain threshold (*look up*) facility.

- Sorting: can the spreadsheet sort columns and rows in ascending or descending order?

- Help! Is there a help facility for on-screen advice? At least one popular product tries to go further and anticipate your wishes. For example, if you propose to split the screen horizontally the program will ask if you wish it to be divided exactly in half. If so, it means hitting just the ENTER key but otherwise you can give a different answer.

- Printing: all packages let you print out the material. But if you have a large spreadsheet that must be printed in sections it could involve a complex procedure rather than, as in some packages, merely specifying the two diagonally opposite corners of the entire sheet.

- Consolidation: combining several worksheets into a single version might be needed, for example in a firm with several departments. Thus check whether information from different models can be merged into one corporate one.

- Protection: can cells be protected from other users making any changes so that they do not mistakenly spoil important parts of the model like titles or formulae?

- Interface: can the package interface with other software such as a graphics package or a word processor?

- Memory: spreadsheets devour memory voraciously. The more powerful the program the more memory it demands. Since the contents of the spreadsheet are held in memory until consigned to disk, your computer's capacity will govern the size and complexity of the spreadsheet that can be devised. Check how much memory the program needs and what is left for your spreadsheets; you may find that you will need a hard disk to handle the type of jobs you will be doing.

All these factors then need to be put together to produce a general value for money judgement. When *Which Computer?* magazine examined 10 of the most popular spreadsheets (*Which Computer?*, December 1984) it reported that in performance and value for money, the best three buys were:

> *Lotus 1-2-3*
> *SuperCalc*
> *Symphony*

Unfortunately, due to complications about who then owned the commercial rights to *VisiCalc*, this pioneering product was omitted completely. If you are considering buying a spreadsheet, do check *VisiCalc* – if only to provide a base line from which to compare the other three products.

Also, there are more books and other related products in relation to *VisiCalc* than to practically any other software package around.

Spreadsheets are a vast field in their own right. But for most managers the best of the products on the market offer fairly similar facilities which differ mainly at the margin.

Graphics

It is often important to turn numerical data into bar diagrams, pie charts and graphs. Most spreadsheets can produce a crude form of illustration but it is seldom impressive.

To turn spreadsheet data into a graphical presentation will usually mean first having a suitable printer (*plotter*) able to draw charts in three dimensions and different colours.

Secondly it may require a separate, graphics software package. Before finally adopting a particular spreadsheet package, or indeed buying a graphics package, test that they are mutually compatible. That is, they can readily transfer data backwards and forwards between them.

Compatibility is not a problem if you decide to buy an integrated package like *Open Access* or *Symphony*. However, even these packages expect you to perform the well known 'floppy disk dance.' To turn your spreadsheet into a graph or pie chart and insert it into a report that you are preparing on the word processor, means that you may have to shuffle between three or more disks several times before achieving the desired result.

There may well be more sense in buying the second generation of integrated software that reduces all the necessary programs to a single floppy disk.

SUMMARY

The spreadsheet is a mixture of electronic blackboard and programmable calculator.

Spreadsheets handle a variety of numerical chores, particularly where figures have to be constantly readjusted.

Templates can be used in spreadsheets to save lengthy setting up tasks.

Around 20–40 hours are needed by a newcomer to master a spreadsheet fully.

Issues to check on include displays, functions, sorting, help facility, printing, consolidation, protection, interfacing and memory requirements.

To turn spreadsheet material into a graphic presentation usually requires a graphics package which must also be compatible with the spreadsheet program.

An integrated package that offers spreadsheet, graphics and other facilities may be a better purchase in some situations.

Stick with the best-selling spreadsheets at this stage.

10 Management Aids

Sales manager Tony Morton is anxious. The report that he wants to put before the board is an important one. It has to arrive there on time. But the first draft on the document is being prepared by his assistant, Benson. On past experience Benson will not meet the deadline.

Tony sits down at his personal computer and inserts the program disk from the new behaviour modification package. He begins describing Benson to the computer. The computer also has a personality description of Tony himself. Eventually the program makes the following suggestion on how Tony might achieve a timely report from his assistant, Benson:

> He prefers recognition for his work to status and money. You can more easily obtain the reports that you need if you make him feel comfortable and relaxed. Never use questioning to demean him. Try to help him focus on the overall departmental goals as well as on his own job and make an effort to relate the two.

Fiction? Not so. A new breed of management aid software is now becoming available that delivers exactly this kind of help to managers who need support in how to achieve their objectives.

Previous chapters have considered word processors, databases and training packages as possible aids to management. But there are a variety of other applications that offer attractive personal gains.

These include desktops, ideas organisers and behavioural tools. There are also special programs for making life easier by performing some of the chores of managing computer files (*utilities*) and communications packages that, together with special equipment, allow data to be transferred from one computer to another, across the world if necessary.

Utilities and communications packages are more advanced tools and outside the scope of this particular book. We will look briefly at the other possible aids to management.

ORGANISERS AND DESKTOPS

In assisting managers to use the computer as a personal tool for improved effectiveness there are surprisingly few well-constructed products that address themselves to the role that managers have to play.

Several applications on the market claim to offer managers help in becoming better organised in various ways, including:

- managing your time

- storing and finding addresses

- controlling projects

- organising your thoughts in a systematic fashion

Desktops

Desktops are a new breed of software package that seem destined to boom. They are accessories to existing programs, adding a number of useful features.

They are called *desktops* because they are meant to help managers turn their computer from a tool used occasionally for a limited purpose, such as a spreadsheet application, into an active extension of their work desk.

Most desktops allow you to switch rapidly from one sort of task to another, while working in harmony with your own existing software. Unlike integrated programs such as *Xchange, Open Access* or *Symphony*, you are not required to learn a whole new complex range of commands and methods of working. Nor do you have to ditch your existing investment in software.

The desktop package is usually designed to sit in between your regular software and the computer's operating system. It behaves almost as if it were the operating system. The effect is to allow you to switch instantly between the desktop program and one or more other programs.

From a manager's point of view this facility offers important gains. If you are mainly into, say *Lotus 1-2-3,* then you can load this into the computer immediately after loading the desktop. From then on you can call on the spreadsheet program whenever you wish. Meanwhile, the desktop also provides useful aids such as a diary, notebook, list of telephone numbers and so on, which you might use during your daily activities at your desk.

Desktops range considerably in price from the all-embracing program that tries to offer managers practically every daily aid they might ever need, to simple packages that just provide a few, highly practical tools.

In choosing a desktop there are several important issues to consider. If it is to control your main software package that you use regularly, you need to be absolutely sure that the two products are totally compatible.

Secondly, if it is to become a daily tool, always installed on the computer before any other program, does it really offer useful facilities that you will actually need? Many facilities may appear attractive, like filing systems, or diaries but in practice you may never adopt them permanently.

If you use only a small part of a large desktop package then it could clog up large chunks of otherwise useful memory. Similarly, a large desktop will have priority for the computer's memory so it is important to check how much total memory you are going to require.

If the desktop does become a way of life you could become extremely reliant on it. If the disk on which it is supplied is software protected so that you cannot make full back-up copies without using a master disk, then should the original software house cease trading it could have serious consequences.

MANAGING YOUR TIME

If you want something done, it is sometimes said, ask a busy person. Most managers are constantly being asked to do things. Consequently, time is always scarce for an effective manager, no matter how well organized. Software applications to help with time management are of two main kinds: diary keeping and activity scheduling.

The diary keeping software applications are usually remarkably simple. The package will normally allow you to enter activities and retrieve them according to date, time, or by some special category which you choose.

The program will also produce a calendar for any month of any year where days have scheduled activities. The user calls up the calendar either as part of a menu of other management aids or as a program in its own right.

Superplanner, which is produced by the American Sorcim Corporation, offers a menu of: calendar, address book, card box, reminders and a facility for altering the various files which the user creates.

By selecting Calendar the current month appears on the screen showing the days and dates. You can then flip through the calendar looking forwards or backwards across the months or jump straight to January or December.

The program allows you to schedule activities by calling up any day in any year; you can jot down meetings or notes in a free form style of entry. The program then marks the scheduled day in the calendar with an asterisk.

Another facility is the ability to select scheduled activities using any criteria that the user chooses. For example, you can code any really important activities with a special mark and all these can be listed later, regardless of date. Similarly if the manager wants to review all dates when he will be meeting a certain member of staff, or visiting a certain site, these can be shown in sequence.

The package is a free form filing system (see Chapter 8) but the use of a perpetual calendar makes it a potentially more helpful tool in some management situations.

To use each of *Superplanner's* facilities though, you must leave what you are currently doing and move on to the next activity. Other packages, like SPI's *Open Access,* use the concept of windows to simulate what happens in real life, when the manager is trying to do several jobs simultaneously!

Open Access will display a calendar for a particular month to which brief notes can be added. But to make an appointment or to jot down a few notes it is possible to call up a different part of the package which is overlaid on top of the original screen. (See Figure 10. 1.)

This opens a window to an appointment card or a scratch pad on which notes can be added. By pressing a single key the window is 'closed' and the calendar returns. Alternatively, yet another window can be created showing a calculator so that the manager can perform computations. (See Figure 10.2.)

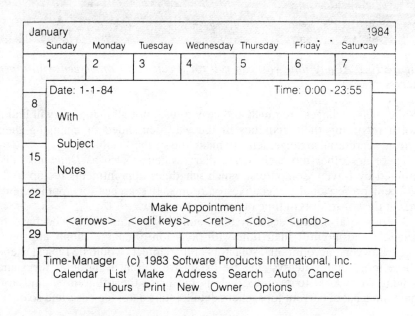

Figure 10.1 Calendar in SPI's Open Access; a window opens on the calendar to allow individual daily appointments to be made

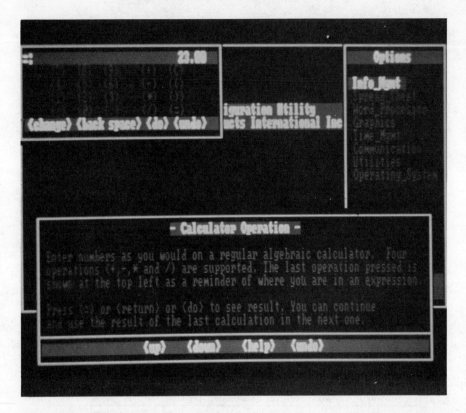

Figure 10.2 At any time you can call for a calculator on screen with Open Access

While such packages are quick and easy to use, not all managers will find it worth recording their activities in the way demanded or changing their current secretarial arrangements to make the systems viable.

There are other more elaborate diary systems, such as *Datebook*, distributed by Raven Computers, which schedules appointments for up to 27 different professionals, executives or rooms. It searches for appointments that fit the constraints of time of day, week or year.

There are also large scale systems aimed at professionals who have to schedule and monitor their time with precision to charge clients appropriately. Lawyers, accountants, solicitors and architects would be typical users. These more elaborate systems are expensive, often in modular form and ranging from £200 to over £350. For that price the program should also maintain a list of current jobs, client details, start date, fee basis and so on.

ADDRESSES

Packages that store addresses are special versions of a filing database system. Indeed if you buy virtually any database system it will do perfectly well for keeping addresses and retrieving these on request.

The address package will normally present a screen ready laid out with fields for name, telephone number and several lines for the address. Information can be added, deleted or altered and there will usually be a limited capacity for selecting on the basis of several fields.

For example, assuming you kept a list of 500 contact names the address package should be able to locate say, all the people named Brown living in Birmingham.

Similarly, if you want to contact the name of a particular doctor in the Address File but cannot recall the name, you might enter: Dr* . This would then locate all the doctors regardless of their actual names.

Computer packages that provide address, diary and other note-keeping facilities present managers with a basic problem of whether and how to alter their normal way of working.

If you buy several different packages for diary, address and note-keeping purposes, swopping between them constantly could prove impractical. An integrated product like SPI's *Open Access*, which combines the various facilities, is more attractive but to be fully effective you may need to keep the computer running all day, instantly accessible. Again that may prove neither practical nor congenial in a small office.

PROJECT CONTROL

Project planning is a specialised activity in its own right. However, most managers regularly have to plan and control projects of varying size and there are numerous computer-based aids available.

The most sophisticated forms of program, involving the full use of critical path analysis and other advanced methods, are not likely to be of much help. They demand a detailed understanding of techniques which are complex even before being transferred to the computer.

However, there are some simplified forms of scheduling programs, such as Raven's *Milestone*, which do use critical path analysis to schedule manpower, money and time. The relationship between these three variables can also be investigated. Thus for example, *Milestone* will calculate the effects of changes in manpower on the expected completion date of a project. It can also produce a chart of the various project activities, shown on the screen or printed out for permanent reference.

Programs such as these place a severe form of discipline on management. But once learned they can be a useful tool for thinking through one's plans in detail, thus helping to ensure effective implementation.

ORGANISE YOUR THOUGHTS

The computer has an enormous capacity for bringing together diverse information and reordering it in a systematic way. The human brain can also do this, often at the expense of the equally important talent for creativity.

At different times managers are expected to think both systematically and creatively. Report writing may demand a creative approach to developing and putting together ideas or information which later have to be ordered in some logical fashion.

When thinking about problems or making plans a manager may consider many ideas, some of which may be related to each other. Seeing the connections may, however, prove difficult. A tool which helps to put creative thoughts into some sensible order would thus come in extremely useful.

Several software products now claim to offer the ability to 'process ideas' in some way. What they usually mean is that ideas or concepts can be recorded by the program in some semi-structured way.

Two specialist products that offer a way of ordering thoughts more logically are *Think Tank* which is produced by Living Videotext of America and the British product produced by Caxton Software called *Brainstorm*.

Brainstorm is the more ambitious of the two. Both products store your ideas in a structure, like a family tree or the kind of outline one used to write at school using Roman numerals and indented headings.

Brainstorm goes beyond this, checking to see if ideas have been used more than once and if so, mentioning this in the margin. It also places them in a tree structure in the appropriate places in the overall ideas list. Thus you can literally see the connections and links between different ideas or information. *Brainstorm* is described in more detail in Part Two.

Ideas processors are not cheap; *Brainstorm* cost over £300 at the start of 1985 and few managers can probably justify this expenditure for themselves alone. But many executives will see the potential of such a product.

BEHAVIOUR MODIFICATION

Several software products are now becoming available that use psychological research to assist managers in highly practical ways.

Sometimes these products offer a one-off form of help, as for example a computerised form of assessing your personal management style with accompanying advice on how to improve your performance. One such product produces a seven page detailed report for the manager and concludes with specific advice along these lines:

> Examine how you can share your ideas with others regularly as
> they develop and take their criticisms as part of the problem
> solving process to gain their acceptance and enthusiastic com-
> mitment.

Another series now on the market is called *The Human Edge*. These adapt some of the findings of psychological research to create a personal tutor.

Take for instance *The Management Edge*. It offers instant consultancy on human relations problems that you might encounter at work. First, you are personally assessed by answering a series of statements about yourself such as:

I often worry too much at work. agree/disagree
I enjoy talking at company meetings. agree/disagree

Next you assess your subordinates using around 90 characteristics such as kind, sarcastic, rigid, uncaring, independent and so on. Much the same process occurs for assessing your superiors, your own managerial skills and your organization.

Having given the computer enough information you can then seek help under various subject headings such as improving communications, increasing performance and motivation, effective discipline, replacement counselling and so on.

Eventually the program prints out some highly specific advice, such as the example at the start of this chapter, about what to do in various selected situations. There are other packages in the series dealing with negotiation, selling, and communications.

The point of these products is that they are not just one-shot learning experiences, they are meant to be continuously used as personal management aids. Whether such computerised help really does change someone's managerial approach is debatable. But the suggestions are based on soundly researched behaviourist principles.

What the software sellers do not reveal is what happens when you follow the computer's proposals on how to handle your boss and he fires you. Just try asking for your money back!

AIDS OR HINDRANCE?

New products are constantly coming onto the market so it is sensible to keep a look out for potentially useful aids. For example, a new breed of software that helps managers to write letters in another language is just now becoming available.

However, apart from the ubiquitous spreadsheet, computerised management aids have been taking a long time to make a real impact on managers' daily lives. Only part of this is due to managers not being computer-minded.

Many of the aids look attractive during demonstration or in the catalogue but prove hard to integrate into daily work patterns. For example, not everyone wants a computer on all day in their personal office. Other aids require regular maintenance of new input so that unless they are kept completely up to date they are useless.

SUMMARY

There are software packages that help schedule your personal time and diary.

Address packages will control names and addresses and select or sort names.

There are some simplified packages aimed at improving a manager's control over projects.

Packages to help organize your ideas are now available.

Behaviour modification programs help managers improve their handling of interpersonal situations.

To make computerised aids effective may mean changing your personal work patterns and reorganising how your office is arranged.

Part Two

Introduction

The purpose of Part Two is to assist managers further in selecting useful packages from the vast range of software now available. Packages described here are not being recommended for purchase. They are suggested as worth careful consideration when making your software selections.

Each package has been used by the author on an Apricot Personal Computer, with a dual disk drive. But all the software is also usable on a wide variety of other machines, including the IBM PC.

However, take nothing for granted. Insist on seeing the package in which you are interested working on the exact type and model of machine that you intend to use, including the printer if possible.

To make the material varied and interesting no attempt has been made to give each package description an identical structure or coverage. The main feaures though are explained, together with comments on ease of use, limitations, documentation and so on.

EASE OF USE

Particular attention has been paid to ease of use since for less experienced managers this factor will count for a great deal in choosing software.

An important aspect of ease of use is what the user must do to get the package up and running on the computer. Many packages, for instance, expect the user to go through an elaborate ritual, not merely of copying disks, but transferring specific files and renaming them.

If you are being asked to pay the list price or near it for a software package, installation should usually be performed by the dealer or distributor. Though installation may only need to occur once, it is still an unsatisfactory aspect of many programs. Other packages manage to arrive completely ready to run, apart from requiring back-up copies, and adding the operating system.

Do not be persuaded by forceful sales talk that getting a particular program up and running is merely a case of answering a few questions that appear on the screen at the start of the program. You may not understand the questions, let alone the answers!

To run one particular package you are given on screen a list of possible machines which work with the package and you must choose one. The Apricot computer though, does not appear amongst the choices!

A call to the software distributors revealed that it was shown under a name associated with one of its components! There was no mention of this vital fact in the manual. Consequently the product reviews in Part Two usually mention if the start up procedure is particularly elaborate, or adequate.

Software changes rapidly; new versions are often produced to eliminate problems that have been identified. Despite this pattern of upgrading, the basic package usually remains essentially the same, with minor amendments and embellishments.

Part Two is thus more concerned with giving managers a feel for what a product is about and what its main attractions and drawbacks are, than a detailed account of the way it works. For totally up-to-date assessments it is advisable to study the computer magazines for their software reviews.

MEMORY

There is no absolute standard for the amount of memory in a personal business computer. Increasingly though, 256K is emerging as a minimum base line which is likely to continue rising over the years. So no mention is made about memory requirements for a package if this is below 256K.

Occasionally though, a package will need more than this, particular the integrated software like *Open Access* or *Symphony*. In these cases the reviews will always mention this fact.

VERDICT

The packages have been examined, not so much for their detailed technical aspects, but from a management perspective. So, apart from the general description and review material, a Management Verdict has also been included.

Like all such evaluations, the Management Verdict is ultimately a matter of judgement. For really detailed appraisals, study the software reviews which are listed in the bibliography, search for the latest ones and discuss your needs with your dealer or supplier.

The Management Verdict is shown at the beginning of each package description as star ratings out of five. The verdict deals with four key aspects of each package:

- ● ease or difficulty of getting started
- ● ease of use
- ● general performance
- ● documentation

The first of these concerns the ease with which one can take the newly arrived software, get it running on the computer and begin to make some progress in actually using it.

The second takes an overall view of how easy or difficult the total package is to use. Highly-experienced users sometimes forget how baffling even simple aspects of a package can be to the newcomer. Even the best instructions occasionally fail to communicate what one is supposed to do next.

Thus the ease of use criterion examines the 30 packages chosen from the stance of a manager who is not a thoroughly experienced computer user.

The evaluation of general performance was based on two distinct aspects. First, how well does the package do what it is supposed to do? Secondly, how does this performance relate to other, reasonably comparable products? No two packages are exactly the same and any comparison, even if based entirely on scientific benchmark tests, is likely to be only a guide to the product's effectiveness under certain conditions.

Since Part Two is not an attempt to conduct a detailed cross-comparison of software the general performance verdict should be interpreted merely as an approximate guide. Detailed benchmark tests are increasingly becoming available through the better computer magazines and these should be used for more precise evaluations.

The documentation provided with a package can be a crucial factor in whether or not the relatively inexperienced manager can make real progress in using a newly purchased product. The Management Verdict on documentation indicates the overall effectiveness of everything that is supplied to help the user, apart from the program itself. However this does not include support from the suppliers.

These four aspects are important for the average manager who is considering the purchase of a particular package but they are not the only criteria for judging an item of software. A general value for money judgement is also possible along with other more elaborate benchmarks.

Similarly, the fact that a package is extremely powerful and presented impressively may not make it particularly suitable for everyday management needs in which software is used as a personal computing tool.

Ultimately, you must make up your own mind about a product and merely use the Management Verdict as a guideline.

SELECTION

The selection of the packages was also based on simple criteria. Products costing more than about £700 were generally excluded, on grounds of cost. Although a large company might not baulk at this amount, many managers in smaller organisations certainly would.

The generosity of the suppliers in providing their products was considerable. But inevitably some packages which could sensibly have been included were omitted because they were not made available.

Similarly, highly specialist packages were mainly excluded and generally the ones chosen reflect the contents of Part One of the book. In other words, the packages are ones which are considered as likely candidates for becoming a practical, day-to-day management computing tool.

Having a practising manager test out the products hopefully provides an overall consistency of view. But the time available for research was consequently a major constraint. Hence the total number of packages chosen was kept to 30. Because a product is not included does not necessarily imply an adverse opinion about it.

However, more packages were examined than are described. Some were simply not good enough, others were considered unsuitable, mainly because of difficulty in using them.

SUPPLIERS

Some of the packages were provided by the original producers while others came from distributors. Each review therefore begins with the name of the firm supplying it. Where this differs from the originating company, then the latter's name is also given.

Finally it is worth stressing that the reviews are for guidance only. The material was accurate at the time of writing but, given the speed at which the software market moves, neither the author nor the publishers can be held liable for differences that may be found in products which are purchased on the basis of reading the following material.

BRAINSTORM

Type:	Organiser (Ideas processor)	
Management Verdict:	Getting started	(4) ****
	Ease of use	(4) ****
	General performance	(4) ****
	Documentation	(3) ***
Supplied by:	Caxton Software Ltd, 10-14 Bedford Street, London WC2E 9HE	
Telephone:	(01) 379 6502	

Brainstorm is regularly bought by many large companies, like Shell, Ferranti and ICL, whose executives have grasped the essential nature of this unusual computer program. It takes messy, disorganised ideas and quite literally helps mould them into a more rational structure.

Imagine that you are writing a report on a major production problem in a factory which you currently manage. You begin by drawing up a list of factors that will have to be investigated as possibly contributing to the crisis. But instead of writing these down on paper you enter them into your *Brainstorm* package, for example:

```
Quality Control
Raw materials
Sabotage
Machine failure
Training
```

As you finish the list, your mind is stimulated by one of the items: quality control, and you remember many more issues around this factor that will need mentioning in the report.

Rather than start the list all over again you merely place the cursor on the computer screen at the heading Quality Control, press a key and the screen instantly clears so that these words only are at the top of the page. You then proceed to add all your current thoughts about Quality Control:

```
Quality Control
    1 Training
        Supervisors
        Quality circles
        Competition
```

While you are doing this, though, one of the items under Quality Control rings another bell in your mind. You therefore break off again to make a further sub-list of points:

Supervisors
No graduates

The size of the computer memory is the only constraint on the number of levels at which information can be stored. Eventually, the complete list can be printed out, with the sub-lists slightly indented to separate them from the previous level of information.

None of this is particularly amazing. Indeed a good word processing package will allow you do almost the same thing. Where *Brainstorm* scores is first its flexibility in handling new entries and rapidly adjusting the lists, and secondly, its capacity to spot and link entries that occur more than once.

As you add the various sub-categories, *Brainstorm* obligingly keeps track of any items that you use more than once. Thus, in the above example a 1 shown against 'Training' warns that there is a link with a namesake, somewhere else in the list.

If the word 'Training', for example, appears in several places throughout the list, then when *Brainstorm* prints out the final results the Training subdivision, with all its accompanying items, will also be repeated in the appropriate places.

This makes for a long and usually messy print out. But the payoff is that you can readily see the connections between the various ideas. These connections may not only trigger new ideas but can cause you to completely rethink the entire structure of the model.

Brainstorm is therefore a mechanised way of ordering ideas that often begin in anything but a logical fashion. Indeed, it is a tool for encouraging creative thinking. When we write lists down on paper the very process favours the linear, sequential approach and rather excludes the creative leaps and unexpected, but perhaps important, connections.

The program frees you from the tyranny of the written list. You can throw ideas onto the screen and worry later about re-ordering them, what their relationships are with each other and what you might have initially omitted altogether.

Brainstorm works incredibly fast and apart from its ability to help order ideas, it can also be used as a database, since in essence it is a free-form filing system with a capacity to absorb endless quantities of text.

USERS

Who might use *Brainstorm*? Practically anyone who ever writes anything down or juggles with facts, ideas or information! Authors, students, systems analysts, programmers, psychologists and managers are ready examples.

Managers in particular will find the program a compelling tool. It is ideal for preparing reports, letters and plans, analysing decisions and problems, for project control and for miscellaneous tasks like keeping address books and diary systems.

Ian Masters, is Treasurer of the International Commodities Clearing House and has been using *Brainstorm* for around seven months. 'If I'm working on a paper which is fairly bulky and have a lot of thoughts which I can't necessarily marshal, it's an invaluable tool.' Masters also uses the package as a prelude to critical path analysis and organising all the different activities. But he is clear about the main benefit of *Brainstorm*, 'It stops you rambling!'

Effective managers usually keep a personal action list or a 'To Do sheet'. To be useful, these must be altered constantly, removing some items, adding others until there is a danger of losing sight of priorities in a welter of detail and scrawled jottings.

Brainstorm transforms the action list. Infinite details can be added to the main structure of the list without clutter, since the program lets you decide to which level of subdivision you wish to go. You can regularly print out fresh, clean action sheets, sometimes in summary form and occasionally in all their mind-numbing detail.

GETTING STARTED

Brainstorm comes ready to run on most computers, and after making the mandatory back-up copy, you merely type in: Brain, and up comes the package logo. After a polite warning that you are enjoying a copyright product, you arrive immediately at the main menu.

There are just eleven simple choices:

> Use, Clear, Xit, Load, Save, Merge, Print, Write, Id. drive, Directory and Kill

Most of these are self-explanatory and certainly easy to learn. You press U for 'Use', and arrive at the start of a new or existing list. 'Clear' rubs out the whole model, while 'Xit' takes you out of the system altogether. 'Print' and 'Write' allow you to produce either hard copy or send the material to disk. 'Kill', deletes a file.

After that *Brainstorm* reverts to using a combination of control and command keys for allowing entries to be manipulated, edited and retrieved. If, as in our example above, you decide to promote the heading Quality Control to head a new list of entries, then you merely place the cursor over that item, press Control R and the words move up to the title section. The cursor is placed ready for the first new entry below.

If you are somewhere deep down in the bowels of the model and want to get back to the beginning, just press Control Q and you return there instantly. Other keys allow you to jump around in a limited way, to Hunt for namesakes and re-order the list.

Should you decide to move a heading that has below it a whole series of subheadings, then all these move with it to the new location. If you kill off such a heading then you obliterate all the subheadings too.

152 Understanding Management Software

Since *Brainstorm* is a tool for creating models these can all be stored on disk and different models can be linked together, using the Merge option, in which case *Brainstorm* works out a whole set of new connections for the combined entries. It is also possible to read the *Brainstorm* file into a WP package to tidy up some of its inevitably rather messy layouts.

DRAWBACKS

Clever though *Brainstorm* undoubtedly is, there are a number of drawbacks of varying degrees of concern. First, the package works by looking for namesakes using an exact match. Ideally therefore, it is best to stick to single word entries at the early levels to maximise the chance of matching being able to occur. This is a limitation since one often writes whole phrases which may vary only slightly each time.

To overcome this difficulty, *Brainstorm* offers a wild card entry system. Suppose you have typed 'United States of America' and later decide to write just 'America', in another part of the model. The package will not link up these two entries.

But if, when deciding to enter 'America', you wonder if there is indeed another such item, then by typing '*America' the program will hunt for anything else that ends in this word. It will then correct your new entry to read 'United States of America'. The catch is that you have to remember that you may have entered earlier something similar.

Secondly, the manual comes with an appendix on how to customise the keys, so that for example, on the Apricot computer you can use the cursor's directional keys, instead of commands like Control E and so on. There are dire warnings not do it yourself, unless you really know how. Insist that your dealer does the adaptation for you as a condition of purchase.

Thirdly, *Brainstorm* has no scrolling facility. As your outline grows, putting out endless tentacles, it is easy to lose track of where on earth you are in the model. You can acquire so many divisions and subdivisions that you may have to keep returning to the beginning just to retain a sense of direction. In place of scrolling the only choice is to print out some or all of the model and use this as a sort of route map.

Fourthly, the package has no calculation facilities – which may not worry some people but more numerate managers may find this annoying. Nor does the package have any really effective sorting facilities, which must surely have been a mistake that some future editions should rectify.

The documentation on *Brainstorm* is hardly inspiring. True, it is well printed and laid out, seemingly having its heart in the right place by starting with a tutorial but this rather peters out.

It doesn't bother, for instance to take you through examples of using the command keys for marking current entries, jumping to marked entries, moving listed items, or listing all or parts of the current list. Instead, you are referred straight to the reference part of the manual.

To be fair, this section is mainly remarkably clear but working examples really do help people get to grips with new programs far more than just terse explanations of what to do.

Finally, *Brainstorm* is expensive at £295+VAT. Few individuals would probably spend this sort of money, though the successful writer Douglas Adams, author of *The Hitch Hiker's Guide to the Galaxy*, apparently swears by it.

Despite the criticisms, this is a refreshingly simple and stimulating product to use. From opening the box to beginning to know your way around it should take no longer than a few hours. If your dealer is prepared to give a proper demonstration and half an hour's tuition, the time scale will be even shorter.

It is definitely a product to try out thoroughly first, before you make a decision to buy. But be warned. Once you begin using *Brainstorm* it tends to be addictive!

References

BIDMEAD, Chris. Brainstorm. *Practical Computing*, July 1984, pp 80–1

BUDGETT, Henry. Having a Brainstorm. *Computing Today*, April 1984, pp 64–5

LEIGH, Andrew. Turn Confusion Into Clarity. *Apricot User*, April 1985, pp 31, 34, 36

RODWELL, Peter. Thinking on the Computer. *Sixteen Bit Computing*, August 1984, pp 28, 30–2

Brainstorm. *Which Computer?*, May 1984, pp 134–5

Database. *Punch*, March 1984

How to Smarten up Your Ideas. *Business Computing and Communications*, April 1984

CARDBOX PLUS

Type:	Database	
Management Verdict:	Getting started	(4) ****
	Ease of use	(4) ****
	General performance	(4) ****
	Documentation	(3) ***
Supplied by:	Business Simulations Ltd,	
	Scriventon House,	
	Speldhurst,	
	Tunbridge Wells,	
	Kent TN3 OTU	
Telephone:	(0892) 863105	

If you like using ordinary index cards then you'll feel at home with *Cardbox Plus*. It's basically an automated card filing system with knobs on.

This package and its predecessor, just plain *Cardbox*, are often regarded as standards by which other products are sometimes judged. When *Cardbox* was launched a few years ago it was hailed as a breakthrough in simplifying database systems. The later *Cardbox Plus* represents further refinement on the original, less flexible package.

Cardbox Plus is exactly what its name implies, an electronic filing system that simulates a conventional box of index cards. So close is the likeness that you can even 'draw' the index card onto the screen and then 'turn it over' and add information on the other side.

The package is a way of keeping a set of records about one set of things, essentially a list rather than a more sophisticated tool for relating all items on the list with items on other lists.

A full blooded data management system allows you to link different files containing entirely different information. Thus for example, if you keep a set of staff records these can be related to another set about their current projects, a history of their pay awards or internal moves.

Cardbox Plus won't do any such fancy relating of data across different databases or files. Instead, it offers great speed in creating new forms of record cards and then rapidly sorting them into virtually any combination that you might want.

TEXT

To the average working manager, a particular attraction of *Cardbox Plus* is its ability to absorb a fair quantity of free form text. This must always be an addition to a card which already has some initial data fields on it. You cannot just create an entirely blank card.

Nor can the free form text be indexed or sorted in any way except as part of a general rearrangement of the cards. But the ability to store and rapidly retrieve large quantities of text is a considerable attraction. You can add up to 8000 characters or around 7–800 words in this way.

Thus the package is ideal for keeping track of publications, mailing lists, abstracts, glossaries, letters, notes, action sheets and simplified personnel records. In fact anything that would normally go onto a conventional index card. Incidentally, the bibliography for this book was created and sorted using *Cardbox Plus*.

GETTING STARTED

To start the program you merely make the usual back-up copy then insert your disk and type '*Cardbox*'. Up comes the *Cardbox* logo, after which you reach the main menu.

The menu divides the operations into two types: primary and secondary. There are just three of the former: various tasks involving the database itself, defining the layouts of the cards (format definition) and various housekeeping facilities (utilities) such as copying and erasing files.

The secondary functions stem from the three main primary tasks. For example, if your choice of primary function is 'Database', then *Cardbox Plus* offers a further six actions. You can:

Use the database. That is, add and manipulate information in an already existing database

Analyse the way a particular database is organised – a rarely used facility

Create a new database

Repair a damaged database

Bulk Load, add record cards from an existing file into another database

Order, permitting the cards to be kept in different sequences, such as alphabetical or numerical order and so on.

If you choose one of these six then the package takes you to the next level of menu and you are again offered a series of choices, executed by pressing one of several single keys.

Learning *Cardbox Plus* is therefore possible in a relatively short time. After one working day you would probably be able to begin putting the package to some practical use. Some of the more complex sorting or layout arrangements for data though, will take much longer to master fully.

There are several attractive features that makes this package a usable management tool. At any time, you can redesign the way information is recorded in fields, which is discussed further below.

Secondly, to allow different layouts of information for printing and presentation purposes, the package uses the idea of a template. Thus for instance, in creating a personalised letter for a mailing shot, you face a blank screen on which the letter can be typed. When you reach a point where some particular item from the database should be inserted, say a person's name or company, you merely press TAB to insert the relevant item, after which you carry on typing in the normal way.

When the letter is printed, the name of the person will be automatically inserted at the right spot with no ugly gaps either side.

STEPS

Using the package can be summarised into six main steps. The first is to decide what your database file will be called. This file holds the database information and also keeps track of all the other subsidiary files for recording how index cards are to be laid out, sorted and so on.

The second step involves a fundamental decision about how the basic index card will look. This is called the native format and is an important decision point. It is at this stage that you decide what fields to adopt, how large each will be, where it should go on the card and what kind of heading (caption) to use. Thus for an employee's number for instance, you might choose an abbreviated heading such as 'Empl. No' or decide to allow space to write the whole heading out as 'Employee Number'.

Unlike some database systems the native format can be changed long after data has been entered onto the record cards. Indeed you can restructure all the fields and devise entirely different formats which allow the data to be laid out in entirely new ways.

Designing the native format is commendably easy. You start with a blank screen and are allowed 26 possible fields in which information can be kept. Each field is given a letter of the alphabet as well as a two letter abbreviation of its main name that will appear on the record card.

Thus 'name' and 'address' might be called A and B respectively, and be abbreviated to NA and AD. On the blank card or screen, the cursor is placed where you want to begin the field and you then press S for Start. Similarly you move the cursor to where the field stops and type E for End.

The heading (caption) is added and you move on to the next field. As each field is defined with its heading, a row of repeating letters appears on the screen in the appropriate place, showing the size allocated:

```
Address: AAAAAAAAAAAAAAAAAAAAAAAAA
AAAAAAAAAAAAAAAAAAAAAAAAAAAAAAAAAA
AAAAAAAAAAAAAAAAAAAAAAAAAAAAAAAAAA
```

To make the card appear neat and tidy, and appear just like a conventional index card, you can then literally draw a border around the card, no matter what the shape. This is painlessly simple and rather fun.

The third step is to save this native format on disk so that it is also available for adding new cards to the filing system.

Step four is to use the native format to begin creating index cards. Having called up the format you merely tell *Cardbox Plus* that you want to ADD data and up comes a blank version of your original format, ready to input information. You can use up to 65,000 cards which is more than enough for managers who intend using this package as a personal computing tool.

Step five involves the various special commands which the package has available. Thus, for example, *Cardbox* will automatically index all the words in a field or allow you to do it manually as each card is filled up with information.

Alternatively you can use a command to SELECT certain cards which can be winnowed out further to form a very specific group that contains the relevant information being sought.

The ease and speed with which cards can be selected should appeal to every busy manager. Suppose that you want to find the index card for an employee called Thompson. Having typed SE for SELECT, you merely type in the abbreviated name for the field, say NA for NAME, then a slash, followed by 'Thompson'.

Almost immediately, the card is before your eyes! If there are six other Thompsons, a note warns that this is 1 of 6 cards. Sets of cards can be pulled out and discarded, leaving others behind in a group, just as would happen with a pile of real index cards.

It is possible to search for items according to certain values, such as all people with an income between £15–20,000, followed by everyone over 35 and then everyone with names beginning with the letter D to K.

These selections are done singly. So cards are called up first by income, then by age, followed by name letter and so on. This may sound cumbersome, but *Cardbox Plus* is so fast that the process seems just like speeding through a set of real index cards looking for certain groups and then narrowing these down till the ones actually required have been found.

Having selected a set of cards, these can be sorted in various ways. For example, by one of the field names, or by ascending or decending order.

During this stage you may decide to create some more alternative layouts (formats) for the information, perhaps omitting certain fields and putting others in new positions. You can have as many alternative layouts as you need.

The sixth and final step is to print out whatever cards or lists you have extracted from the database in the chosen format. The only problem here is that you must define some of the print commands at the earlier step four. Doing so now will lose the latest selection of cards and you will have to begin again.

DRAWBACKS

Cardbox is not a sophisticated full database management system. It is strictly a file management system. Despite this it is quite elaborate enough for general management purposes.

It is possible to make various criticisms of the package at the detailed level. For example, you cannot call up a directory of files; instead you must ask for a file with a generalised title like *.* which will then produce a list of all files available.

Similarly, the package will not perform any calculations. Nor are some of the routines particularly easy to remember, though the program prompts do their best to help. For instance, the options for printing are rather complicated.

There is also no way of storing some of the more complex commands for later, repetitive use. Reviewers have found other minor annoying features too but generally the limitations will not bother a manager who is using the tool for personal computing work.

MANUAL

The manual is printed to a high standard and presented in an A4 ring binder. It has a clear but rather limited tutorial together with a sample file on disk to manipulate and practice selections and other commands. The tutorial is certainly enough to get you well on the road to using the product.

The manual itself is mainly jargon free, covering the facilities in enough detail to solve most problems. There is also a useful appendix on how to design a database. One of its suggestions is that you try to answer these questions:

What information do you want to store and who puts it in?

How do you organise the information into fields and who retrieves it?

How is each field indexed? What questions will be asked and what sequences will be required?

SUPPORT

Cardbox Plus seems well supported by the producers, who appear very committed to their product.

It is not particularly cheap, which raises the question of what you want the program to do. It is worth assessing carefully whether a full database management system would not be preferable, even if a bit more expensive.

On the other hand, the program is a very powerful package and its sheer speed and flexibility combined with relative ease of use, make it a tool that most managers would probably find more than adequate for their everyday needs.

References

BAGSHAW, Eric. Data at Your Fingertips. *Business Computing and Communications*, October 1984, pp 26–8
Database. *Punch*, October 1984, p 100

CONDOR

Type:	Database	
Management Verdict:	Getting started	(4) ****
	Ease of use	(3) ***
	General performance	(4) ****
	Documentation	(4) ****
Supplied by:	Granite Chips Microsystems, 21 Bon Accord Street, Aberdeen, AB12EA	
Telephone:	(0224) 571825	

Condor arrives with a monster manual that may well deter the average manager from going any further. This would be a mistake. *Condor* is a powerful database management system (DBMS) which tries hard to make the many facilities offered as simple to use as possible.

There are no complicated installation arrangements. Self-effacingly, the package is started by typing: DBMS, instead of *Condor*. Then, after the usual logos and licence number statements, you are faced with a blank screen, the word: Ready and an enigmatic A>> prompt.

What do you do next? Unless you know your way around *Condor*, you would probably not get far, since this package is command-driven. To make things happen the manager must understand precisely what instructions (commands) are possible and how to give them.

There is some occasional on-screen help in the way of simple questions and choices, made by selecting single keys. But familiarity with commands is essential for using *Condor*. One attraction of the package though is that commands are in ordinary English and easily developed into more complicated sequences of instructions.

There are about 40 such commands many of which are easy to remember, such as: Abort, Define, Delete, Display, List, Rename, Sort and Update. Others, like Empty to eliminate all records in a file may be used infrequently. It is possible to go far with just a few such commands before graduating to more complex ones as familiarity is gained with using the package.

Condor is a full database management system, that is, you can connect records in one file with those of another even if they have completely different layouts and field names. Thus you can link records as and when you need to, instead of creating one giant, cumbersome record system.

GETTING STARTED

Condor works by using three files for each set of records. There is a file for the way that fields are laid out (format), another which defines whether these fields are alphabetical, numeric, date and so on, and finally a file for holding the actual data which the manager wants to record.

To start a file, for example, you must decide initially how the data will be laid out and defined. Changes can be made later if necessary. The file is given an eight letter name such as 'Customer', and you instruct *Condor* that you wish to: Define Customer. A blank screen then allows you to put the various fields where and how you want. You can have up to 127 fields. The process of deciding the layout of the record and the field definitions is quick and painless. Learning is a matter of hours not days.

To put data into the customer file you merely type: Enter Customer and up comes the record card which you have designed and specified. It is blank, ready for information to be added. Listing the results is equally simple. For instance, to create a report of all customers shown by their names and city you would merely enter: List Customer by First.name Last.name City.

Selecting records is again straightforward, for example: Select Customer where First. name is Taylor. However, *Condor* does this by creating a temporary file called Result. To see it you must give another instruction: List result. This is inflexible and at times irritating.

The program will sort the contents of a file so that you can show your information in a variety of ways. Up to 32 fields at once can be used for sorting, though this can take a considerable time. For instance, to sort 1000 records using two criteria for locating 50 records, can take nearly half an hour.

Other features such as calculations, making relationships or links between different files, simultaneously adding or altering information to whole batches of files, are all handled well by *Condor*.

LEARNING

Familiarity with part of *Condor* makes it easy to understand the rest since its general approach to helping the user is consistent. A manager committed to learning and using this package should be at home with many of the more useful features within a few weeks.

The documentation supplied is certainly substantial. It consists of a well presented, three-part user guide which becomes progressively more advanced and a detailed reference guide. The latter includes a full list of error messages, a glossary and an index.

This package is usable by someone who has little or no computer knowledge. But busy managers need to be aware that it demands hard work in mastering working through the three tuition sections. Having done so though, *Condor* is a rewarding product to use.

References
High Flying Database. *Sixteen Bit Computing*, March 1984, pp 52, 54, 55
LANG, Kathy. Database Comparison. The Story So Far, *Personal Computer World*, January 1985 pp 140–1, 143, 202, 203

DATAMASTER

Type:	Database	
Management Verdict:	Getting started	(4) ****
	Ease of use	(4) ****
	General performance	(4) ****
	Documentation	(4) ****
Supplied by:	Sapphire Systems Ltd,	
	180 Cranbrook Rd,	
	Ilford,	
	Essex IG1 4LX	
Telephone:	(01) 554 0582	

DataMaster comes with a well produced tutorial disk that operates almost like a film. You can speed up or slow down the material so that you can choose your own pace. The tutorial is designed like a sandwich course: you complete a module then practise examples provided in the manual.

By the time you have completed the tutorial you should be able to put *DataMaster* to work. Well, that is the theory! In fact, the package arrived with a faulty disk which refused to work and a somewhat embarrassed Sapphire Systems man had to change it.

It is a measure, though, of the ease of using *DataMaster* that even without this disk it is possible to get the system working quickly and relatively painlessly by following screen instructions and regularly dipping into the exceptionally well produced manual.

US CONNECTIONS

DataMaster is one the bestselling products of its kind in America, where it is called *DataEase*, with some justification.

Most database systems for personal computers are merely the equivalent of an electronic card index box. Each card is a record and records can usually be sorted and selected in various combinations. But if you have another set of records there is often no way of linking the two together.

For example, as a manager you might keep a set of basic records on each of the staff for whom you are responsible. But the record card might get unwieldy if you also tried to keep track of each person's holiday and sickness history. A second set of cards might be needed for that.

But what happens when you want information on sick leave together with facts about salary and date of joining? With many computer database systems it means extracting the information from two or more separate record systems and combining these to produce the desired result.

DataMaster allows you link one set of records with another so that what appears to be a series of separate files of records can be made to work as if they were one giant record card.

Thus the program handles several files at once, which can save enormous amounts of time in keeping material up to date. Information which is entered in one record for instance, can also be automatically fed into other sets of records. Similarly, you can ask for information to be extracted from several files at once.

GETTING STARTED

DataMaster comes ready to run on your computer and usually on two disks, plus the tutorial disk. It is just possible to squeeze the package, excluding the tutorial on a single, double sided disk.

It is also necessary to instruct the package about the printer that you are using. This could cause a few problems if your machine is not listed among the options, although a universal version is provided. However, as supplied, the manual did not reveal this and it took another special call to the producers to discover this fact.

Using *DataMaster* involves three distinct stages: designing data records (forms), entering data, all of which is held on one database and designing and generating reports.

First, you must decide how the record card is going to look, just as if you were doing it with pen and paper. You start with a blank screen and begin typing in the various kinds of data that are going to be kept on the record. For example, you may decide to start with:

```
Name
Title
Department
Date of Joining
Salary
Current Project
```

This is typed exactly like this onto the screen, in any layout you wish. Next you return to the beginning, place the cursor just after the word 'Name' and press the key for Field.

The package then puts you through a simple question-and-answer routine. Even experts approve of this approach; it ensures that you cannot easily make a mistake in defining what is an essential aspect of using a computer-based information system.

If you are using the six items above you will be asked by *DataMaster* whether the information in each will be text, a mixture of numbers and letters, just numbers, sterling, a date or a telephone number and so on.

It is also necessary to say how long each field or item of information is likely to be. Since you can use around 250 characters per field, there is plenty of room for more elaborate types of information.

You can have as many layouts of information (forms) as you want, subject only to your disk capacity. In building up these layouts though, you have to do your homework carefully. It is easy enough to alter your rough draft of the record card, but once you start using it for live information any changes may be more difficult and affect the database.

It can also take a considerable time to make the alterations. For example, to add one new field to a set of 1000 records can take *DataMaster* two and a half hours.

Where *DataMaster* scores is the speed with which you can set up a relationship between two different sets of records or files. Having chosen the Relationship menu, a simple form appears on the screen which requires the names of the two files that are to be linked.

Next you must define as equal at least one field in each of the two files. In fact, up to three fields can be made equal in this way. This process allows you to search for data in both files at once and bring them together as a single answer.

Entering data is equally straightforward since the form you have just designed appears on the screen awaiting the information to be inserted. When you are satisfied with the record card you merely press a single key and it is entered onto the database.

It is when you come to modify or delete an existing large record that *DataMaster* seems to falter. It takes far longer than it should for this particular package to make the adjustments and you may become impatient waiting for it to complete the job.

You are strongly advised to have a demonstration of this particular aspect of the package since it may be crucial in deciding whether it is a practical long term proposition.

REPORTS

DataMaster provides two types of reports. The first is a predefined one that can be used regularly and the second an ad hoc enquiry. Again the program scores strongly in its ability to help the user define complex questions without a knowledge of programming or using elaborate codes.

You can quiz the database merely by answering *DataMaster*'s own questions. For example, if you wanted to list all male employees with a salary over £7000 you would reply to various *DataMaster* choices and end up with:

```
for Employees
with Sex=Male and
Salary>7000
list records
Name
```

When you become familiar with *DataMaster*'s special way of searching the database you can choose not to use the step-by-step menu way of building up an enquiry and type the query straight in.

Although the query language feels strange at first, the menu approach rapidly teaches the user what it is all about. Once learned, the flexibility and range of data searching makes the package an extremely powerful one.

DOCUMENTATION

The A4 manual is well designed and there are plenty of examples of how the screen will appear under different conditions. The writing is particularly clear and easy to follow.

There is also a separate, smaller and more specialist manual on how to produce different types of reports and how to use *DataMaster*'s special query language. There are dozens of working examples which not only provide a good model for defining your own questions but which demonstrate clearly how to use the query techniques.

Where both documents are weak is that the use of examples has become a substitute for clear statements about the rules for using the program.

DRAWBACKS

A particular drawback of this package is the way that it actually looks on the screen. There is a mess of thick, highlighted prompts and menus. It is quite difficult sometimes to decide which keys they refer to.

There is not always a clear statement from *DataMaster* as to what it is doing and an inflexibility sometimes in allowing the user to abandon a particular operation. You may have to complete a routine simply in order to delete the material and start again.

A more serious limitation concerns the ability to call up more than one record at a time from different files to examine the contents. While the package will allow you to extract practically any combination of information from sets of records into a single answer, this must occur using the query language or a predefined reporting arrangement. By contrast, some competing products let the user view two records simultaneously, using the windows concept.

If you intend to keep a large number of records on the database and also propose to have a whole series of files likened to each other, then updating records could prove unacceptably time consuming.

The drawbacks to *DataMaster* though are heavily outweighed by its ease of use and power. Managers looking for a database system that they can reasonably expect to begin using in a few days and which they will not also rapidly outgrow will find this package worth investigating.

References

LANG, Kathy. DataMaster. *Personal Computer World,* May 1984, pp 242–3, 245–6
Database Packages. *Business Micro*, November 1983, pp 31, 32, 35–6
DataMaster. Which Computer?, April 1984
WOOLEY, Ben. The Rivals in Friendliness. *Apricot User*, February 1985, pp 36–8, 44–5

DATEBOOK

Type:	Diary	
Management Verdict:	Getting started	(5) *****
	Ease of use	(5) *****
	General performance	(4) ****
	Documentation	(4) ****
Supplied by:	Raven Computers, 28-32 Cheapside, Bradford, West Yorkshire BD1 4JA	
Telephone:	(0274) 309386	

Keeping track of appointments and scheduling meetings for a busy executive can be a minor nightmare. If there are several such people to be assisted in this way then the task can consume hours wasted in fixing and refixing meetings as situations change and new requests for appointments, conferences and access time are demanded.

Datebook is an automated diary. It is designed to speed the process of keeping track of personal schedules and to handle the inevitable process of change. The typical manager's diary can rapidly become an unreadable scrawl if many changes have to be made to planned meetings. Also, it is helpful to start each day with a neatly printed list of the forthcoming events. Creating such a list with *Datebook* is easy and equally simple to amend.

The package can handle the appointments of up to 27 managers by grouping them together in nine blocks of three. Alternatively, if there are limited room facilities for meeting, the system can be used for scheduling their use. It could also be used for keeping track of equipment that is loaned or hired out.

INITIAL DECISIONS

If the diary is for more than one person the first choice must be how to group them into blocks of three. This applies if instead of managers' names the system is being used for room bookings.

Next it is necessary to select the earliest time that an appointment can be made. *Datebook* uses a 12 hour day and the earliest time must be expressed as an even hour, that is 9.00am, 10.00am and so on.

The next crucial choice is the time interval on which the diary system is to be based: 10, 15, 20 or 30 minutes. The intervals are governed by how finely you want to schedule your time. All appointments must be made in multiples of the chosen interval. Once selected, this cannot be altered without losing all the appointments that have been entered.

After this, by pressing single keys you must define your normal working hours. For example:

```
(B)egin work   = 8: 00
(S)tart lunch =12: 00
(F)inish lunch= 1: 00
(E)nd work    = 5: 00
```

The limits set are used when *Datebook* searches for appointment openings. However, they can be ignored with a specific instruction to do so.

It is also necessary to define your normal working days from Monday through to Sunday. These can also be ignored if you deliberately choose to do so when making an appointment.

The final set of decisions that must be made in creating the diary system concerns the number of days ahead that the diary will schedule. This depends on the number of people handled by the diary system and the capacity of the floppy disk.

For example, a 126K disk can handle 1600 appointments for one person spread over 140 days. Alternatively, where appointments need not be scheduled very far in advance the disk could store 120 appointments each for 12 people spread over 28 days. The manual contains a formula for calculating appointments and days in advance in relation to disk space.

The screen display shows a list of diary times for one to three people broken down into the time intervals selected. At the bottom of the screen are a list of menu options.

GETTING STARTED

There are no complicated commands to learn since every task in using the diary is started by pressing one of the letters shown in the menu. These allow the user to (S)chedule, (C)ancel and (M)odify an appointment.

Other options include a facility for finding out if there is any time free in a busy schedule, moving around the diary from (T)oday to (N)ext day or some time in the (F)uture.

There is also the ability to print out a day's appointments as well as displaying any appointments that somebody else has with the manager. This allows a person to ring up the manager's secretary for example, and ask, 'I've forgotten when I'm supposed to come, can you remind me please?'

Putting appointments into the diary is straightforward and altering them is equally simple. You are given several choices that include naming the person with whom the appointment is to be fixed, the time, the reason and the proposed length of the meeting.

Datebook also keeps a special list of up to 40 appointments that were originally scheduled but which for some have reason have been cancelled and are now in limbo. These can be rescheduled when time is available.

The Future list is a convenient place to put appointments that are scheduled beyond the diary's current range of dates. Each day that

Datebook is run, appointments in this list move one day closer to being within the normal range. When they come within range they are automatically removed from the list and put into the proper day's schedule.

The conference-scheduling facility is a powerful tool, assuming that the diary is serving a group of people who might meet together. After specifying a time and date together with the length of the conference *Datebook* will reply with one of four options.

`Each one's appointment schedule must be examined.`
(This searches through to check if each person is busy and also if there is another time that day when they are free.)
`Everyone can attend at the date and time shown below`
`All can attend between xx:yy and uu:vv`
`There is no time that day when all can attend.`

Once everyone is free the conference is scheduled by a single key stroke and similarly it can be cancelled later if necessary.

DRAWBACKS

Datebook is an electronic diary which is vulnerable to a number of problems. It is easy to cancel items irrevocably or, through some disk failure problem, lose important schedules. Thus it is essential to keep constantly backing up the data, continually making copies, since one mistake could throw into chaos the plans and schedules of many busy managers.

The system is most effective when it is working for several people rather than just one. If it is used for one person the screen remains annoyingly divided up into three sections.

There is limited space for putting in the title of a meeting. This may not matter too often but could prove a problem occasionally. Although it is possible to scroll through the diary or go to a specific day the inability to look at, say, a whole week at a time without first printing this out is restricting.

Probably the major constraint that the system faces is the need for it to be constantly running on the computer. If the package is justified in the first place then it will probably need to be accessed with great regularity.

This package would therefore be mainly effective in conjunction with a hard disk, since otherwise the diary would virtually block the computer for other uses. Alternatively it might be worth buying a dedicated machine just for handling the diary. This would only be justified if it was serving perhaps a dozen or more people.

As a tool for a single working manager *Datebook* would probably not be entirely appropriate but shared between several people it could be an effective time saver.

Produced by: Organic Software,
                 6049, Douglas Blvd,
                 Suite 17, Roseville,
                 CA 95678
                 USA

EVERYMAN

Type:	Database	
Management Verdict:	Getting started	(2) **
	Ease of use	(3) ***
	General performance	(4) ****
	Documentation	(3) ***
Supplied by:	Vector International Ltd,	
	6a Lower Teddington Road,	
	Hampton Wick,	
	Kingston-upon-Thames,	
	Surrey KT1 4ER.	
Telephone:	(01) 943 1257	

Everyman is not for everybody. It is a sophisticated database management system that puts to shame some of the facilities which big mainframe machines offer managers. To master it, though, takes dedication and more time than can be spared by many busy executives.

Using the package you can create a file containing many different sorts of records, each with different layouts and information, and then link them all together. Thus data can be entered in one place and then shunted to dozens of others, being manipulated on the way or altered automatically, without the user having to do anything.

An example of this in action is a personnel record system in which the basic details of an employee are added to an individual Employee Record Card. Other types of records, such as training, history of pay awards, departmental and corporate summaries, and so on, can then draw on this basic information.

A RELATIONAL DATABASE

Chapter Eight explains in some detail the difference between a simple record system and a relational database. *Everyman* is much closer to being a true relational data base than the majority of products that are currently on the market.

Most packages keep records in a file and, apart from some minor changes, the contents remain fundamentally the same, though layouts can sometimes differ. There is usually a limit to the amount of record linkage that is possible.

By contrast, *Everyman* does not care what the records contain, that is, what their structure is, as long as the user can define how they are to be linked. Nor is the number of links restricted.

GETTING STARTED

Disarmingly, *Everyman* arrives on a single disk. But making it ready for regular use is complex and the makers apparently assume that dealers will make any necessary amendments until you are confident enough to run the installation program yourself.

You can, however, start without that and with the special tutorial provided on disk and in the manual begin quickly discovering how *Everyman* works.

A set of records and the relationships between them is called by *Everyman* a 'project'. This is essentially a model; its creation, though initially simple, may deter some managers from going further.

You must define in detail exactly what you want to record, how the items will link to each other and the precise nature of these relationships. Some data, for example, will be derived from calculations performed when the card is created and the value stored in the item permanently.

Other data may not be part of the card itself but may be recalculated each time the record is updated. This is not retained, only the formula for the item is stored.

SAMPLE SYSTEM

Suppose a personnel officer wants to keep employee records on the computer. He might need one set giving details about each individual, another summarising the picture in each department and a third for the corporation as a whole.

All the separate files and records would need to link together to form a coherent whole. This task was once far beyond the abilities of the non computer specialist. With *Everyman* it is possible to develop such a system yourself.

The structure showing the links between the separate files is created on screen, using *Everyman*'s unique method of drawing. (see also page 122).

Individual records are then designed for the employee, the department and the corporation overview. All three types of records can be viewed simultaneously.

The structure diagram is read from the bottom up, so that the EMPLOYMENT box stems from the EMPLOYEE and DEPARTMENT boxes or records.

By placing the cursor in a particular box and pressing RETURN, you go to the relevant file and either begin designing the record card or, if the system is live, start adding data.

Installing the detailed relationships between individual items across different types of record cards is not easy and requires the use of *Everyman*'s special commands. In essence, you are learning a simple form of programming.

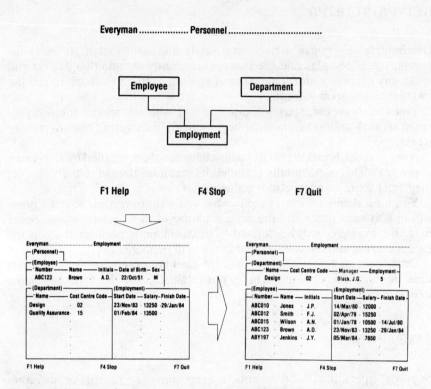

Figure E.1 A simple personnel system with files linked, using Everyman by Vector International

Any database usually passes through three distinct stages: design, testing and going live. A nice *Everyman* feature is that these stages are incorporated into the system. The fields on the cards or their relationships can be altered during the first two stages. Once the project goes live though, changes are possible only at the expense of losing the data already recorded.

Everyman will not permit any variation in how a record is laid out. It uses a universal format of one line for each record. Rather than spending time designing layouts therefore, you can concentrate on defining the variables, not wondering where to put the items on the card.

However, this standardised entry form may rule out *Everyman* for many applications where you want to copy the look of existing manual records.

Entering records is straightforward but the database must be live at this stage, not being tested. To select which cardbox to use, just place the cursor in the box on the screen and press RETURN. The record card arrives and to enter the actual material the cursor is simply placed on a new blank line and the data typed in.

REPORTS

Producing reports is not exactly *Everyman*'s strength. Indeed the manual describes the various steps almost apologising for their apparent complexity. The process can in fact be simplified using what are called 'drivers'. These are actually sequences of operations which are remembered by the package. You type them once and afterwards the package will repeat them on a single command.

The program can also 'learn' a specific set of key entries that the user has made and reproduce them on demand. This can save time if, for example, you want to call for a regular report on a topic.

HELP

Asking for help produces one or more screens full of text usually relevant to the current point reached in the program.

DOCUMENTATION

There is a hefty 200 page tutorial which takes you through various examples of using *Everyman*. This is followed by around 300 pages of manual. Both show frequent examples of what the screen will look like in various situations. The material is well laid out, typeset and printed to a high standard. The index is comprehensive and fully cross-referenced.

A small reference card gives an overview of the keystrokes for moving around the program and also the keyboard layout, but it is of limited value.

LONG TERM INVESTMENT

Everyman is powerful and innovative, but a package that will mainly appeal to managers who already have some familiarity with database systems and want a product that challenges their ingenuity.

In 1984 IBM announced that *Everyman* was to be the first European-developed product to be distributed internally throughout its own network, a rare accolade.

Although it is hard to master fully unaided, you are unlikely to outgrow this package in a year or so. Consequently, spending time to learn it thoroughly may be a justifiable investment.

References

BAGSHAW, Eric. Data at Your Fingertips. *Business Computing and Communications*, October 1984, pp 26–8

LANG, Kathy. Data Management on Micros Comes of Age? *Sixteen Bit Computing*. July 1984, pp 47–8, 50, 54, 56

LANG, Kathy. Everyman. *Personal Computer World*, 1984, pp 251–3, 256, 258

LANG, Kathy. For the Record. *Business Computing: The Survival Guide*, VNU Business Publications, 1985, pp 63–6

PIPER, Robert. Find Your Facts More Easily. *Micro Decision*, August 1984, pp 47, 48, 50, 52, 54

FILES and FOLDERS

Type:	Database	
Management Verdict:	Getting started	(3) ***
	Ease of use	(4) ****
	General preformance	(3) ***
	Documentation	(3) ***
Supplied by:	ACT (UK) Ltd, Shenstone House, Dudley Road, Halesowen, West Midlands, B63 3NT	
Telephone:	(021) 501 2284	

This package is aimed straight at the new computer user. It makes little or no concessions to those who might be familiar with software of various kinds. *Files and Folders* assumes that you do not know very much about anything and it goes on from there.

There are no complicated commands to learn. Everything, starting with the master menu, is strictly controlled by choosing from the clear English statements:

Get a Folder, Revise a Folder, Make a Folder, Make a Report, Other Functions, File Cabinet, Master Exit, Help

In addition, what comes up on the screen is the image of a real file card or folder, complete with projecting title tab, to be filled in with a suitable heading.

The package also uses the special function keys available on computers like the IBM PC and the Apricot PC. Thus each of the above English style commands is issued by pressing just one of seven keys. On the Apricot, six of these commands actually appear as words on the special LED micro-screen.

What *Files and Folders* offers the manager is a system for creating fairly structured records for such tasks as stock control, sales, general ledger, client data and other information that can be put into carefully defined fields.

GETTING STARTED

On the version used here, the package consisted of three separate disks. In fact two disks are needed to use *Files and Folders* and you have to put the right files onto your own working disks.

Accompanying the rather smart, cloth-covered container and professional looking manual was a rather tatty list of selected files that have to be put onto the appropriate back up disks. This somewhat tarnished the image of a well-thought-out new user's product. But once over that hurdle, starting up merely involves typing 'Openfile', to reach the main menu.

Because the underlying principle of *Files and Folders* is to take nothing for granted about the knowledge of the new user, the approach is always to go for the clearest way of presenting how to get from A to B. While this approach is helpful at the start, it can quickly can become rather cumbersome once you begin to know your way around.

But how *do* you get to know your way around? In most packages there is a carefully produced overview that explains the way the whole product works. Usually, this is supported by some kind of flowchart or tree, showing the menu choices. It's a sort of route map for computer users.

There is no such help in this package. Instead, the best way of getting into it is to work your way through the excellent tutorial. This is impeccably clear and at times quite chatty.

You begin by indicating that you want to 'Make a Folder', which is this package's term for a file. The layout and contents of the file are designed on the screen as you go. First you type in the title of the item, say 'Name', then press the key for 'Start a box'.

A box is *Files and Folders* way of talking about a field in a language that just about everyone can understand! You move the cursor along for the number of characters you need and then press a key for 'End Box'.

The caption must then be typed into the box itself and you are offered various choices for defining the field, for example whether it is to be numerical and if so to how many decimal places, whether it has a date or time and so on.

You can insist that certain fields be treated as unique so that, for example a number or name entered into them later cannot be repeated by mistake.

A further choice is to make some of the fields depend on previous ones. For example, suppose you list the price of something in one box and the quantity sold in another. A third box, representing Value, could be calculated by multiplying the other two together. *Files and Folders* lets you do this with an easily understood Maths function that can also test the formula before using the folder for live data.

RECORDS

The records for *Files and Folders* are laid out systematically and defined carefully at the start. They can be changed later in terms of layout and fields but, as with most databases, this is generally not a good idea once you have plenty of data already recorded. For example, to add one new field to each of 1000 records may take over 20 minutes.

One useful feature that the package offers is the ability to link various sets of records that are currently held in separate files. You can have up to three files open simultaneously and up to eight linked together. All files that are linked, though, must be kept together on the same disk or 'Filing Cabinet', as *Files and Folders* calls it.

What the linking facility offers, for instance, is that when you come to fill in the name of someone on a record card, their address which is held elsewhere on the database can be automatically transferred to the current card on which you are working. Thus data placed in one one part of the data base, can be switched to another location when needed.

Another helpful feature is the way that *Files and Folders* guides the user in the creation of mailing lists, including positioning the text in just the right place on the computer paper. There is even a screen image of a printer page, complete with perforations on either side, to make the task more realistic.

DATA MANIPULATION

Locating records is straightforward, just a matter of typing in the item you want, say the name of an individual, pressing the 'Search For' key, and the package will find the record virtually instantaneously. You can also sort the data by up to five fields at a time. However, you must have defined the items on which you want to sort when devising the original folder.

Data can be listed on the screen or printed out in two main ways. First you can print it out line by line so that for example, records can appear showing:

```
Name......Title.....Price......Quantity....
Name......Title.....Price......Quantity....
Name......Title.....Price......Quantity....
```

Or you can completely rearrange the data so that it comes out in any format you choose, for instance:

```
Name...............
Title..............
Price..............
Quantity...........
```

However, there is no way of storing a sequence of selections which can mean some annoyingly repetitive work when perhaps twice a month you want to make complex sorts.

DRAWBACKS

The price for trying to simplify the database management task significantly is a package which inevitably suffers from a range of drawbacks. These may only become apparent and indeed a matter of concern, once you gain real experience in using *Files and Folders*.

The software has different levels of menu and there is no way of jumping around from one place to another. You have to laboriously go from where you are to the next level and so on. Thus for example, you can find yourself pressing EXIT not just once but several times before you can finally get back to the master menu or leave the program altogether.

The file linking facility demands that you establish the various relationships as you begin creating the structure of the whole database. However, in practice the need to create links may only emerge later with regular use.

Perhaps the major limitation is that you are restricted to a maximum record size of around 1600 characters. This may prove rather limiting for some management purposes and the system is primarily aimed at applications where there are clearly defined fields.

MANUAL AND SUPPORT

The manual for *Files and Folders* comes in an A5 ring binder and is typeset. It is well illustrated and continually reproduces what your computer screen will look like at various stages of using the package.

The page layouts have been made particularly clear with bold headings, reproductions of what the function keys will do at different times and an imaginative use of bold type to emphasise various points and instructions.

The 80 page tutorial *Getting Started* is excellent and only a really experienced user might perhaps criticise it for occasionally becoming rather pedantic.

The package is well supported by the current distributors.

Produced by: Starcom Computer Corporation,
                    15446 Bel-Red Rd. Suite 340,
                    Redmont,
                    WA 98053,
                    USA

References

LANG, Kathy. Files and Folders. *Personal Computer World*, December 1984 pp 204–7
LANG, Kathy. For the Record. *Business Computing: The Survival Guide*, VNU Business Publications, May 1985, pp 63, 64, 65, 66

FRIDAY!

Type:	Database	
Management Verdict:	Getting started	(5) *****
	Ease of use	(4) ****
	General performance	(3) ***
	Documentation	(5) *****
Supplied by:	ACT (UK) Ltd,	
	Shenstone House,	
	Dudley Road,	
	Halesowen,	
	West Midlands, B63 3NT	
Telephone:	(021) 501 2284	

The whimsically named *Friday!* database package is for people new to microcomputers. This includes managers who do not have the time to learn complex packages, such as *Friday!*'s parent, *dBase II*. The latter is a bestseller, but few managers with duties that take them out and about have time to master it.

So Ashton-Tate, makers of *dBase II* have converted part of it into *Friday!*, to produce a less enigmatic and demanding product.

While *dBase II* has been criticized for being unfriendly, that is not giving much user guidance, its offshoot goes to the other extreme. *Friday!* is replete with menus, sub menus, prompts, questions, and requests for confirmation of proposed action. The package certainly passes the flying blind test, in which you can virtually abandon the manual and only steer by what appears on the screen.

This package is basically a simple, one-at-a-time system. That is, it only handles records in single sets. There is no way to link these to others for constructing a more elaborate database.

GETTING STARTED

There are two floppy disks, only one of which is required regularly. The other contains working examples used during the tutorial.

The opening menu is starkly simple:

```
A- Enter Data
B- Retrieve Data
C- Other activities
D- Leave

What do you want to do ? [ ]
```

Any of the first three leads to yet more menus and choices. It is hard to make a mistake.

Many users worry about what is happening after they have given an instruction to a program. Perhaps they have ruined the computer, maybe the program is being erased, possibly the data is being lost. *Friday!* keeps you informed with brief comments such as, 'One moment please, creating your file' or 'Saving your screen layout'. These are reassuring to all but the most experienced user.

At any stage you can return to the main menu, without first passing through other layers of choices. This makes for fast operating and leaves the user with a sense of having events under control.

If there are no files yet created, then the system automatically sets up one. This is the equivalent of a blank form on which are defined the fields in which information will be stored.

The layout for defining the fields, their length, name and so, on is fixed by the program so as to minimize the mistakes during this important process. Afterwards, you may reorganize how the form will be laid out.

To create your own form you are shown a grid on which to place the various fields. Though easy to use, it becomes tedious after a while and is less satisfying or flexible than, for example, the approach taken by *Cardbox Plus* (see page 154). The first field in any *Friday!* record is normally the unique one that is used by the package to conduct its fast searches.

Once you have completed the setting up process a few times it becomes exceptionally fast to design a new database system from scratch. Having defined the fields and their layout you automatically go into the next stage of entering data. Once the data is entered the database is ready for use.

If later you change your mind and want to add more fields *Friday!* lets you do this without the risk of losing data already entered. This is particularly useful since *Friday!*'s users may have limited experience of designing databases.

FEATURES

Too much should not be expected of a package such as this which does not aspire to offering the facilities of more sophisticated products. Browsing and searching for specific records is simple but if you want to conduct a more targeted form of search it is not so easy.

To obtain a report from the database there is either a quick presentation of information using a standard *Friday!* layout, the contents of which you may select from the fields available, or you can create a customized report. The latter require more time to design and involve instructions, using phrases such as 'Employees '$'! (Keywords).

The makers of *Friday!* claim that searches can be conducted with English style commands but the reality is not always that simple.

This package handles up to 60,000 records but each is limited to 1000 characters, divided between 32 fields. While the record capacity may not worry the average manager wanting a database for personal use in the office, the field and character restrictions may prove more irksome.

There is a danger that one will like *Friday!* enormously at first, but with experience, find that it is too limited. For example, helpful though all the menus and prompts may be, they could eventually become irritating and time consuming.

Another example of such limitations is the primitive system for creating personalized standard letters. The method used by *Friday!* is almost absurdly cumbersome.

DOCUMENTATION

Friday!'s documentation is impeccable. The actual text reaches a standard of clarity to which few other manuals aspire. It is superbly designed, printed in two colours and presented in a high quality ring binder that folds into a desk easel.

A unique feature is that every prompt on screen has its own reference number at the top right which can also be found in the manual. If you need help while using *Friday!*, detailed advice in the manual is nearly always available and highly relevant.

To help users gain an overview there is a well constructed flowchart (see Figure 4.2 on page 174) plus a fold out sheet summarizing all the commands that may be given to *Friday!*

Finally there is a separate glossy book called *Through the Micromaze* which uses excellent graphics to explain the basics of microcomputers.

This package will appeal to managers who want an easy way into database systems. Many will react to its simple approach with 'Thank heavens it's *Friday!*' Others, brooding over the weekend, may conclude that they will quickly outgrow it.

Produced by: Ashton-Tate Ltd,
Cofferidge Close,
Stony Stratford,
Milton Keynes,
MK11 1BY

References

LANG, Kathy. Friday! *Personal Computer World*, July 1984, pp 132, 133–5
LANG, Kathy. For the Record. *Business Computing: The Survival Guide*, VNU Business Publications, May 1985, pp 63, 64, 65, 66
LEWIS, Mike. Friday! *Practical Computing*, June 1984, pp 110–1

GRAMMATIK

Type:	Grammar Check	
Management Verdict:	Getting started	(5) *****
	Ease of use	(4) ****
	General performance	(4) ****
	Documentation	(3) ***
Supplied by:	Raven Computers, 28/32 Cheapside, Bradford, West Yorkshire BD1 4JA	
Telephone:	(0274) 309386	

When managers write reports they often forget the small details. Punctuation, cliches, and a mixture of vague, misused or excessive words can spoil an otherwise good report.

Even long memoranda can suffer from a variety of grammatical errors or overworked phrases. While successful managers do not have to produce literary works of art they are expected to be above average in their written communications.

Grammatik is a computerised way of checking written material for obvious errors and some less obvious ones. The program can highlight these kinds of mistakes:

Archaic usage, that is words like 'upon', which have fallen into disuse

Commonly misused words, like 'advice', instead of 'advise'

Overworked or trite phrases like 'down to earth'

Redundant phrases like 'seldom ever' or 'join together'

Improper usage like 'must have'

Vague words like 'fairly' or 'very'

Wordy phrases like 'all of' 'in terms of'; these can usually be replaced with just one word

Grammatik will also check for inconsistent capitalisation, for example, missing capitals at the start of a sentence. It notes any words that seem to have been written twice, like the the, and it traces dubious punctuation. It also recognises a variety of abbreviations such as: Jan, wk, av, oz, dept, govt, mins and so on.

A particularly useful feature is the suggestion of alternatives. For instance, if it finds the phrase 'a number of', it will mark this as wordy and suggest that instead you use 'several', 'many' or 'some'.

There are two other features. The first is a word and sentence analysis. Unique words are listed, followed by a frequency count of the rest. Words used more than once, twice, three times and so on, are shown in rank order.

For large quantities of early draft material this facility can help to identify possible themes and help arrive at a relevant structure of the main points. With long nearly completed reports it can help reduce excessive repetition.

The second facility is a check on sexist words and phrases. *Grammatik* will suggest that you change words like chairman to 'chairperson' or 'man hours' to 'person hours'. It could be useful to a local government officer preparing reports to a women's committee.

GETTING STARTED

This package is usually incorporated onto your word processing disk. Once a piece of text has been drafted, you call up *Grammatik* by typing GMK. You are then offered a menu of choices which are selected by typing single keys.

You may decide to dispense with the punctuation check, or require errors to be listed on the printer, or decide whether or not each identified error should be marked in the text.

The name of the file to be checked is typed in, together with another file name to hold the newly marked text. If necessary, this last action can be handled by *Grammatik* automatically.

It is strangely satisfying, sitting back and letting *Grammatik* whirr and click its way through your text, sending errors to the printer as they are found. A typical chapter of this book took about three minutes to process but it varies, depending on how many errors the program finds.

When the check ends, the program states how many problems it found, followed by some helpful statistics about the text itself. The latter are a useful guide to style.

Amongst the facts which the program lists are the average length of sentences and words, and the number of 'to be's' and prepositions. Short sentences and words, and a low number of 'to be's', compared to the total number of sentences are all accepted ways of judging text for readability.

Suppose that you want to avoid jargon or to break the habit of overusing the word 'but'. With *Grammatik* you can define a list of such words or phrases to be monitored. Up to 400 user-defined words can be added to create a personalised checker.

Since *Grammatik* knows nothing about the meaning of words, some detected problems will be correct in certain situations. However, the detection of many errors suggests that the document needs revision.

Although the package is easy to use, it may not prove entirely compatible with your word processor. It was originally designed for using with *WordStar* and does not work entirely satisfactorily with, for example *Superwriter*. It checks the text but spoils the indenting arrangements. So test *Grammatik* first, if possible, or get the dealer to confirm in writing that the package is entirely compatible with the WP system which you use.

Although *Grammatik* will also produce a profile of the words used in text this facility is not designed for excessively long documents. Using a computer with a 512K memory, for example, the software will not handle a document of 120 pages (roughly 30,000 words) in one go but will ask for the material to be split into smaller chunks.

Grammatik comes as a single disk and a 22 page manual in an A4 ring binder. Text reproduction is rather poor but the actual instructions are straightforward.

You can be using *Grammatik* within half an hour of starting. It is a tool many managers will find extremely reassuring to have available.

Produced by:　　　　　　Aspen Software Company,
　　　　　　　　　　　　New Mexico
　　　　　　　　　　　　USA

HANDS ON MICROCOMPUTERS

Type:	**Tutorial**	
Management Verdict:	**Getting started**	**(5) *****
	Ease of use	**(5) *****
	General performance	**(2) ****
	Documentation	**(2) ****
Supplied by:	**Microcal Ltd,**	
	Pilgrim House,	
	2-6 William Street,	
	Windsor,	
	Berks. SL4 7BA	
Telephone:	**(07535) 53828**	

Hands-on experience is what counts in getting acquainted with computers. This package attempts to give you just that, namely a practical chance to use the keyboard and become familiar with some basic computer ideas and jargon.

There are three modules of disk-based teaching, each of which can be completed in about half an hour. The main approach is to provide some facts and then gently quiz the student to check for comprehension.

The three modules deal with:

hardware – screen and keyboard, the processor, memory, disk storage and printers

information processing – disk storage, applications, word processing, financial planning and databases and programming languages

operating systems – functions, CP/M, MS-DOS, PC-DOS

Throughout the tutorial it is possible to recap and to select which module to work on. There is a brief manual which illustrates such items as a daisy-wheel, a typical computer arrangement with printer, keyboard, disk drives, processor and hard disk unit, and how disks are write protected.

There is a brief practical demonstration of word processing, a spreadsheet and the concept of a database. By the end of the tutorial the user should be familiar with the key ideas about computers.

There are however some severe limitations to this particular package. Apart from its brevity, the interaction between student and computer is confined to occasionally posing a few questions to be answered. Otherwise there is little difference between reading the text on screen or a book. Indeed, a book might be preferable since the amount of interactive learning is limited and screen layouts are often unimaginative.

The package is extremely cheap and, being aimed at the complete novice, is kept short. It is mainly jargon free and is a way of reducing a newcomer's fears by offering a chance to use the keyboard and to acquire a sense of controlling the machine.

Produced by:

Microsoft Corporation
10700 Northup Way,
Bellvue, WA 98004
USA

HANDS ON MS-DOS

Type:	Tutorial	
Management Verdict:	**Getting started**	**(5) *******
	Ease of use	**(5) *******
	General performance	**(3) *****
	Documentation	**(3) *****
Supplied by:	**Microcal Ltd,**	
	Pilgrim House,	
	2-6 William Street,	
	Windsor,	
	Berks. SL4 7BA	
Telephone:	**(07535) 53828**	

This computer-based training package teaches you to use the MS-DOS operating system in a painless, practical way. Not everyone though, likes this method of learning. It's impersonal, demanding a degree of self-discipline to complete the seven disk-based modules of tuition.

To make it seem less clinical, the package regularly calls you by your name, which you type in at the start of the course. 'Good! That's right John', or 'Whoops! You've got them both wrong Peter. Let me help you out' is the kind of chatty approach injected occasionally throughout the tutorial.

The package should normally arrive ready for your immediate use without any more preparation. After typing in your name the program checks whether you are registering as a student for the first time. If so, you are assigned a number which you then quote whenever you want to use the tutorial.

AIMS

The package teaches the use of these MS-DOS facilities:

    looking at files and directories
    simple file operations like renaming or deleting a file
    copy disk files and listing them to the printer
    control and function keys
    formatting disks
    labelling disks
    system generation
    copying and comparing disks
    chkdsk and recover
    additional facilities such as pipes and filters, multiple
        directories and changing the prompt command

USING THE TUTORIAL

There is a brief, 29 page, high quality manual supplied which supplements the program. Most of the training material therefore appears on the screen.

Once you are using the package you can usually choose from various options such as recap, obtain help, continue or end the session. As you progress, the program remembers where you have reached. So, when starting a new session there is a choice of carrying on where you left off, restarting the module at the beginning, or skipping to some other part of it, or even choosing an entirely different module.

The opening session consists of too much text, which is not much fun to read. But once the program begins simulating what happens with a real disk, the learning process becomes more testing.

The simulated part of the display is shown at the top half of the screen and the instructions are given below. Make a mistake and *Hands On MS-DOS* will ask you to do it again. If you repeat your mistake you are not asked to do it again but instead you are given a new explanation and then asked to repeat the action.

There is a sense of really using *MS-DOS* when the results of giving a command appear, as expected, on the screen. The shift from simulation to the real thing therefore, is easy. There should be little difficulty putting the learning into practice.

The presentation on the screen is not exciting or imaginative but the text is usually crystal clear and the average manager will probably advance through the course at a brisk pace. The complete course should take around three to five hours, depending on the pace of the student and the number of mistakes made.

This inexpensive package should get the beginner off to a flying start and save a wasteful struggle with just the *MS-DOS* manual.

Produced by: Microsoft Corporation,
                      10700 Northup Way,
                      Bellvue, WA 98004,
                      USA

References

TEHAN, Patricia. Training 1: Learning from a Disk. *Apricot User*, May 1985, pp 59, 60, 62

LOTUS 1-2-3

Type:	Integrated software	
Management Verdict:	Getting started	(5) *****
	Ease of use	(4) ****
	General performance	(5) *****
	Documentation	(5) *****
Supplied by:	ACT (UK) Ltd,	
	Shenstone House,	
	Dudley Road,	
	Halesowen,	
	West Midlands, B63 3NT	
Telephone:	(021) 501 2284	

Spreadsheets put business microcomputers on the map. Since then, packages have been pouring onto the market. There are over 60 from which to choose.

Few accountants worthy of the name now manage without one. But it is surprising how many managers have yet to discover the joys of spreadsheeting. For some it appears a specialist tool. For others it is for occasional use. But a common question asked is, 'What else can it do?'

Lotus 1-2-3 made a loud noise when it was introduced a few years ago. Vigorous sales promotion communicated the message that here was an easy to use spreadsheet which included a database system and both could rapidly convert data into graphs.

These integrated facilities appealed to accountants and businessmen alike. The product made huge profits within a year, taking the Lotus Development Corporation into the financial record books.

Since then, competitive products, all offering varying forms of integration between different types of programs, have been in frenetic pursuit. Lotus itself maintained the pace by expanding the capabilities of its original product, producing the equally innovative *Symphony* (see page 232).

So what happened to *Lotus 1-2-3* ? Surprisingly it has gone from strength to strength. Whenever carefully conducted tests are published by sceptical computer magazines, the same answer keeps emerging: *Lotus 1-2-3* is fast and easy to use.

Amongst the many companies that have made this package into an essential management tool is Unilever. Managers in its perfume and fragrance offshoot, PPF Limited, can now obtain speedy answers to questions like, 'What happens if we sell 25 tons of this perfume at such and such a price?'

The company's 50 page five year plan is regularly produced on *Lotus 1-2-3* and the program is popular with staff, including one accounts clerk who had never used a microcomputer before and now handles complicated tasks using the package.

Banks are also big customers. Barclays for instance, uses it for management services to customers.

FIRST STEPS

Lotus 1-2-3 comes with five disks. Of these, one is a tutorial, and the second is only used when you want to print graphs. The fourth contains useful programs you may need occasionally. But the core of the program is on a single, system disk. Because Lotus 1-2-3 is copy protected, the fifth disk is therefore a spare systems disk.

To install the package on your computer is exceptionally easy. It all happens automatically after you give a simple command. All you need to do is insert disks until the installation program is completed.

The manual then suggests that you begin with the electronic tutorial. This is a minor masterpiece, setting the standard for many other software products to follow. It consists of six modules:

Module 1   Getting Started
Module 2-4 Loan analysis work sheets
Module 5   Handling a database
Module 6   Graphing

These will take about a day to complete if you do not rush, studying what happens and perhaps running through some of the modules again.

After the tutorial, the need for a one- or two-day course will be much reduced. It would probably be better to begin using Lotus 1-2-3 for real work tasks and perhaps attend a medium level course. Not everyone perhaps would agree with this view. Simon Moores, Lotus trainer with Drake International, warns that 'you don't become productive with Lotus to start with'. He suggests that it takes from 50 to 100 hours before users can create their own spreadsheet models.

The success of *Lotus 1-2-3* has created in its wake an enormous training industry. There are more choices for training than any other package currently on the market. Courses are available for beginners, for those with some basic skills and for advanced users. There are also a vast number of books available on Lotus 1-2-3, which is always a useful indication of a product's popularity.

GETTING STARTED

There are two ways to begin. The simpler uses the essential product facilities and has help facilities every step of the way, plus certain safeguards so that new users cannot easily erase data by mistake. The alternative is to use the full system immediately.

There are extensive help facilities on screen, in fact virtually a full manual on disk. Whatever you are doing within *Lotus 1-2-3*, relevant advice is available.

There are more than 200 help screens available. If you choose a topic for help there may be several other advice screens available from there. However, evidence from regular users suggests that they do not see the help facility as a vital one.

Control

Lotus 1-2-3 is controlled by a mixture of choosing from menu options and giving specific commands. There is no way of abandoning the menus as in some packages and some users do become frustrated with all the choices.

The screen is kept as uncluttered as possible and to give the commands you press the slash key(/), at which a main menu appears:

```
Work sheet Range Copy Move File Print Graph Data Quit
Global, Insert, Delete, Column-width, Erase, Titles, Window, Status
```

Selections are made either by moving the cursor over one of these items and pressing RETURN or by using the first letter of the word itself. Once you become used to this latter method, moving around *Lotus 1-2-3* is extremely fast.

SPREADSHEET

The main part of the package is the spreadsheet which has theoretically half a million separate cells available. A more realistic limit, governed by available computer memory, would be between 10–15,000 which is more than enough for most management purposes.

You can vary individual column widths, protect cells from being altered by mistake or by less competent users, split the screen in two and work with different sections of the spreadsheet, merge spreadsheets, print them and so on.

The idea of the spreadsheet is no longer new, so that much of what *Lotus 1-2-3* offers is typical of many other products. But it has many useful features that are not always available elsewhere.

Unlike some spreadsheets, it can detect the difference between words giving a cell a title, such as 'Sales', and a numerical entry. You do not have to warn the package that you are entering a number. In fact the package handles text well enough for it to be used as a rudimentary word processor, though it is not designed for that purpose.

The ability to use formulae is an important aspect of the spreadsheet concept. *Lotus 1-2-3* has plenty of these available, dealing with statistics (such as standard deviation), finance (such as Net Present Value) and dates (such as being able to calculate the difference between one time period and another).

On all objective tests the package handles re-calculations speedily. If your spreadsheet is a modest sized one, then do not blink, you will miss the changes and wonder if they have occurred! Larger models though can be slower.

LESS TYPING

What makes *Lotus 1-2-3* particularly attractive to many users is the Macro facility. This stores sequences of key strokes for future use. It is an alternative to typing. Sequences are stored and given a single-letter name. They start when that letter is pressed in conjunction with the CONTROL key.

Many types of action can be initiated automatically, including the creation of spreadsheet layout. Thus for example, you could create your own template for regular use.

The facility will type a sequences of figures, including a formula, create a graph and interact with the user to allow them to enter figures manually and even to make decisions about what to do next.

Though this is a powerful tool in the hands of an experienced user, it is not easy for the beginner to use. It should be considered a facility to explore once the basics have been mastered.

GRAPHICS

Spreadsheet numbers can be quickly converted into a visual presentation using the graphics program. This draws bar charts, line graphs, block diagrams and graphs with two sets of variables, such as sales and profits. There is no ability to create three dimensional graphs which is a popular executive toy these days. However this is hardly an essential tool.

Creating graphs with *Lotus 1-2-3* is straightforward but it is not up to the standard set by Psion's *Xchange*.

To print the graph, it is necessary to store it first on disk and then use the separate Printgraph disk. It is cumbersome compared to the rest of the package.

DATABASE

This is the weakest part of the package. Even the tutorial disk makes a meal of this feature, leaving one wondering if learning it is justified. There are so many other good systems which can also use data taken from spreadsheets like *Lotus 1-2-3*.

The database is created on the spreadsheet grid. Thus each field occupies a column and each record occupies a row. Adding records is just a case of putting new data into the cells across the row.

Similarly, it is easy to add a new field later without upsetting the whole structure of the database. This is in marked contrast to more conventional database systems where adding a new field is either impossible or time consuming.

The database can be sorted and searches made for specific records. But this is not one of its strengths and many managers may decide to rely on other systems for such help.

DOCUMENTATION

When it was launched some years ago the *Lotus 1-2-3* documentation established a new base line from which to judge material produced for all other management software.

The manual remains good by comparison with many other products. It is well structured, clearly written, lavishly illustrated and well printed. The index is substantial and there is a particularly helpful special index showing all the commands in a 'tree' fashion so that their place in the overall program can be readily established.

It is a pity though that all this useful material is stuffed into an ill-designed ring binder that prevents easy turning of large chunks of pages at a time.

Finally, there is a separate quick reference guide that summarizes the commands, explains the functions keys, how to use Macros and other facilities.

ROLLS ROYCE

Apart from the limitations mentioned previously, *Lotus 1-2-3* is a particularly heavy user of computer memory. At least 256K is needed and even this may not be enough in some situations.

The package is priced at the upper end of the market, but then it offers more and works better than many, newer products. There are many cheaper spreadsheets on the market that are more than adequate for the average non-accountant's use. Despite its age though, *Lotus 1-2-3* remains the Rolls Royce of the spreadsheet world and some people will always want the best.

Produced by: Lotus Development (UK) Limited
                Consort House,
                Victoria Street,
                Windsor,
                Berkshire, SL4 1EX

Telephone: (0753) 840281

References

FOREMAN, Michael. Triple Attraction of Lotus 1-2-3. *Micro Decision*, December 1983, pp 47–50

HAWKINS, A. Look Beyond 1-2-3. *Apricot User*, March 1985, pp 66–7, 70, 72

LIARDET, Mike. Lotus 1-2-3. *Personal Computer World*, November 1983, pp 132–5

VAIL, Simon. Sniffing Out The Right Formulae. *Micro Decision*, November 1985, pp 126–7, 130

The Best Spreadsheet. *Which Computer?*, December 1984, pp 99, 101, 103, 109, 112, 113

As easy as 1-2-3. *Which Computer?*, January 1984, pp 163, 165

Computer Tutors. *Which Computer?*, June 1984, pp 86–7, 89

Lotus 1-2-3. *Which Computer?*, May 1985, pp 57, 61, 64, 66

MICROFILE

Type:	Filing System	
Management Verdict:	Getting started	(5) *****
	Ease of use	(5) *****
	General performance	(3) ***
	Documentation	(2) **
Supplied by:	Lutterworth Software, 126 New Walk, Leicester, LEI 7JA	
Telephone:	(0533) 550822	

Learning to use the average database usually takes several hours and often days or weeks. The manual alone will normally be dozens of pages long. You have be prepared for a steady slog to acquire a good working knowledge of the package.

Not so *Microfile*. This low cost product which sells for under £50 comes with a manual produced on the equivalent of two sides of an A4 page of paper. There is no product hype with *Microfile* which makes no giant claims to be all things to all computer users. It is the equivalent of an electronic card index box. There is a sample database on the disk with 20 records on it. By playing around with this you quickly discover the potential and limitations of *Microfile*.

GETTING STARTED

There are no elaborate start up procedures. Just make a back up copy of the disk, preferably also containing a copy of the operating system, and you are ready to start.

Type 'Filesys', and *Microfile* immediately arrives to ask 'Do you want to set up a filing system?' If you say 'no', then you are immediately returned to the operating system. This can happen often if, for example you make a serious mistake, such as trying to create a new filing system using the name of an existing one.

Once you have named your new file, *Microfile* goes straight to the point by asking 'How many fields do you want (1–16)?' After this, each field must be given a label and a length. The latter must not exceed 40 characters including the label.

The limited number of fields and their lengths would not be acceptable for some applications. But equally, the card index systems which many managers maintain may only possess a dozen or so fields.

Having defined the fields, *Microfile* checks 'Is everything all right?' Either way, you return to the operating system, since if you are not satisfied you must start all over again, while if you like the results then the program records your file definition on disk and returns you to the operating system.

USING THE FILING SYSTEM

Once the file is ready for use you start from the operating system and type 'File'. *Microfile* arrives and asks for the name of the file and you are straight into nine main choices:

1. Add   (a record)
2. Amend   (a record)
3. Batch   (alter or amend records in batches)
4. Delete   (a record)
5. Examine   (the database)
6. Format   (choose a layout for printing or displaying records)
7. Print   (all or some of the records)
8. Search   (for a record)
9. Sort   (records)
0. Quit

To start any of them you press the appropriate number and the rest is just a case of answering a few simple questions posed by the package.

The sheer simplicity of *Microfile* is a pleasure to use. But it is important to realise that there are severe limitations on how the package works and what you can actually do with it. For example, when you come to add items into a record there is no facility for deleting a wrongly typed letter or number. Instead you must erase the entire field and start again.

The restrictions imposed by the package become more apparent when you want to inspect the database in some way. The Examine option is merely a chance to demand a particular record by number, if you know what that is in the first place.

The Search facility is extremely basic. You can demand to see records based on data held in one or more fields but you cannot lay down any conditions such as everyone who lives in Sheffield or London. Nor can you ask for everyone with a salary of, say, over £8000. Search will identify a batch of records but these can only be viewed on the screen or printed out, they cannot be sorted any more, nor can they be sent to another file for rearranging.

The Sort routine itself can hardly claim that title. Using whichever field you choose, all it does is to rearrange the existing record cards from A to Z. It will not work in reverse, from Z to A. No other kinds of sorts are possible.

Record cards can be changed in bulk, for example if you want to enter the current date, using the batch command. You can also create an alternative, temporary format so that just some of the fields can be printed out with varying amounts of spaces between them. This allows a standard letter to be produced using the addresses on the record cards, together with a salutation, such as 'Dear John'.

There is a top limit of just over 32,000 record cards but this package is definitely not aimed at a large record application. But as a fast, easy to use electronic card index system it will attract managers who want instant results.

References

LEIGH, Andrew. The Pocket Money Software Suites. *Apricot User*, July 1985, pp 24, 25, 28, 30

MILESTONE

Type:	Project management	
Management Verdict:	Getting started	(5) *****
	Ease of use	(5) *****
	General performance	(4) ****
	Documentation	(4) ****
Supplied by:	Raven Computers	
	28/32 Cheapside,	
	Bradford	
	West Yorkshire BD1 4JA	
Telephone	(0274) 309386	

A favourite NASA technique to control the launching of space vehicles is Critical Path Analysis. It was developed in the 1950s to aid planning and development of the Polaris missile.

Though seldom working on the giant scale of NASA or major defence contracts, most managers plan and control projects of varying size and complexity. Like NASA, they are concerned with organising manpower, money and time to make projects or tasks happen on schedule, in the most efficient way possible.

Critical Path Analysis (CPA) treats a whole job as a series of smaller tasks. Before some of these can be started, certain others may first have to be completed, hence the critical paths which directly influence the outcome. If certain tasks are done too slowly or not completed, the whole project may be slowed or halted.

Many organisations now use CPA to control the development of large scale development, purchasing, documentation, delivery and product testing. But this kind of analysis requires a large mainframe or minicomputer. Only experts tend to make use of such facilities.

Milestone is a simplified form of CPA which runs on the average business personal computer. It comes on a single disk with a commendably short manual of just over 80 pages.

The package creates a project schedule on the screen. The first step is to break down the job into its component parts and make several simple decisions such as:

what time scale to use, for example, hours, days, weeks, months, quarters or years

project start date

names of the various project activities (jobs)

how long each activity should take

dependency: that is, whether the start of an activity depends on the
completion of other activities, and if so, which ones

At each stage of the project you can also record the manpower implications
shown as skills required, and the costs.

The most important decisions when using *Milestone* concern the dependencies. The package needs to know whether there is any relationship
between the start of an activity and the finishing of any other. You can make
any one single activity dependent on the completion of up to nine others. If
it needs more than nine dependencies, the job must be broken down into
smaller components.

In theory, the number of jobs or activities in each project can run into
thousands. Few managers will use more than two or three score. The
amount of computer memory available governs how many activities *Milestone* can control. With 64K it holds 190 jobs and with a business personal
computer the number may well exceed 500.

ON SCREEN

What appears on the screen is a series of arrows showing the time that each
project takes. The basic form of schedule is shown in the diagram, which
illustrates ten stages of laying a small street sewer.

The double thick arrows reveal the critical paths. If any of these activities
are slowed down or speeded up, the whole project schedule alters.

```
First Street Water Main, Revision 1, 3/26/85
Prepared by Andrew

                                Feb                  Mar                     Apr  Apr                May
Job Description                 6    13   20   27   5    12   19   26   2    9    16   23   30   7
                                0    1    2    3    4    5    6    7    8    9    10   11   12   13
     1 Purchase the pipe        O---------->.........>    .    .    .    .    .    .    .    .    .
     2 Dig 1st part of trench   O---------->.........>    .    .    .    .    .    .    .    .    .
     3 Purchase fittings        O====================>    .    .    .    .    .    .    .    .    .
     4 Lay 1st part of pipe     .    .    .    .    >=========>   .    .    .    .    .    .    .
     5 Dig 2nd part of trench   .    .    >---->..............>   .    .    .    .    .    .    .
     6 Fill 1st part of trench  .    .    .    .    .    .    >---->....>    .    .    .    .    .
     7 Lay 2nd part of pipe     .    .    .    .    .    .    >=========>    .    .    .    .    .
     8 Fill 2nd part of trench  .    .    .    .    .    .    .    >==== >   .    .    .    .    .
     9 Repave street            .    .    .    .    .    .    .    .    >==========>   .    .    .
    10 Repair sidewalk          .    .    .    .    .    .    .    >---->.... ..........>   .    .
    11 Project completed        .    .    .    .    .    .    .    .    .    .    X    .    .
              Operating Engineer=1    1    1    0    0    0    1    0    2    3    3    0    0    0
                       Laborer=3      3    3    0    4    4    6    4    2    0    0    0    0    0
                        Welder=0      0    0    0    2    2    2    2    0    0    0    0    0    0
          Total manpower level=4      4    4    0    6    6    9    6    4    3    3    0    0    0
                  Manpower cost=2.5K  2.5K 2.5K 0    3.5K 3.5K 5.5K 3.5K 3K   3K   3K   0    0    0
                   Direct cost=75K    0    5K   0    13K  0    10K  5K   10K  30K  0    0    0    0
               Total cost=77K         2.5K 7.5K 0    16K  3.5K 15K  8.5K 13K  33K  3K   0    0    0

Symbol - Explanation
>----->    Duration of a normal job
>....>     Slack time for a normal job
>====>     Duration of a critical path job
>::::>     Duration of a completed job
*          Job with zero duration
O---->     Job with no prerequisites
>----X     Job with no successors
```

Figure M.1 Using Milestone's critical path analysis facility to schedule laying a street water main

Milestone offers a choice of whether to calculate the critical path. This is a helpful option since often a manager may merely want to use the system to show the time scales for a variety of different, unconnected projects.

At the bottom of the screen are several choices. You can decide to add, erase or insert a job. Also the whole schedule can be modified by changing the arrangements for each activity, for example its dependencies.

Though you can alter the starting date of the project the selected time scale cannot be readily changed once the projects or activities have been entered.

The package will also produce a series of reports summarising how resources are being used, the starting, finishing time and duration of the activities, whether these have been completed, and an indication of any slack time in the system.

An important reporting facility is the ability to produce a print out of the entire time schedule, no matter how large this may be. It is printed on computer paper in sections which can then be taped together to produce a complete picture of the project.

EASE OF USE

The attractions of *Milestone* are the ease with which you can learn to use it and the power that it places at your disposal.

John J. Christensen, for example, works at the Boeing Aerospace Company in Seattle with access to some of the most sophisticated computers in the world. But when he starts a new project he runs a test schedule through a microcomputer.

He uses *Milestone* regularly and once the package displays a firm estimate of material and manpower costs, he finds that the schedule becomes a driving force behind the project and its focus. 'People are expected to measure up to it. What's interesting, is that even though the whole process takes only about an hour's work, the finished reports look like you had to put much more into it.'

Milestone is entirely controlled by a simple menu that is rapidly understood and requires no learning of codes. The package is interactive, that is, you can keep altering the contents of a particular project to test what happens under different assumptions.

The interactive nature of *Milestone* is of particular benefit to managers who are not familiar with breaking projects down into the form needed for CPA. You can start with just one or two activities and create the schedule as you progress, using each development to spark off other thoughts about possible activities which ought to be recorded.

By pressing S for Sort, and R for Re-number, the activities can be re-organised and automatically re-numbered into the most logical sequence.

DRAWBACKS

Since *Milestone* does not aspire to being a comprehensive CPA system it naturally has some limitations. It is not possible, for example, to record a fraction of a task indicating that it has reached, say, half way through completion.

Secondly, it does not attempt to provide a system for allocating resources, or for incorporating probabilities about how long individual activities might take.

Thirdly, the descriptions of the individual tasks must be kept short when in some situations a longer title might be desirable. The final drawback is the inability to alter the time schedule once this is created.

These limitations are a small price to pay, though, for a powerful scheduling system that is rapidly learned and generally flexible in use.

SUPPORT

The package is an American one and distributed by Raven Computers. The latter maintain a regular customer support service which is generally available during working hours.

Produced by: Organic Software,
                        6049, Douglas Blvd,
                        Suite 17, Roseville,
                        CA 95678
                        USA

References

LEIGH, Andrew. Time your Tasks, Move After Move. *Apricot User*, June 1985, pp 50–52, 54

THE NEGOTIATION EDGE

Type:	**Organizer (behavioral science)**	
Management Verdict:	Getting started	(5) *****
	Ease of use	(5) *****
	General performance	(5) *****
	Documentation	(2) **
Supplied by:	Thorn EMI Computer Software	
	Thomson House,	
	296 Farnborough Road,	
	Farnborough,	
	Hants, GU14 7NF	
Telephone:	(0252) 543333	

Every manager occasionally negotiates. It may be with other managers, at formal trade union meetings, with clients or simply with subordinates. Obtaining what you want is a rare skill and effective advice on how to succeed is worth paying for.

Increasingly computers are being used to produce what are called expert systems. That is, the know-how of one or more specialists is drawn together into a computer-based system for providing advice and information.

Expert systems try to provide through the computer the benefit of access to people who really know what they are talking about in a particular field. In the most elaborate systems you can ask questions and use the knowledge stored in the computer to produce facts and suggestions.

In the simpler systems you can obtain the equivalent of informed coaching about how best to proceed or a set of facts which the imaginary expert in the computer considers that you will find helpful.

The Negotiation Edge, by Human Edge Software of Palo Alto, California, is part of a series of computer-based advice systems available for the microcomputer dealing with, amongst other topics, selling, management and communications.

The package comes on two disks and with a manual that will hardly be used since the program is virtually self-sufficient. Presumably to avoid the appearance of selling just a couple of disks, there is also a brief appendix on the fundamentals of negotiation.

The points made though are much the same as in any guide to successful negotiation: types of negotiation, persuasion and power, negotiating authority, using questions, using adjournments, and so on.

The real benefit of *The Negotiation Edge* only starts when you insert the program and output disks and begin to tap the expert at your disposal.

USING THE NEGOTIATION EDGE

The package works by first asking you a series of highly personal questions about yourself. You indicate whether you agree or disagree with various statements such as:

I usually arrive early for an appointment
I enjoy talking in front of a group
It's not whether you win or lose that matters but how you play the game
I like things best when they are somewhat confused and the correct approach isn't clear
Winning is all that matters in negotiations
I like to have power over others
I am concerned about the welfare of others
People usually have hidden motives when they negotiate

There are some 90 such questions and you must answer each, one way or the other. Depending on how well you know yourself, you should complete the personal profile within about five or ten minutes. It is possible to alter the answers, either as you progress or later, since the computer stores your profile for regular use.

Next, you give the name of someone with whom you are intending to negotiate. You then answer a different set of equally personal probes about the person with whom you are intending to negotiate. This time you have some 90 different adjectives with which to agree or disagree as to whether they are an accurate reflection of the other person's behaviour and personality.

Thus you must agree or disagree that the person is:

kind, sarcastic, rigid, ruthless, inquiring, aggressive, controlling, charitable, conventional, cautious and so on.

Finally you are presented with eighteen specific questions with which you must agree or disagree, such as:

Peter Jones has a shortage of time for completing the negotiations
I lack enough time to complete the negotiations successfully
I have never negotiated with Peter Jones before
The power to control the proceedings is equally divided between us.

There are nearly twenty of these more factual statements to assess, including whether you and the other person are part of a negotiating team.

Based on this information the computer then draws up a behavioral profile of both parties, using well researched findings from human and social psychology. The two profiles are used to produce a strategy report suggesting how you should proceed to negotiate with the other person.

Answering all the questions is fun but also thought provoking. The computer takes only a few seconds to begin producing its analysis and if you have reservations about this information being stored on disk, you can always erase it at the end of the session!

THE OUTPUT

The Negotiation Edge produces a three to ten page strategy report, though the average size is about five pages. It starts with a brief overall assessment of how the two parties relate in terms of negotiations. For example, two extracts from reports produced by the program on real people commented:

> Both Peter Jones and you will approach the meeting in a serious fashion. Being an easy-going person, you should have few difficulties in negotiating with him. Bear in mind he is most impressed with hard facts and figures.

> Miss Jane Morton and you have quite different negotiating styles. You are confident of your positions and express them forcefully. She tends to worry about her actions and lacks your initiative in presenting new ideas. She negotiates best when the issues under negotiation are defined prior to the meeting.

These initial remarks are followed by an opening section which deals with two aspects of negotiating:

> the anticipated position that the other person is likely to take
> tactics and strategy

Here the advice is equally specific such as:

> Keep sarcasm and criticism to yourself. Your type of humour is not likely to be appreciated by Miss Jane Morton. Sarcastic comments only harm your relationship and make the possibility of reaching an agreement unlikely. Even if such remarks are appropriate, it would be best to focus your attention on the issues at hand.

Other advice follows on what to do during the negotiations, under such headings as:

> Avoid threats
> Appear cooperative
> Watch for bluffs

Then a closing section advises how to bring the negotiations to a successful conclusion. Brief paragraphs offer suggestions under topics such as:

> Stop short of walking out
> Know when to let up
> Check the fine print
> Use humour to divert Mr Peter Jones

The report concludes with some simple summary statements proposing the negotiation Game Plan.

Having produced a profile the program is at an end unless you want to give it another one to draw up. Thus the package is meant to be a tool for managers, available when they need it. It is able to give fast, practical advice on new negotiating situations.

Unless you have a vast amount of negotiating to do the package is unlikely to be used continuously since once you have used it for the various people with whom you must deal it cannot offer any further help. However, as you change your approach and perhaps alter your perception of life, it is possible to alter your own profile and likewise to amend the profile of the other party.

The most obvious weakness is that many negotiating situations are not with one other person but a team of people. The package makes the reasonable assumption that there will always be a chief negotiator in such situations. However, this person may not always be the real force in the proceedings. If there is such a key individual though, yet another profile could be created with a further report.

Similarly, if you want advice on how to get on with your boss the program will produce equally good advice but it tends to assume that you are negotiating a business deal.

IN THE STARS

The basic issue concerning this remarkable program is whether the advice is good and what happens if you do indeed follow it. Certainly the reports it produced during testing were reasonably accurate assessments of the people in question and how they were known to react in negotiating situations.

But is *The Negotiation Edge* merely a pale computer copy of the Delphic Oracle, dishing out pleasing but ultimately unclear advice? Is the package merely an electronic form of horoscope, fun but not to be taken seriously?

On balance the verdict must go in favour of the software package. It produces credible and at times specific suggestions on what managers should do to improve their chances of success in negotiating.

If you are already a seasoned negotiator then perhaps the package can be dismissed as irrelevant or at best only of marginal help. But it will be welcomed by those who are less practised in the art and would like some practical ideas to try at the negotiating table.

Using this package there is a reasonable chance that you will do better at negotiating than without it. And like all good advice, you do not have to take it.

Produced by: Human Edge Software Corporation,
2445 Faber Place,
Palo Alto,
CA 94303,
USA

NOTEBOOK

Type:	Database Management (text orientated) System	
Management Verdict:	Getting started	(5) *****
	Ease of use	(4) ****
	General performance	(4) ****
	Documentation	(3) ***
Supplied by:	Raven Computers, 28–32 Cheapside, Bradford, West Yorkshire, BD1 4JA	
Telephone:	(0274) 309386	

This database system will appeal to managers who have quantities of messy information to store, sort, organize and retrieve. Material does not need to be neatly classified, since *Notebook* handles large quantities of text and gives instant access.

It is suitable for personnel files, customer and mailing lists, product descriptions, client records, legal documents, briefs, research notes, abstracts, bibliographies, address books and so on. In fact, anything that can be stored as text and which requires rapid sorting, selection or retrieval can usefully be handled by *Notebook*.

LEARNING NOTEBOOK

The main features of the package can be learned in an afternoon. It has no complicated commands, all instructions are presented as options in the various menus. Records are entered just like using a word processor and are edited on the screen.

In theory, you can even use your own word processor to create the text for *Notebook*, which has a facility for importing 'foreign' material into the system. However, this facility refused to work with *Superwriter* and it seems advisable to ask to see this function actually working if you plan to import material in this way.

For busy managers with insufficient time to plan their database in detail, the fun of *Notebook* is that there is no need to reserve a fixed amount of space for each field or item of information. Indeed, you can create just one field headed, for example, Text, or Miscellaneous. Having done that, the field then expands dynamically to absorb the data or information which is typed in.

Later, if you want to add another field to the record card, this is easily done with a few key strokes. However, you cannot alter the basic order of the established fields without an elaborate procedure.

Each record can contain up to 20 fields and, depending on the computer, each field stores up to two pages of text. In practice, this means that on the average business personal computer, Notebook will absorb around 40 pages of text on each record card. The number of record cards is only limited by disk capacity.

EXTRACTING

Having entered data, either in an organised way under various field headings or simply as text in one giant field, you can then sort and select records in a highly flexible way. Selection has been reduced to a highly simplified form of menu choices. It is practically impossible to go wrong in the step by step process of defining the items for retrieval.

The strength of *Notebook* emerges as its ability to define any word or phrase in a large body of text under the selection heading: Contains. Using this choice, you merely type in the text you are seeking, and the whole database is rapidly scanned to find the item(s).

The power of the selection facility is considerable, it is the equivalent of having every word or sentence indexed. The limitation is that you cannot readily obtain a multiple selection such as requesting a run of records containing the names Jones OR Smith OR Thompson OR Houseman. To achieve this you would have to find all records containing Jones OR Smith, and create a file for these, then repeat the process for the other two names, finally merging the two files into a single one.

Sorting too is reduced to its essentials in an effort to make it trouble free. You merely press O for sOrt, and then choose on which field heading you want to conduct the sort. The final choice is between sorting the records in ascending or descending order.

Each time a sort or selection is conducted the retrieved material is stored in what *Notebook* calls a 'View'. This is an index of the material and in turn can be re-sorted and additional material selected from it.

DELETING

The producers of *Notebook* have paid particular attention to the dangers of deleting records and whole databases by mistake. A record is marked for deletion by pressing a single delete key, but it remains in the database and can be 'un-deleted' at any time.

The deleted record will not print out and remains available to view, taking up space. Similarly, if you edit a record after it has been entered in a database *Notebook* makes a new copy and puts the old one in a special file.

To eliminate deleted records and special files finally, hence reclaiming the disk space, it is necessary to reorganise (Compact) the database. Reorganising not only permanently erases deleted records forever, but rearranges the whole database for maximum efficiency. It also places a back-up copy on disk. This is a reassuring, fail-safe measure. But it also doubles the amount of disk space needed for each database.

If a database is large, this doubling of disk space required would be severely limiting. So *Notebook* provides a special program called Compact. This allows the database to be reorganised without also creating the backup files.

PRINTING

The material in the database can be readily printed out, either in the original layout or in special ones defined by the user. Though this latter process is easy to follow it is unnecessarily cumbersome.

Standard letters or labels can be produced in which information is drawn from the database. Compared to some products on the market, setting up these arrangements in *Notebook* is commendably simple.

DRAWBACKS

The speed and simplicity of *Notebook* makes it an ideal executive tool. Its handling of free form text is excellent and most facilities are quickly grasped and learned. The price of these benefits though, is that in some areas the package is inflexible. For example, make a typing mistake in defining what database you want to use at the start and you have to quit the program and start all over again.

Another drawback is the inability to select a series of records by giving a list of references. Similarly, though the package can erase certain files, there is no such facility for deleting databases.

Nor can you inspect what databases are available. The logic behind this seems to be the perhaps unreasonable expectation that most users will keep a separate disk for each database. It does, however, ensure that erasing a database can only occur as a deliberate action, right outside the normal workings of the package.

In fact, to conduct these tasks it is necessary to use the commands available from the computer's normal operating system. While this is not difficult, it can be a time waster.

Finally, although *Notebook* is geared for handling text it does not handle wordwrap. That is, when you get to the end of a line you must do a carriage return, just like a traditional typewriter.

DOCUMENTATION

Notebook comes on a single disk with a 144 page manual. The latter is in an ordinary A4 ring binder with text reproduced from the original typescript. The manual begins with a product overview, then a brief guide to installation, followed by a tutorial section consisting of 20 different exercises. The disk has a sample database to use with the exercises.

Completing the exercises is quick and sufficient to get you started with confidence. The remainder of the manual is a reference section and a helpful final series of worked examples, such as setting up and printing an address database, writing form letters, handling special printing problems and so on.

Produced by: Pro/Tem Software Inc,
814 Tolman Drive,
Stanford,
California, 94305,
USA

THE NUTCRACKER SUITE

Type:	**Simple text editor**	
Management Verdict:	**Getting started**	**(5) *******
	Ease of use	**(5) *******
	General performance	**(4) ******
	Documentation	**(4) ******
Supplied by:	**Lutterworth Software,**	
	6 Cromwell Close,	
	Walcote,	
	Lutterworth,	
	Leics. LE17 4JJ	
Telephone:	**(0455) 4259**	

The man who tried to give away real pound notes on Westminster Bridge had difficulty finding anyone who believed that it was a genuine offer. *The Nutcracker Suite* is not free, but at nearly the same price as a box of ten disks it may seem too good to be true. But this package is a worth a second look.

The program does not aspire to being a full blown word processor. But then many managers simply do not need the power and range of such systems. Some of the simple tasks, like typing a quick memo or an envelope address, can nowadays take longer than using a traditional typewriter. All the stages of calling up the program, which demands a date and often irrelevant other facts, typing the text, saving it, possibly formatting it to obtain the right kind of layout, then printing it, can be time consuming.

The Nutcracker Suite eliminates the more fancy routines of word processing and lets you use the computer almost exactly like an electric typewriter. Indeed, one facility it offers is the ability to type directly, line by line, from your micro to the printer, while still retaining all the benefits of editing on screen.

You have the option of whether to save the text and can make multiple copies with pauses for manually inserting the pages, or the whole process can be handled automatically with the paper being fed through continuously.

PROGRAMS

There are merely three programs that make up the suite. E(dit) allows you to type text onto the screen, including the line by line transfer to the printer. P(rint) enables you to call up a piece of text, a set of addresses or other material and have it printed in the usual way. Finally S(et) permits the user to choose some simple requirements for how the printer will perform. If your printer can handle the various options, there is a choice of producing the print in either large or condensed size, in bold, italics, with adjusted left margin and so on.

There is also a facility for sending other instructions such as justification commands to the printer. These must be typed in the standard computer code (ASCII) that most machines understand.

COMMANDS

The Nutcracker Suite is designed to be learned in minutes not hours. With a machine like the Apricot or the IBM PC, the package makes full use of the special function keys as well as the cursor direction arrows.

There is therefore hardly anything to master. For machines that do not respond to the special keys, or for people who prefer pressing letters for controlling what happens on the screen, there are half a dozen control commands listed.

TEXT HANDLING

Although the package can type continuous lines of text without needing a carriage return (wordwrap) this is an optional mode since the program is not meant for large quantities of material. It can only absorb 640 lines of text or about 10 pages of typing.

For longer documents the text must be split into several files and then combined for printing. Since few managers regularly type their own lengthy reports, this limitation is not necessarily a serious one.

Similarly, although lines can be deleted, there are no commands for eliminating complete words, sentences or paragraphs. Instead everything works line by line. To erase a word therefore, means either deleting it letter by letter, or moving the cursor over it using the space bar.

Probably the most confusing thing about the package is that it shows a screenful at a time, like real pages. In other words, you cannot scroll up through the text. But then a 10 line memo will not require such a facility.

The other irritating feature is the need to switch between an Editing mode and an Add mode merely to make certain corrections. The package is strictly a line by line product and if you want to go back three lines it means changing mode.

Nor can you move whole blocks of text around. Instead, material can be transported one line at a time. If it becomes laborious then it is time to call up the proper word processor. Text typed using this program can be read by most good word processors so that if the job becomes more complex than originally expected, you can always switch over to the more powerful WP package.

The Nutcracker Suite arrives in a neat plastic container accompanied by a manual on 16 pages slightly larger than the size of a 3½″ disk. It is well written and conveys the important messages with a brevity that will make many managers offer a silent but sincere vote of thanks.

This is a package for small typing jobs and is in no way a substitute for a real WP package.

References

LEIGH, Andrew. The Pocket Money Software Suites, *Apricot User*, July 1985, pp 24, 25, 28, 30

OPEN ACCESS

Type:	Integrated Software	
Management Verdict:	Getting started	(3) ***
	Ease of use	(4) ****
	General performance	(5) *****
	Documentation	(5) *****
Supplied by:	Software Products International, 13 Horseshoe Park, Berkshire, RG8 7JN	
Telephone:	(07357) 4081	

Open Access is an integrated product which, more than most, tries to offer the whole gamut of potentially useful applications for the working manager. Thus it contains modules on:

spreadsheets
information management
word processing
time management
graphics
communications

Monster software packages like this need to offer something special. Their cost, the time needed to learn them, the fact that they tend to displace other packages already being used and perhaps mastered with great effort, and finally their requirement to be built into a manager's work pattern, all mean that deciding to buy and use them is a long term commitment.

GETTING STARTED

The package comes on two floppy disks with additional tutorial and 'get you started' disks. It can be run with either two disk drives or one, with a hard disk. The main programs are called up from disk as they are needed, rather than held all the time in the computer's memory.

Because the various applications of *Open Access* are not all fighting each other for memory space, they are more powerful than some of the other products on the market that put all the program into memory at the start. However such programs are also sometimes slower in operation than is occasionally desirable.

To run the package you will also need 256K of computer memory and additional colour facilities if the graphics package is to be used. Colour plays an important part in the presentation throughout the package but it is certainly not essential.

If you are a beginner with management software and want to exploit the potential of *Open Access* fully it is definitely best to let your dealer install this particular product. But it is not essential and you can go a long way with it without worrying about this aspect, although you might find yourself frequently swapping disks.

COMMANDS

One of the attractions of integrated packages, particularly to a manager who is not already committed to one or more other products, is an economy of learning. Throughout *Open Access*, for instance, many commands are common and it is thus easier to master the basics of each separate module than it would be with entirely different products.

Included in the package is a template which fits over the appropriate keys to remind the user what pressing them will achieve. The two most important ones are the DO and the UNDO keys. Together, these control many of the actions which you will want to start or reverse. Throughout all the modules there are menus from which you choose the options either by highlighting the particular item with the cursor or pressing the first letter of the word.

Early on, you learn that *Open Access* uses windows to increase the amount of information which the screen holds. (See page 137.) However, this is mainly help information rather than actual data from the various modules.

Help is offered at two levels. The first offers guidance on what the menu choices mean. The help window opens by being overlaid on the original information on the screen thus temporarily covering part of it. You can then scroll through this help file and see what amounts to a page or so of clear guidance.

This facility is thus sensitive to the particular choices you are currently facing. There is always highly relevant advice available at the touch of a key.

If you press HELP again, another window opens with detailed facts about what certain selected keys will do on your particular brand of computer. It is therefore possible to make rapid progress with the software without excessive reliance on the manual.

Suppose at this point that you need to make a quick calculation. By pressing another key you can open a third window which shows a simple form of calculator, and you can complete your computation. (See page 138.)

TRANSFER OF DATA

Although there is good use of windows in *Open Access* for helping the user, it is not possible to freeze your current job and switch temporarily to another by opening a window on a different task. For example, you cannot be using the word processor and temporarily open a window on the electronic note pad, make a few jottings and return to where you left off.

To move data between one module and another is also cumbersome. It is first necessary to export it to a special file and then import it into the new place. If you transfer data from the spreadsheet into the word processor you end up with just a block of material, not a spreadsheet facility along with it.

SPREADSHEET

On offer from the spreadsheet are an impressive 3000 x 216 cells or over half a million. Few managers need this and the computer memory would probably be filled long before all the cells were eventually filled.

Data entry is easy and entries can be underlined, emboldened and justified left, right or centre. Up to six windows can be opened for viewing the spreadsheet though nowadays this is not an unusual feature.

One particularly useful facility is goal seeking. You decide the results that you want from the spreadsheet, then make the package work backwards until it finds the figures that would achieve this end result.

Some useful built-in formulae will also be appreciated by financially minded managers.

WORD PROCESSING

This is a full WYSIWYG system. That is, what you see on the screen is what you get on the final page. Compared to some other integrated packages on sale, this word processor is particularly powerful and pleasantly easy to use.

It will accept up to 32,000 characters per document which is more limiting than it may sound. If you intend to produce long reports regularly, this WP package may not be ideal for your purposes, though of course documents can be linked together to form a single large one by joining up files and other such devices.

Text which is typed to the screen is automatically saved periodically without user intervention. This is a failsafe method for insuring against some disaster, like a power failure. But some people prefer only to save their document right at the end of all the typing and editing, so it is worth thinking carefully about which approach you want to be stuck with for the next few years.

To print a document is rather complicated. You are greeted with a whole series of choices to make. Considering this package is aimed at busy managers the approach is surprising.

In the version tested there was no spelling checker, which may not matter for some users but it is a facility that many people quickly learn to appreciate if, as in many WP products, it is included.

DATABASE

The success of the famous *dBase II* package, has lured even the best software producers to try and create comparable products. What they ignore is that the majority of ordinary managers will never want or need such a powerful program.

The price for such power is complexity of use and the *Open Access* database is no exception. However, compared to many similar products it is far easier to learn and use.

The database system itself is a capable of handling more than one file at a time which, together with the special query language makes for a powerful facility. Up to 32,000 records can be filed though it is possible to link up to five files using key fields to allow much larger quantities of data to be manipulated.

The reporting capabilities of the package are sound, relying on the user to define how the material is to be laid out. *Open Access* comes close to offering what its name suggests. It is a product geared to managers and its success in the market place suggests that managers know what they like.

TIME MANAGER

The advantage of this time manager system is that it is integrated into the overall package. Thus there is no reason why it should not be available at any time without complicated disk swapping.

The module consists of a calendar showing all the days of the month, into which you can insert a brief two or three words as a reminder. The main purpose though, is to allow you to choose the day you need by rapidly moving the cursor to the right date.

You can call up different parts of the time manager, such as the page for making an appointment or the page for recording an address and telephone number, and a small note pad for making jottings about the particular day in question such as 'things to do'.

The program will produce a daily schedule of your appointments to be printed out each morning and will automatically schedule appointments that occur regularly on a daily, weekly or monthly basis.

Another useful feature is that if you want to prevent your lunch hours being booked up, or stop appointments before 9.30 in the morning then you can reserve certain hours for particular activities.

GRAPHICS

The graphics are limited in the kinds of charts it can display, namely bar, line and pie. However these can be produced in various formats, including several different types on one screen and three dimensional ones.

Graphic displays can be drawn from existing data and saved for later use. Thus you can create, in effect, a slide show of different presentations which can be an effective tool for managers who want to get their message across using the computer.

The creation of graphs in *Open Access* is not as simple as, for example, Psion's *Xchange* and it will take some practice to do it well.

COMMUNICATIONS

This module was not tested but is claimed to be able to transmit data to other machines over the telephone system and mainframe equipment. *Open Access* can also accept data from national information networks.

Figure OA.1 The Open Access kit

DOCUMENTATION

There is a get-you-started document which runs through a simple demonstration of each module contained on the getting started disk. It also explains clearly how to prepare work disks and make the system ready to run on your computer.

The second manual is a bumper volume that gives details of the system and a tutorial dealing with the examples contained on the tutorial disk.

The third volume is a reference manual describing all the commands and error messages. Finally, there is a pocket reference card containing a summary of the commands and other key information.

OVERALL

Open Access is solidly aimed at working managers and much thought has been given to making it thoroughly attractive to have up and running all day as a regular tool.

The product is well supported and regularly updated, though if you do not own an IBM you may wait a long time for the latest changes to arrive for your particular machine.

The components of *Open Access* would separately add up to around £8–900 and since it costs well below that it offers an attractive deal.

However, its main power comes from running all day and being used as a whole by a manager rather than swapping to other types of programs. This can be restricting but as a practical tool for a manager not deep into microcomputers *Open Access* is worth serious consideration.

References

BAGSHAW, Eric. One for All. *Business Computing: The Survival Guide*, VNU Business Publications, 1985, pp 73, 75–7
BRIGHT, Peter. Open Access. *Personal Computer World*, June 1984, pp 162–4
HAWKINS, A. Look Beyond 1-2-3. *Apricot User*, March 1985, pp 66–7, 70, 72
PIPER, Robert. Putting Your Office on Disk. *Micro Decision*, June 1984, pp 51–2, 56
Having it All. *Which Computer?*, June 1984, *Which Computer?*, July 1984, pp 102–3, 105–8

PALANTIR

Type:	WP and Speller	
Management Verdict:	Getting started	(5) *****
	Ease of use	(4) ****
	General performance	(4) ****
	Documentation	(4) ****
Supplied by:	Palantir Ltd,	
	Columbia House,	
	69 Aldwych,	
	London WC2B 4DX	
Telephone:	(01) 242 6284	

'New lamps for old' has been around as a marketing offer for a long time. Sensible people are rightly cautious about such temptations, or variations on the same theme. Nevertheless, during 1985 users of Microsoft's *Superwriter* word processor were attracted by an offer that many found hard to resist.

In exchange for their existing *Superwriter* package, plus a nominal charge of under £100, the producers of the *Palantir* word processor and speller sent their own product. The latter was said to be worth more than £350. Dissatisfied customers could have their money and their *Superwriter* back.

Palantir is a well established American product, aimed at serious users. It is a package with several interesting features, including an easy to use approach to advanced word processing.

The package is mainly what-you-see-is-what-you-get (WYSIWYG) so that, for instance, underlining, bold and highlighted text all show on the screen.

GETTING STARTED

Palantir is on a single disk, ready for immediate use on many computers. After making the mandatory back-up copy and storing the original, there should normally be no trouble in going straight to work.

There is a standard opening menu of ten choices including edit, read, save, back-up, print, help and so on. There is also a useful reminder of how much disk space is left. Knowing that 85 per cent of available space has been used helps avoid the dreaded warning 'Disk Full'!

There is a help facility which is only accessible from the menus and is not always strictly related to the problem area which the user is facing.

To instruct *Palantir* you can mainly choose from a menu or press the special function keys. But commands can also be issued by typing in a simple letter. This makes the process quicker, once you are used to them. The speed of learning *Palantir* will certainly appeal to many busy managers. Most of the main functions can be mastered in a day or so.

USING PALANTIR

Typing and editing is straightforward, but there are two disappointing aspects. There is no specific command for erasing single words. For this you must place the cursor on the first letter and move it to the end, having indicated an intention to delete. This is cumbersome and for large documents excessively slow.

Secondly, once text is altered it will need rearranging (reformatting) so that material is laid out properly without excessive gaps between words and sentences. This process does not happen automatically, as in some packages. Again, busy managers may find this chore irritating.

Reading a file currently on disk, saving text and making back-up copies are all variations on the same process which *Palantir* handles through simple menu choices.

Similarly, the File menu offers various options for erasing, renaming and copying documents. The most notable option is the Inspect feature which allows you to review a retrieved document without filling the memory with the whole document.

Typethrough is a *Palantir* feature which is absent in many comparable WP packages. With it you can communicate directly to the printer, as if your keyboard and printer had become an elaborate typewriter. This will appeal to some managers who want to put an address on an envelope or add a post script to a letter quickly. The feature is marred though, by a total inability to alter the text in any way, once it is on the screen.

The main benefit of Typethrough is the ability to send commands direct to the printer so that it can perform tasks which the WP package does not normally permit.

There is a good search and replace facility so that words or phrases can be found and changed either singly or en masse. Similarly, more complex arrangements are possible for moving blocks, which are always highlighted so that text to be shifted can be clearly seen.

Another useful advanced feature, which an increasing number of WP packages offer, is the ability to remember a series of words or phrases and then recall them to the screen at the touch of a couple of keys. *Palantir* calls this facility a 'Lexicon', others know it as a Macro.

Each Lexicon or Macro can store up to 250 characters, enough for entire sentences or short paragraphs. There can be 36 different entries in any one file and it is possible to create a series of such files, though only one can be used with each job without elaborate rearrangements.

Many managers will find this facility a real boon. It can eliminate endless chores such as filling in the details of a memo (name, addressee, reference number, circulation list etc), devising standard letters, act as an aide mem-oire and so on. This feature though, takes some practice to use correctly since the creation of a Lexicon must be done perfectly to make it work.

Similarly, the mail merge facility, which permits *Palantir* to print form letters, will also take considerable practice. But compared to many other packages on the market its methods of creating such documents are far easier and the manual is particularly well written at this point. A worked example using a mythical manager called Rudge, who must organize the company picnic, is gradually developed to show how to create a complex mail out system.

Palantir is able to cope with documents of any size since it does not keep all the material in the computer memory. Instead it refers to the disk when necessary. Few managers will personally want to type giant documents but total flexibility on document size is a feature which may be sorely missed if absent in a WP package.

SPELLER

Spelling is not the forte of every manager and avoiding such petty mistakes is crucial if a report or memo is not to appear slapdash and lacking in credibility.

The *Palantir* spelling checker, which is usually sold along with the word processor, comes on a separate disk and with its own manual. On a double-sided disk with over 700K capacity, it is possible to fit the WP package, the speller and the operating system, which makes for a handy and powerful tool. The speller can also be used with other word processors and is a formidable product in its own right.

The speller uses 96K of memory and will devour 256K if available. This will enable the enormous 60,000 word dictionary to be loaded into the computer memory and thus to check the text more rapidly.

There are numerous facilities, only some of which may be permanently useful. The five most helpful can transform your spelling approach.

First, the package will identify all suspect words which it cannot locate in its large dictionary. The latter has been carefully researched and refined, not simply compiled from a standard publication. It will then show the suspect words in their context by giving a brief extract from the material.

Secondly, it will offer a series of guesses about what the word should actually be. Usually three guesses are offered but more can be requested.

Thirdly, in contrast to some spellers, which will identify and mark the mistake in the document, but not alter it, *Palantir*'s speller automatically inserts the corrected word. This is a great time saver.

Fourthly, you can use the extensive dictionary like a conventional one, looking up words about which you are uncertain. The difference is that the speed of finding your word is much faster and you can give the speller just a vague idea of the word you have in mind.

Finally, the speller has a list of common spelling mistakes, such as teh instead of the, and will automatically make the correction.

Other facilities include being able to add words to the dictionary and also create bespoke dictionaries for specialist purposes.

The effectiveness of this speller is heavily governed by the available computer memory since the dictionary is broken down into four files. If these cannot be loaded into memory together, then conducting a full word check will take longer.

The checker is more elaborate than many managers will need but it is certainly an efficient tool, particularly for long documents.

DOCUMENTATION

The extensive documentation has simple tasks mainly at the start; more complex ones are reserved for later sections.

There is a series of lessons using material contained on disk. But this is merely used to demonstrate the package and aid practice. It is not an interactive tutorial.

On balance most managers will find it equally preferable to work through the well-written manual since all the sections are clear and are commendably brief.

The manual itself is typeset and well organised with protruding tabs for easy reference. There is a well-constructed index and a separate one for the several appendices. Included in the latter are a series of worked examples showing advanced features such as creating form letters, producing labels and so on. A list of error messages is also provided.

Also supplied is a detailed pocket reference guide, specific to the particular computer being used, but unfortunately there is no flow diagram giving an overall idea of how all the commands and menus fit together as a whole.

There is a set of sticky labels to add to the keyboard to remind you which ones do what, until you are familiar with all the various commands.

Palantir will suit managers who need a powerful word processing package that is easy to master and is not overloaded with facilities that will probably never be used.

Reference

The Best Word Processing Package. *Which Computer?*, February 1985, pp 93, 95–6, 98, 100–1

QED+

Type:	Desktop	
Management Verdict:	Getting started	(2) **
	Ease of use	(4) ****
	General performance	(3) ***
	Documentation	(2) **
Supplied by:	Quantec Systems & Software, 230-236 Lavender Hill, London SW11 1LE.	
Telephone:	(01) 228 7507	

QED+ is a breed of software called a desktop. These are designed to provide managers with useful daily tools while still letting you work with your other software. Like most desktops, *QED+* allows you to switch rapidly from one sort of task to another, while working in harmony with your own regularly used packages.

QED+ has been described unkindly by one critic as a juggernaut. It is certainly closer to the style of an integrated package like *Symphony*, than to the cheap and cheerful *Sidekick* by Borland, which is mainly only available for the IBM computer.

INSTALLATION

Installing *QED+* is not for beginners. The process is complicated, made more so by the fact that the software is copy protected.

After the installation procedure you must have your own, newly formatted disk with all the *QED+* programs on it. But this disk will not work unless you first place into the second drive the original master disk supplied by Quantec.

QED+ is mainly controlled by choosing from menus (menu-driven) with the options often appearing as windows overlaid on the existing screen. But there are also various command instructions, such as: press CONTROL F, and use of the computer's special function keys.

SWITCHING

A key feature of *QED+* is that you can switch instantly between it and one other program. This latter program can also be changed, using *QED+*'s configure menu, to one of nine others of your own choice.

To jump from *QED+* to another program is instantaneous. You merely press CONTROL 7 and land immediately in the other software. For example,

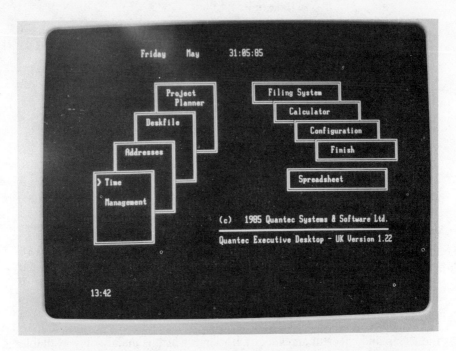

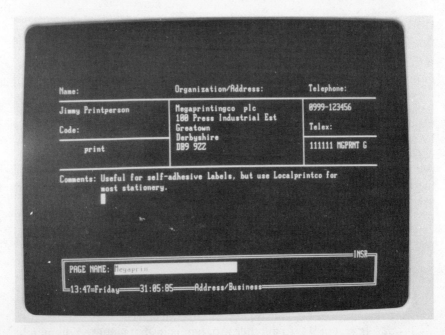

Figure Q.1 The QED+ menu as it appears on screen. The second picture shows a typical address book page from QED+

this description of *QED+* was written while using *Superwriter* and simultaneously switching back and forth between the two.

From a manager's point of view this facility offers important gains. If you are mainly into, say *Lotus 1-2-3*, then you can load it immediately after *QED+*, demanding the spreadsheet program whenever you wish. Meanwhile, *QED+* also provides useful aids which you might use either regularly or occasionally.

TIME MANAGER

To access this part of *QED+* you move the cursor prompt into the Time Management Box of the master menu and press RETURN. You are then offered the choice of basically three facilities: a diary, a journal and an events record.

It would be interesting to discover how many truly busy managers would have time to use all three programs, even though each is easy to use.

Diary pages are divided into four. One part shows the individual appointments that day. Entering a time and explanation of what the appointment is about is straight-forward. You can make appointments in units of 15 minutes or as single hours. However, there is no facility for a meeting at say, 11.35 or 2.40.

The second section holds comments and the third records key events which will also be transferred automatically to the calendar. A fourth box contains reminders which cannot be accessed from the diary but which stem from items in one of the other two time management facilities, namely the appropriate day in the Journal or the Events record.

Finding an item in the diary merely involves selecting the Search option then typing up to 50 characters. *QED+* will search the diary pages and locate the relevant item or items immediately. Though placing an item in the diary is fast, it could be argued that a conventional diary is faster and less bother.

The Journal or day book is more akin to a notebook. On the lefthand side you can record items of importance and on the right side there is space for reminders about these items or any other matters. These reminders are also automatically shunted into the correct place in the relevant diary page.

The third element of the time manager is an events record enabling you to have an item such as 'Management Team Meeting' appear regularly in the same slot every month in the diary. There is room for 32 events in every event file page.

There is also a two month calendar and key events from the diary are shown in the appropriate dates.

ADDRESS BOOK

The *QED+* address book is a simple electronic filing system for recording names, addresses, telephone numbers and brief comments. There are in fact three different types of address book: business, personal and places or organizations. It is impressive but perhaps more elaborate than many managers will require.

You can also choose to print a label so that it appears within a page correctly positioned for an envelope placed in the printer. There is a facility for generating a telephone list in alphabetical sequence with *QED+* displaying up to 20 numbers at a time. If you have a modem you can also use the address book with its telephone numbers to dial them automatically.

The address book will prove useful to managers but it would be sensible to ignore the complexities of having several different books running at the same time. The labelling and other options will be of practical help, once the database has built up to a significant number of entries.

DESK FILE

The desk file is an electronic notebook with considerable potential. It will appeal particularly to those without time to master more complex database systems. Basically this is a free form filing system which imposes few constraints on the user.

The system allows you type a page of text at a time, that is 20 lines of 78 columns or roughly 200 words. If you have created a number of such pages and then use the search facility, *QED+* will ask 'Look For?'

You can then use up to 50 characters of text as the basis for the search, or merely just one or two. *QED+* will hunt for text with the relevant items. If there is more than one page then you can examine the others too.

Alternatively, this module of *QED+* can be used to create more structured files using a form creation facility. This is more complicated to use but lets you design and store standard layouts for memos, petty cash, pay slips or anything else that needs a structured approach.

It is also possible to transfer information from the address book straight into the form. This facility allows busy managers to create quick letters or memos which, with minimum effort, can be immediately addressed, perhaps with a large circulation list of names.

Large amounts of miscellaneous data can be stored and retrieved without complex codes or searches. However, there is no sorting facility or any of the more usual facilities associated with a database system. Text both in this module and the others can be converted to telex characters.

The desk file will appeal to managers who want an easy filing system which is quick to learn and easy to use.

PROJECT PLANNING

The inclusion of a project planner in *QED+* makes the product good value for money when this particular facility is taken into account.

The CPA system included in *QED+* has been reduced to its simplest. It is difficult to make a mistake and the speed with which one can create a bar chart diagram is commendable.

Up to 150 tasks can be included. For each the program will calculate the earliest and latest, start and finish dates. It shows how much slack time exists in the schedule and which tasks are on the critical path. The latter is also highlighted on the bar chart display.

This scheduling system is so easy to use that many managers who have never used CPA before will find themselves quickly turning to it regularly for planning their more complicated activities.

One drawback is that when you are detailing a new task, it is not possible simultaneously to see the other tasks already scheduled. Thus you cannot easily create the project schedule directly on the screen as you go along, since you will quickly forget the name of the previous tasks. The alternative is to keep producing a revised hard copy.

The rather messy bar chart display uses highlighting for the critical path and other graphic devices for non-critical tasks and slack days.

The planner provides a workman-like tool for the many managers who have no need for a more elaborate CPA system.

CALCULATOR

The *QED+* calculator can be summoned whenever you are editing some text. A window opens on the screen, always in the same place, and you have a conventional calculator with five separate memories. Also helpful is a print option which activates the printer so that all entries are typed as hard copy, like a till roll.

After the calculator has been closed, you can also insert the last result into any text that you are editing.

FILING

Imagine that you are a manager whose clerical support has suddenly let you down. Perhaps the clerk has left or your secretary has acquired flu. You urgently want to find a document but are not sure where to look amongst the mass of cabinets and files.

The *QED+* filing system can transform your previous dependence on others. The system is basically a computerized method of keeping track of all your physical, not computer, files and the documents stored in them.

As the physical documents are filed away a record is made in the *QED+* filing system under one of the 1000 available headings. The program will then search for a title to tell you in which file a document is stored or even list all document titles which contain a key word, such as 'Budget'. It will list their file location and date filed.

Although it may take careful planning to develop a suitable framework for the files, the results can save much time in locating urgently needed documents. This alone may justify the effort of building the system.

HELP

There is an excellent help facility which is related directly to the area of *QED+* in which you are working. This help facility appears as a window which can be scrolled through to read the complete advice.

It is also a two layer facility. If you press help again, this time also using the CONTROL key, then the window changes to give advice about what the various function keys do.

Other features of *QED+* include an ability to take information from one part of the system and use it quickly in another. For example if you are running *Lotus 1-2-3* you can transfer up to 20 lines from either the top of the sheet or the bottom to anywhere else in *QED+*. The process is exceedingly simple and will be welcomed by managers who want to create a report taking material from a spreadsheet, a graphics package and address list and incorporate them into a single document on a word processor.

MANUAL

The 100 page *QED+* manual is an example of overkill. On the one hand, as indicated earlier in relation to installation, it makes assumptions about the knowledge of the user. On the other it is often tediously repetitive and pedantic, for example, explaining on innumerable occasions the meaning of highlighting an item in a menu and how to select it by moving the cursor.

The menu-driven approach plus the help screens makes reference to the manual unnecessary on most occasions. It is only needed for the special commands such as transporting data from one part of the system to another and other more complex operations.

The manual has plenty of illustrations of the *QED+* screens and contains a comprehensive index; there is no difficulty in locating instructions when you need them.

OVERALL VERDICT

To obtain the best from *QED+* you need a hard disk system and plenty of memory, otherwise you are in for frequent disk swopping if you regularly use more than just one main software package.

Another requirement is a willingness to integrate it fully into your current work style. Indeed the latter will probably have to change significantly (hopefully for the better) for *QED+* to be totally effective as a management aid.

At times the software is cumbersome and at others delightfully simple. The ability to switch between it and other programs makes it a product worth investigating. Also the ease with which data can be transported from many different sorts of software makes *QED+* a helpful program almost in its own right.

To sum up, *QED+* has much to offer, but take time to decide exactly how much of it you are likely to use.

References

POUNTAIN, Dick. All Within Easy Reach. *Business Computing: The Survival Guide*, VNU Business Publications, 1985, pp 78, 80–2
LEIGH, Andrew. Desktops=Integration. QED?, *Apricot User*, August 1985, pp 34–37

SNOWBALL GUIDED LEARNING COURSE

Type:	Tutorial	
Management Verdict:	Getting started	(5) *****
	Ease of use	(5) *****
	General performance	(3) ***
	Documentation	(1) *
Supplied by:	MicroGuide Limited, 14–18 Low Pavement, Nottingham.	
Telephone:	(0602) 581020	

Snowball Guided Learning Course is an easy to use tutorial consisting of 31 units of tuition. The first 26 units develop skills in learning each letter of the keyboard interspersed with consolidation units.

The package demands 100 per cent accuracy in the practice sessions for the letters, the numeric keys and in handling uppercase and special characters.

The speed sessions are not geared to any specific standard but merely provide instant feedback:

You have typed at 25 WPM ; with 6 mistakes. You therefore have a keyboard speed of 16 WPM. Well done! Practice will improve your speed and accuracy.

The five speed tests start with a one minute practice and build up to a five minute session.

Accompanying the single disk is an A4 ring binder which converts to an easel for propping up on the desk. It contains a set of student progress charts for recording results and the text for practising speed. Few managers will bother with the manual or find it particularly helpful.

The package is geared for use by a training section which is teaching typing skills on conventional typewriters. For example, the speed tests instruct the student to use a carriage return key which is unnecessary on the computer when typing. Similarly there is a considerable supply of student progress charts.

SPELLBINDER

Type:	Word Processor	
Management Verdict:	Getting started	(4) ****
	Ease of use	(3) ***
	General performance	(4) ****
	Documentation	(2) **
Supplied by:	Sierra Systems, 6 The Greenway, Epson, Surrey.	
Telephone:	(03727) 22890	

Spellbinder has been around a long time. It is a word processor with knobs on. To see what a really sophisticated WP package can achieve it is worth checking this product.

The issue for managers, however, is whether they will ever use half its impressive features. Though not a difficult package to learn initially, the more advanced routines require plenty of time to master.

GETTING STARTED

Unless you have an uncommon computer you should be able to obtain *Spellbinder* already tailored to your needs. You may, however, have substantial trouble with the printer and it is important to ensure that you see it working fully on exactly the same model that you will be using regularly.

The package is command-driven; that is, to make things happen you will have to give instructions, usually in the form of one or two letters of the alphabet. It also makes good use of the computer's special function keys.

To switch between editing or creating text and giving commands, you must press the CONTROL key and the letter Q. Repeating this returns you to editing. Most other actions which you need to perform are variations on this theme.

What *Spellbinder* offers is more of everything. For example, some word processors will only allow the cursor to jump a character, a word or a line at a time. *Spellbinder* lets you choose between these options, plus jumping by sentence, by paragraph and to special markers that you may place throughout the text.

Similarly, the printing facilities are substantial. The permitted choices cover styles of print, spacing, line widths, justification, handling hyphens and so on. You can print titles on every page, number pages and even specify different left margins for odd and even numbered pages to make your document look more attractive. Using these features, however, can prove difficult and often confusing.

The major disadvantage is that what you see on the screen is not what you get (WYSIWYG) from the printer. You can view the text just before printing to check its appearance but this is time consuming.

MACROS

Macros are special programs designed to automate and simplify frequently-performed tasks. For example, if you regularly write to the members of your team, then using a macro can produce an instant, personalized memo but with the circulation list added at the bottom.

Or if you have a number of phrases or sentences that must be used regularly, then a macro will remember and produce them exactly where required at the touch of a single key. If you want to print a number of files one after another without interruption, it can be done with a macro. You merely call up the relevant program and the rest is easy.

Other macros in *Spellbinder* handle the process of taking text from one file and inserting it into a different one. Thus you can create correspondence from a file of standard paragraphs or phrases, or construct contracts from a list of previously approved clauses.

For more advanced production of personalized material some macros work with a database while others will prepare labels, sort items from a master file in alphabetical order, perform arithmetic operations on numbers already in your text, automatically print text in two columns and create forms.

Spellbinder was one of the first popular software packages to offer macros, many competitors having since evolved their own versions. Using macros is not always easy and occasionally requires managers to virtually become computer programmers. But the simpler macros are a delight to use. With just a few keystrokes you can initiate what would otherwise be tedious and repetitive tasks.

ELECTRIC WEBSTER

This part of *Spellbinder* allows you to check for typographical and grammatical errors. These are compared against a 50,000 word file based on Webster's dictionary.

Spelling and grammar checks are conducted separately. Both can be customised to meet your special needs, for example, to handle technical phrases or include words not found in the dictionary provided. The check does not cope well with plurals although the root word may be there.

The grammar check alerts you to errors such as double negatives, wordy phrases and common misuse of words. It will locate words or sentences which are longer than you specified and highlight slang, cliches and repetition.

These errors are displayed with an indication of the fault and a suggested alternative. Errors can be corrected while checking, rather than having to locate them in the text for alteration. The ability to identify wordy or trite phrases ultimately depends on someone choosing them for incorporation in the program. Checkers that do this work can therefore differ considerably in what they consider to be unacceptable.

After the grammar check, *Spellbinder* provides information on the average length of your phrase, sentence and paragraph, and additional statistical information on the number of words, corrections made and so on.

These facilities may seem a superfluous luxury for many managers who only type brief memos themselves. But they provide a reassuring check that the quality of longer documents, for which the individual executive is personally responsible, reaches a high standard.

HARD TO BEAT

The Electric Webster underlines the comprehensiveness of *Spellbinder* which is hard to beat in terms of the sheer number of things that it can do.

It comes on two disks, the second being the spelling and grammar programs. Together with the operating system, both can fit on a double-sided floppy disk. To start working with *Spellbinder* takes only a matter of seconds from inserting the disk in the drive.

The documentation with the package is beginning to show its age and needs updating. The reproduction does not match the rest of the product and the print size is too small. There are few illustrations of screens and the text is overcrowded, making the manual a daunting read.

There is a six page appendix masquerading as a quick reference guide and a much needed glossary of terms. The index is only just adequate.

However, if you take word processing seriously, *Spellbinder* could be what you are seeking. When compared with many other WP products it offers as much or more. You just need to be sure that more is what you really need.

Produced by: Lexisoft Inc,
                    Box 1378,
                    Davis,
                    C.A.95167,
                    USA

References

LANG, Kathy. Text Play. *Business Computing:The Survival Guide*, VNU Business Publications, 1985, pp 50, 51, 54, 55
The Executive Path to Word Processing. Business Computing & Communications, September 1984, pp 48–9, 51, 55, 57

SYMPHONY

Type:	Integrated Software	
Management Verdict:	Getting started	(3) ***
	Ease of use	(3) ***
	General performance	(4) ****
	Documentation	(5) *****
Supplied by:	Lotus Development (UK) Ltd, Consort House, Victoria Street, Windsor, Berks. SL4 1EX	
Telephone:	(0753) 840281	

The manager who is thinking of buying or using *Symphony* must make a fundamental decision, 'Am I prepared to commit myself to using this product for the next few years?'

To build *Symphony* into an everyday working tool means a long term, personal devotion to becoming familiar with this powerful and all embracing package. Its potential is considerable, but the vast array of commands and function keys demands several months of solid use before they become second nature.

Symphony is an enormous spreadsheet or grid, to which the user can add material in a wide variety of ways. The spreadsheet or grid consists of over 8000 rows and more than 250 columns. The result is a workspace that exceeds 2 million cells. In reality, however, the workspace size is governed by the amount of RAM memory available on the Microcomputer.

This mammoth grid can be used as a conventional spreadsheet, a database, a word processor, for business graphics and for communications. All material is stored in the single spreadsheet. By pressing a single key for Type, you can switch between one application and another, for instance from word processing to a database, or between a spreadsheet and graphs.

Thus the package is an integrated one in which managers merely have to learn one main set of instructions to complete a wide range of computer tasks.

Symphony is meant to be the successor to the company's runaway success *Lotus 1-2-3*. When *Symphony* was launched, users of the earlier program were tempted with offers to exchange their existing product for the new one, at only £200.

Apparently the scheme was not a winner and stories circulated about disappointed customers asking for their copies of Lotus 1-2-3 back. (For *Lotus 1-2-3* see page 187.)

GETTING STARTED

Symphony has a special software protection device against copying. To start you must always use the special Program disk provided. After making back-up copies and completing a slightly elaborate procedure for turning what begins as the original Help and Tutorial disk into the vital Program disk, you answer some basic questions about your computer system.

The package is then ready to use. You can either plunge straight into making it work, using the excellent documentation, or instead become a *Symphony* student.

The tutorial lesson disk is an outstanding example of how to help new users get to grips with a software package. It is fully interactive, that is, the user is constantly required to make things happen to working examples on the screen.

It is virtually impossible to make a mistake during the tutorial and the approach is sufficiently varied to retain the user's interest. There are modules on each of *Symphony*'s six main facilities and each has two or three separate lessons.

The entire tutorial takes several hours to complete and each is fairly intensive. Most managers would spread this over two or more weeks. It normally requires at least two run throughs of a module before a user can confidently apply the lessons to a live situation.

In addition, when using the product there is a comprehensive help facility which can be called up at any time. The help screens are virtually a manual in their own right. Even if you get stuck it does not take long to discover what to do next.

USING SYMPHONY

Having started the program, the user sees a grid which is a window onto the spreadsheet. It is labelled in the bottom righthand corner.

Above the window on the right is a single, highlighted word indicating the type of work environment. For example, Sheet for spreadsheet, Form for a database, Doc for word processing, Graph for business graphics and Comm for communications.

Pressing function key F9 on an IBM PC, or the HELP key on an Apricot, produces a menu along a blank line at the top of the screen. Various options are then listed which can be chosen by either typing the first letter of the relevant word, or by moving the cursor along the line to highlight the relevant choice and then pressing RETURN.

There are always English style menus available and in many instances single word commands are also expanded into a brief descriptive sentence when the relevant menu word is highlighted by the cursor.

By pressing the function key for Switch, it is possible to move between a word processing job and say, a graph. Thus a manager writing a report can change the window from Doc to Graph and incorporate this second window into the report.

The advantage of such an approach is that, instead of moving data around, the user merely alters the characteristics of the window which the data is occupying.

Dozens of windows can be opened up and shuffled around, like cards. Also, windows can be variable in size, moved about on the screen, stored and so on. All windows, though, are merely viewing places for looking into the giant spreadsheet. Confusion can easily arise with a large work area containing say, a database in one corner, a couple of spreadsheets elsewhere, a few graphs and a letter or two.

SPREADSHEET

The spreadsheet is *Symphony*'s main strength, since it is based on the best selling *Lotus 1-2-3* product. The latter's facilities are incorporated and improved in *Symphony*.

Copying, moving and erasing cells, ranges and blocks is simple; with a little practice it is possible to turn spreadsheet material into graphs, pie charts, block diagrams and so on.

The package will be attractive to managers who want a powerful planning tool and are less worried about the finer points of other applications.

WORD PROCESSING

The word processing facility is exceptionally easy both to understand and to use. As with the rest of *Symphony*, menus and online help is always available. However, there is a heavy reliance on function keys for some tasks and this makes using the WP program cumbersome.

But all the normal commands are available to insert, delete, make block moves, search and replace, format for letters and reports. There is also a merge facility to take information from the database and put it into standard letters.

DATABASE

The database uses the spreadsheet layout, each row being treated as a record and each cell as a field. Creating a database is slightly more elaborate than more conventional products, but the gain is greater flexibility and sometimes faster entry and definition of headings and so on.

To avoid errors you can require that each entry to the database be inserted as a number, label, date or time of day. Records can be sorted in ascending or descending order with just a few key strokes.

There are no major restrictions on the size of field or records and the database can be searched using virtually any combination of criteria.

The major limitation is that the entire database has to be held in the computer memory. Since the whole package is a heavy user of memory, if you are anticpate using *Symphony* for extensive database activities then it may be prove necessary to expand your computer's memory radically.

The graphics facility allows you to turn spreadsheet or database material into charts of various kinds. These can be automatically updated when the data changes and can be browsed through like any other stored material.

A useful feature is that, using *Symphony*'s zoom facility, a small graph created from a spreadsheet can be expanded to fill the entire screen.

OTHER FEATURES

To simplify some of the work of using *Symphony* it is possible to teach the package to perform routine tasks automatically. Macros consist of a column of entries, or formulas which can be given a single English name. Pressing one key and entering the name makes *Symphony* execute all the commands in the macro.

Similarly, the Learn feature switches on a facility that remembers each key stroke, storing it automatically. The whole sequence can then be recalled and repeated. Simple labels, headings or a complex series of events can thus be readily duplicated on command.

DOCUMENTATION

The package arrives in an oddly shaped plastic moulded case divided into two compartments. The first contains the documentation, while the second holds a plastic, book-like device, which opens to reveal the disks and their storage wallets.

There can be few products on the market with such good documentation, except the same producer's *Lotus 1-2-3*. The package contains:

an extensive 100 page, spiral-bound introductory booklet for the specific machine on which the package will be used

a 300 page, spiral-bound, How-To manual, which describes how to use commands without explaining the commands themselves

a 430 page, spiral bound, reference manual

a 60 page glossary which defines words and phrases

a 15 page Quick Reference Guide

an update leaflet with the latest corrections or additional information

a keyboard guide to stick above the function keys for easy reference

Figure S.1 No shortage of documents with Lotus Development's Symphony package

Many of these are lavishly illustrated, all are written in crisp, clear English, and printed to the highest standards. Although the documentation is over-whelming at first, it is not excessive, given the sheer scope and potential of the entire package.

MEMORY

During a work session the computer temporarily stores *Symphony* and any data which you enter, into the machine's random access memory (RAM). To use the package you need at least 512K of RAM, which is more than the average business personal computer possesses.

It is a crucial limitation and if you are thinking of choosing *Symphony* it is important to realize that you may have to spend perhaps another £250–300 to add the additional memory.

Ideally, there should be even more memory than 512K. *Symphony* is a product firmly aimed at the future, when most personal computers will have memories measured not in thousands of bytes but in millions (megabytes).

Finally, the package is expensive. This, together with the time that it will take to really learn well, is why choosing *Symphony* is to make a long term investment in more ways than one.

References

BAGSHAW, Eric. One for All. *Business Computing:The Survival Guide*, VNU Business Publications, 1985, pp 75–7

JADRNICEK, Rik. Symphony, A Full Orchestra Version of Lotus 1-2-3. *Byte*, July 1984, pp 121–3, 372–3

TEHAN, Patricia. Training 1:Learning from a Disk. *Apricot User*, May 1985, pp 59, 60, 62

Integrated Software. *Which Computer?*, July 1984, pp 102-3, 105-8

Lotus 1-2-3. *Which Computer?*, May 1985, pp 59, 61, 64, 66

TOUCH 'N' GO

Type:	Typing Tutorial	
Management Verdict:	Getting started	(5) *****
	Ease of use	(5) *****
	General performance	(5) *****
	Documentation	(N/A)
Supplied by:	Caxton Software Ltd, 10–14 Bedford Street, Covent Garden, London WC2E 9HE	
Telephone:	(01) 379 6502	

There are mixed views about the need for managers to learn typing skills. It certainly helps to be dextrous on the keyboard if you are going to be a regular computer user. But just two fingers are enough for tapping in commands. Many managers feel that they have no need for mastering typing.

Yet the need for typing skills is likely to increase, not decrease, in the next few years. Even if computers do accept rapid dictation and respond to a wide range of verbal commands, the keyboard is likely to remain the main means of communicating to them for many years.

As managers become more proficient at using tools such as spreadsheets, simple database systems, word processors and so on, they will probably type material themselves for others to tidy up and re-present. Computers are also increasingly being used by managers for communication purposes and they will be typing in such material themselves, not delegating this task.

Typing skills are traditionally concerned with words, but today's manager will also be familiar with the numeric keyboard for calculations. Here too, typing skills can be important and a time saver.

QUICK LEARNING

In the last few years a revolution has occurred in the teaching of typing skills. It is no longer necessary to pound away at a machine while studying a book or receiving verbal instruction.

Nowadays you can sit at your computer and, in about a week, become thoroughly proficient at typing. *Touch 'N' Go* is a disk-based typing tutor that offers over 60 lessons to make the user a proficient typist of both letters and numbers.

The attraction of *Touch 'N' Go* is that it offers a systematic approach to your becoming so familiar with all the keys that typing becomes instinctive. It also regularly monitors your speed and accuracy.

For example, in typing a simple repetitive line of the word 'friend' you are expected to get it completely right first time, doing so at the equivalent of 30 words per minute. *Touch 'N' Go* will therefore insist on a repeat of the exercise if anything is typed incorrectly or at too slow a pace. The lessons are subtly graduated so that imperceptibly, the tasks become more difficult.

The variation in speed and accuracy requirements are helpful, for instance, when you are requested to type more complicated lines of text or numbers. The package is more tolerant of small mistakes during complicated tasks but ruthlessly demanding about the simple ones.

Where the student stops each time is recorded on disk. It is therefore possible to take regular breaks from what, inevitably, is a boring, repetitive process.

To counteract the boredom the package relies on providing regular feedback. The latter lies at the heart of effective learning and *Touch 'N' Go* uses this fact effectively. Not only does it instantly report on speed and accuracy after a line or so has been typed, but at the end of a session you can type R for Results and receive an instant analysis of each part of the module.

A table is presented which compares accuracy and speed achieved, against the desired standards. An overall average for the module is also given. It is both challenging and satisfying to be told one's results in detail and so quickly, making *Touch 'N' Go* compulsive to use.

The suppliers claim that the keyboard can be mastered in 24 hours, that the student can achieve a speed of 40 words per minute, an alphabetic accuracy of 95 per cent and a numeric accuracy of 100 per cent.

Much depends though on the student's persistence. Few people are going to complete the 60 or so lessons within a single 24 hour session. Thus it is likely to take about four or five days with frequent breaks between lessons.

The package is simply a disk in a cardboard sleeve. There is no manual, everything being contained on the disk itself. It is easy to use, inexpensive and works.

TRENDISK

Type:	Database	
Management Verdict:	Getting started	(4) ****
	Ease of use	(5) *****
	General performance	(2) **
	Documentation	(2) **
Supplied by:	Microtrend UK, Council Chambers, King Street, Pateley Bridge, Harrogate, N. Yorks. HG3 5LE	
Telephone:	(0423) 711878	

There are few database products which pass the flying blind test. This involves using a product's main features after a once-only read of the manual with no other resort to the documentation.

Trendisk relies entirely on menus for selecting commands. Flying blind reveals that it is a database system which is exceptionally easy to learn and use.

Having typed TDMENU the main choices arrive in this form:

```
Finish working with Trendisk ................0
Creating or deleting a file  ...................1
Processing an existing file....................2
Searching for information in a file ..........3
Report Generator  ...........................4
Printing labels (e.g. for addresses)  ........5
Performing numeric operations with a file ....6
Sorting a file into a new sequence ............7
Stereo file Handling ........................8
Data file backup ...........................9
Please select an option by typing the appropri-
ate number
```

This approach is maintained through the program and it is hard to get lost or stuck. By typing HE you can call for help, though the assistance is usually a menu not detailed guidelines.

Creating a file is fast. *Trendisk* asks in which drive the data disk can be found and whether you wish to create a new file. You are also asked to enter your name, and then a password of exactly five letters.

The password facility can be a nuisance but you can give five letters such as XXXXX, if you want to avoid a specific word being used. Forget the password, though, and you could have problems, since *Trendisk* insists on having it typed precisely. For example, it will not recognise kevin, instead of Kevin.

Type NE for new and after providing a file name, you are ready to begin defining what will appear on the individual record card. There are just three concepts to understand: the item (field) name, which can be up to 10 letters, length of the item (up to 10 numbers or 50 letters) and type, that is, whether the item is numeric (N) or alphabetical (A).

Records can only have 25 items and there can only be five files on each floppy disk. Equally restricting is the inability to alter the record card once it is defined and data has been entered. If you want to make changes the only way is to start right from the beginning, which places a high premium on careful planning right from the start.

Item two on the menu, in which you process an existing file, offers a series of easy to understand choices such as browsing through a file, adding or deleting a record, displaying the record items and so on. To give these commands you merely type two letters, such as BR for Browse, EX for examine and in a short while these commands become second nature.

Trendisk stores the records in the order in which they are created so if you want them in any other order they must be sorted. However the package has a restricted sorting capacity; it can only put the records in ascending alphabetical or numerical order.

You can search the records using three key items which must be defined in advance. This is limiting and so is the facility for laying out the records for printing purposes. To do more sophisticated layouts the package can be linked to a word processing package – a clumsy and indeed expensive solution.

The report-generating command is only able to produce the material in a standard format although you can print out selected parts of the record.

Like the rest of the product the manual for *Trendisk* is clear and easy to follow, though the material is not always presented in an entirely logical sequence. There is a 'getting started' section which is far from being a tutorial.

It is simplicity which makes *Trendisk* attractive. If you have any fear of manuals or complicated software, then this product could be an attractive proposition. But it could leave you wishing that you had compromised more on ease of use in favour of a more powerful package.

References

Trendisk. *Which Computer?*, February 1984

TRENDTEXT/2

Type:	Word processor	
Management Verdict:	Getting started	(4) ****
	Ease of use	(3) ***
	General performance	(3) ***
	Documentation	(3) ***
Supplied by:	Microtrend UK,	
	Council Chambers,	
	King Street,	
	Pateley Bridge,	
	Harrogate,	
	N.Yorks. HG3 5LE	
Telephone:	(0423) 711878	

Trendtext/2 is a deceptively powerful package. You either quickly learn to love it or as speedily conclude that it is definitely not for you. One test where it received what might be called a pass mark was the flying blind check.

Push *Trendtext/2* into the disk drive and see if you can make it work. Ignore the manual and discover how far you can get. On that basis the package is reasonable, though not exceptional. You need to discover, for example, that merely to make anything happen and not get stuck with an apparently immovable letter 'E' for Editing, it is necessary to press two keys simultaneously.

Perhaps it seems unfair to subject the package to such a crude evaluation but it does give a good feel for how hard or otherwise the software will be to use.

Having discovered the basic method of operating though, the rest is commendably easy. Most of the normal WP functions can be performed with limited reference to the manual. There are, however, no help screens other than the menus.

A feature of the software that many people will dislike is that each time you make a correction you cannot then continue typing. Instead, you must remind the computer that you are once again putting in new material. What may seem a minor quirk in programming could drive some people to distraction. There is sense, though, in this arrangement. It prevents all sorts of errors which other WP packages permit which then require unravelling.

Trendtext/2 provides various other useful facilities that some managers may find helpful. It will produce a table of contents from the original material, assuming that you have marked the appropriate items as you went. Similarly, it will create an index and sort this into alphabetical order, a feature that is missing on many comparably priced packages.

The package will perform selective searches and the process seems reasonably easy to master without endless attempts at getting it right. It provides a word count, a facility that, while useful, is hardly essential. More helpful would be a spelling check, which is surprisingly absent. To compensate there is a facility for mailing standard letters and other routine tasks.

The package is attractive on the screen. Everything is clearly laid out, with information on the name of the document, whether you are in editing or another mode, and the current line number. All of this can be helpful or unnecessary, depending on your point of view.

An attractive feature is the ease with which you can set tabs, line lengths and make numbers align around the decimal point to give a neat appearance.

Trendtext/2 copes with long texts, in sharp contrast to many other WP packages that decide enough is enough and insist on giving you a new page from time to time. The software relies on a large memory available in the computer. It uses this until full, then saves the material on disk, after which it continues to accept more text.

If you make a mistake with *Trendtext/2* you usually receive an incomprehensible answer and the lack of help screens makes it difficult to get out of trouble without a careful reference to the manual. For example, text can apparently be completely lost if you mistakenly give instructions to print it when the printer is switched off and you happen to have a full disk. Aborting the whole process obliterates the text permanently.

DOCUMENTATION

The package consists of a single disk and a manual in an A4, three-ring plastic binder. The latter is cramped, with the pages not always flipping backwards and forwards with the ease one is entitled to expect. The typescript text is printed in offset and therefore not the easiest to read. Considering the price, this seems parsimonious but not uncommon.

There is a useful 'Read Me First' overview which explains the main facilities. There is nothing that seriously aspires to being a new user tutorial taking you step by step through all major tasks. Nor are there any sample files on disk for practising sort routines.

The manual is well tabulated and indexed, with jargon free explanations. Worked examples are scarce, but enough to explain major functions.

There is no rapid summary card, which is a pity as these are real time savers. There is however, a set of coloured stickers which can be fixed to the keyboard to help you remember the various commands. By the time you have decided where each goes, it is probably quicker to learn by straightforward practice.

The suppliers, Microtrend, offer advice and help. At least one reputable computer magazine has reported that when this was tested without the firm knowing who was calling the response was a good one.

References

LANG, Kathy. Software File, Word Processor Round Up. *Sixteen Bit Computing*, February 1985, pp 37–9, 41–2, 46, 47–8
Trendtext/2. *Practical Computing*, March 1984

THE ULTIMATE DIARY

Type:	Diary System	
Management Verdict:	Getting started	(5) *****
	Ease of use	(5) *****
	General performance	(3) ***
	Documentation	(2) **
Supplied by:	Lutterworth Software, 126 New Walk, Leicester LEI 7JA	
Telephone:	(0533) 550822	

A diary on disk is the kind of idea that appeals to software companies. A simple program, easy to write and just as easy for the user to understand.

But do you actually want to keep your diary on a computer? Does it offer any real advantages? Frankly, if all you want to do is record your personal schedule then a computer is a waste of time. A simple traditional diary is quicker and more efficient.

But if you have a host of regularly occurring events with specific activities to be undertaken, then a computer system might be a help. Also, if your secretary or clerical assistant has to keep the diary of several busy managers it may be useful to consign all the material to a computer. Any changes that have to be made can be rapidly altered and a new schedule produced at the press of a few keys.

The Ultimate Diary is a modest little package that is not much more than an electronic record card system. Indeed what comes up on the screen once you type in 'Diary' is the layout of a record card showing:

```
Subject Reference No
Event or Action
Notes and Comments
Date and Frequency
```

Apart from the reference number, which is controlled by the package, you type in the rest. For frequency you have several choices. Events can be tagged as:

```
Every 1-9 weeks
Every 13 or 26 weeks
Every 1-9 months
Every nth weekday, for e.g., every second
Tuesday
Every 1-9 years
```

This facility is missing in more expensive diary-keeping systems currently on the market. With many of them you are restricted to recording regular events in a cycle of a week, a month or a quarter. This takes no account of the manager who wants say, to visit several places every six weeks.

Adding, deleting and changing events is fast and easy though you need to know which reference card to call up by number. If you do not know then you can either scan the file card by card, backwards or forwards, or ask to Find a specific item.

The Find facility will search for any part of the original data entry, looking for all matching items. If you are uncertain whether you have an appointment with a Mr Rodman or Redman then you search for R?dman.

The package will also produce various reports which summarise the state of your diary. It will report events on a daily, weekly or monthly basis. If the report is requested just for the screen then you only see one event card at a time and must work your way through each one. Using the printer though, all the relevant events are printed out along with their reference number.

DRAWBACKS

There are number of diary systems on sale and while this one scores on its speed, cheapness (under £50) and ease of use it has severe limitations. For instance, it will only accept 36 characters for the subject matter and 45 for the events and notes. You cannot therefore type much information into each card.

Secondly, it will not actually show a whole monthly calendar with the events marked at the appropriate place or even an indication that an event is due on a particular date.

More limiting still is the inability to show a series of activities that happen on a single day without first printing this out or viewing each relevant record card in turn.

Diary systems are a matter of personal taste. This one is fast and easy to use. It is cheap enough for you to try out and not feel bad if it turns out not to be the one you want. But before making a commitment to a computerised diary system it would sensible to see one in action worked by someone who uses it regularly.

WORDCRAFT

Type:	Word Processor	
Management Verdict:	Getting started	(4) ****
	Ease of use	(3) ***
	General performance	(4) ****
	Documentation	(3) ***
Supplied by:	Dataview Wordcraft	
	Radix House,	
	East Street,	
	Colchester,	
	Essex CO1 2XB	
Telephone:	(0206) 869414	

Unless you are into complicated mailing programs it is doubtful whether, as a busy manager, you will use half of what this package can actually do.

It is widely available for many different computers, has been around for several years and has certainly stood the test of time. The company that produces it has a consistent record of updating the product but not so frequently that you are constantly learning new routines and codes.

That is just as well, since like most other WP packages aspiring to offer a comprehensive range of facilities, the number of codes and routines which you need to learn can be daunting.

Basically *Wordcraft* can do three main tasks. First, it provides standard word processing facilities so that you can create and edit text easily and in a very similar way to how a normal typewriter operates.

Secondly, it will let you take text from one place and combine it with material in another so that you can produce standard letters for mailing shots and similar tasks.

Thirdly, it will check your spelling against a large dictionary of words and highlight within your text just where you went wrong. You then have the choice of either doing something about it or enjoying the rare pleasure of telling the computer that it got the spelling wrong and would it please amend its dictionary!

This only happens though, when you have used a word which it does not recognize, either because you have got a larger vocabulary in your head or have used a jargon word which it needs to learn.

GETTING STARTED

Starting up *Wordcraft* is easy, though you may have problems encouraging it to talk to your printer, depending on the latter's make. But this should only prove a minor difficulty and the producers or their dealers seem well used to handling this kind of problem. Insert your master disk (or rather a copy of it so that the original is carefully preserved) and the rest is automatic.

You merely type in a command, WORDCR, up comes an introductory page and with that you're in business. You go straight to a nearly blank screen which is ready for you to start typing. If you are stuck you can ask for help and there is a range of useful advice messages that in most cases should get you out of trouble.

EDITING

Unlike some word processing packages *Wordcraft* keeps you fully informed of what is going on the whole time. You don't, therefore, start with just a blank screen. Instead up come a series of lines that give the date, name of the document which you are typing, the title of the file in which it will be saved and further information about chapter number, columns, lines and pages.

Most of these prompts are only occasionally helpful and at times positively distracting. But it does gives a sense of being in charge of events, rather than leaving you wondering whether all those words popping up on the screen are really just plummetting into the computer equivalent of a black hole.

A particularly thoughtful feature is the way that *Wordcraft* can, if you wish, display at the bottom of the page the currently available tasks that it will undertake when you press certain pre-selected keys. These 'function' keys save you performing a more elaborate button bashing routine, for which the majority of managers will surely give a silent offering of thanks.

What appears on the screen is mainly what you get when you eventually print out the text. But there are a variety of instructions which are located in the text for printing purposes which you do not necessarily see. For anyone new to Wordcraft this can be confusing. But as with most WP packages, rapid familiarity through regular use soon puts the issue into perspective.

A highly irritating feature of the package is the way that it suddenly decides that you have come to the end of its available page. During a normal typing session this seemed to occur after around 55 lines and can be disconcerting. One minute you are happily tapping away and the next there is a blank screen. Your first thought is 'What happened?', followed by a sudden panic that the previously typed text might have vanished into obscurity. But play around with the arrow keys and back it all comes.

Saving all the text onto disk is just a matter of giving the material a file name, and telling the computer which disk drive to use. If you forget to specify a drive name then *Wordcraft* rebels and won't record your precious text. But that is probably a rather better arrangement than happens on say, *Superwriter*, where failure to tell it what disk drive to use can inadvertently lead to it putting the material on the wrong disk, leaving you wondering where to find it!

Recording the material onto disk is virtually instantaneous. You will receive a reassuring confirmation that the the material has been filed 'OK'.

Getting it back is just as simple and the time that it takes to find and display the document would keep most managers happy no matter how pressed for time they might be.

Once you have typed some material you will doubtless want to move text around quite a bit. After all, that is the whole point of word processing; the computer can do it quicker than if you have to either retype text or physically cut it up and paste it together in the right order. *Wordcraft* does this chore with just about the minimum number of instructions.

MAILINGS

Wordcraft can do some fancy routines in the way of producing personalised letters, mailing shots and allowing you to draw on standard paragraphs to develop special documents where repetitive phrasing is required.

A new facility that the makers have recently introduced is to turn the package into a sort of database in which you store information, sort it and recall it in much the same way that other much more sophisticated systems perform.

The only problem is that actually using this facility is not particularly easy. By the time you have messed about with various combinations of keys you will probably wish that you had stuck to using some specialist package.

On the other hand, if you can master the instructions it does mean that, in conjunction with the rest of the facilities offered by *Wordcraft*, you have a very powerful range of facilities at your disposal.

WHAT THEY SELL YOU

Wordcraft consists of a systems disk which contains all the crucial instructions to the computer for word processing, plus a second disk on which there is the spelling facility along with a tutorial.

The tutorial is perhaps the most disappointing aspect of the product and, to be frank, probably won't be much help to most managers. It is hardly surprising that *Wordcraft* have implicitly recognised this and introduced an interactive, self-contained training course, based on audio cassettes.

You train to use *Wordraft* by listening to the tapes while operating the computer, following instructions as they are given. But this package may not be available for your particular computer and of course you will have to pay extra for it.

The three documents provided are an installation guide, an operator's reference manual and a set of self instruction work cards. These can be arranged into an easel so that they can sit by the computer and be flipped over as you work through them.

When you reach the last card you turn the easel round and start working through the reverse side. Sounds a good idea? In practice, it is thoroughly annoying, since you will probably want to keep flipping backwards and forwards only to find half the text is upside down! About the most useful tool is the fold-up small reference card which summarises all the commands and thus makes them highly accessible just when you need them. The manual is typeset and in large enough print size to avoid the reader becoming myopic. There are also clear examples of how to do various tasks. But it is a long way from being a really user-friendly guide to the product and the self-instruction cards are no substitute.

The manual is not tabbed for easy reference and the index is hardly comprehensive. There is no glossary or list of error messages, which many beginners would normally find helpful. Purists will also criticize it for not actually showing practical examples of some of the codes and messages and layouts that appear on your screen, which can be a reassuring form of feedback.

Each of the documents provided comes in a spiral-bound form so that you won't lose any of the pages. The whole is contained in a tough, fabric-covered box which should survive the rigours of office life for many years.

HOTLINE HELP

If you get stuck using the package what do you do? A careful reading of the manual will usually get you out of trouble. But it can be very time consuming to establish why something is not apparently working properly.

Dataview *Wordcraft* sells through many dealers so it is worth ensuring that whoever supplies you, offers a proper response on the telephone to your queries. The publishers also run their own hotline telephone service from 9.00 a.m. to 5.00 p.m. Monday to Friday. It offers both information and advice on sorting out your package so that it will do what you want it to do. For the registration fee of around £65 in early 1985, you receive a registration card and the number of the hotline service together with your own unique reference number to use when calling for advice.

The fee covers one year's service, which also includes a regular newsletter containing helpful information about getting the best out of *Wordcraft*. Don't expect too much though, since it is also a way of reminding you about how good the company is at its job.

There is not much you can't do with *Wordcraft* if you have got the time to work out how to do it and there are few features which will leave you feeling truly baffled, which says a lot for it.

References

LANG, Kathy. Watch Out Wordstar!, *Sixteen Bit Computing*, March 1984, pp 32, 35, 37
LANG, Kathy. Text Play. *Business Computing:The Survival Guide*, VNU Business Publications, 1985, pp 50, 51, 54, 55

WORDSTAR

Type:	Word Processor	
Management Verdict:	Getting started	(3) ***
	Ease of use	(2) **
	General performance	(4) ****
	Documentation	(4) ****
Supplied by:	ACT (UK) Ltd,	
	Shenstone House,	
	Dudley Road,	
	Halesowen,	
	West Midlands, B63 3NT	
Telephone:	(021) 501-2284	

Once *WordStar* almost meant word processing. Anyone who knew about WP was likely to have heard of, or come across, the ubiquitous American package. This is hardly surprising as over three million copies have been sold around the world.

Nowadays there are dozens of competing products and *WordStar* has been having an increasingly tough time overcoming its reputation as a difficult to use program. An entirely new version called *WordStar 2000* has been produced which is said to overcome the complexity of the older package.

To encourage sales of the older product it is being sold along with add-on packages such as a spelling checker, a mail merge program and so on, all at temptingly reduced prices for the combined product.

Since *WordStar* is so well known, many managers will naturally wish to consider whether this is the right package for them. If three million other people are using it, this together with the volume of independent knowledge, allied products, books and training courses still makes it an important possible choice for a working manager.

Depending on your computer, *WordStar* arrives on one, two or even three disks. For most business personal computers it is likely to arrive on two disks.

LEARNING WORDSTAR

The popularity of *WordStar* has spawned many products to help users master the package. There are recorded cassettes, tutorial disks, training courses and numerous books and articles.

The producers of this package have created their own tutorial which is sold as a separate product and is not considered here. Despite all the paraphernalia the actual tutorial manual which comes with *WordStar* is sufficient to help most people get a good start. It is well written and divided into three parts. There is a short course of six lessons which should take three or four hours to complete and deal with typing ordinary letters. The next six lessons at the intermediate level take about four or five more hours and cover formatting pages, special headings, rearrangement of text and so on.

The extended course, lasting about seven or eight hours trains the user for producing longer documents, mail merge, form letters and other facilities.

GETTING STARTED

Installing *WordStar* on your particular computer is not particularly easy, though this aspect may well be handled by the dealer. Once ready for regular use, you merely call up the package by typing WS. As with all packages, this part can be made automatic by using the computer's operating system.

MENUS AND COMMANDS

After the initial licence material information, the first screen that you see is the opening menu. This is a daunting sequence of columns headed 'Preliminary commands','File Commands' and 'System Commands'. Under each of these are various letters to press to perform different operations, such as D to open a document file, or R to run a program and so on.

If you choose to open a document by pressing D, you arrive at an even more formidable set of choices also placed in columns 'Cursor Movement','Delete','Miscellaneous'. Again by pressing the letters which are listed you can perform other relevant operations.

This is how the rest of *WordStar* works, by dozens of commands which are issued by pressing one, two or sometimes three keys. With computers like the Apricot and the IBM PC the special function keys reduce some of the button bashing to a single key depression.

FEATURE-FILLED

WordStar is packed with features, many of which are rarely likely to be used by the busy manager. There are nearly 150 different codes required to action these features. To control the cursor, for example, there are 20 possible commands.

However, *WordStar* is a powerful program for word processing and once the main commands have been mastered is certainly not as difficult as many critics have suggested. With regular use this package comes into its own; used only occasionally, it would be like owning a Ferrari to go shopping once a week in the local village.

Amongst the better features of *WordStar* are the way that it reproduces on the screen what will usually appear on the page, including underlining. It has powerful options for organising how material will be moved around, filed and retrieved, and is particularly strong on choices for how the final layout of pages will look.

There are good facilities for finding a word or string or words in a text, as well as the ability to replace words throughout a document, either selectively or universally.

A particularly useful aspect is the four different levels of help on screen that it can offer. At level three all menus and explanations are shown, and these are gradually simplified and reduced until at level zero, all explanations are suppressed.

Thus as you gain familiarity with *WordStar* you can gradually drop an increasing amount of the sometimes distracting guidance.

ADD-ONS

One attraction of *WordStar* is the number of available add-on products. For example, *SpellStar* is a spelling checker and *StarIndex* allows the user to create a table of contents, lists of figures and tables and special layouts for reports that can be automatically generated as you type the original material.

DRAWBACKS

There is a definite learning threshold to overcome with all software packages and *WordStar* is no different. However, this package's threshold is probably higher than many managers will want in return for the positive benefits of a powerful program.

To type a quick memo with this program, for example, is exceedingly cumbersome compared to some of the simpler packages now available. The displays on the screen are a monument to a different age when design played little part in the thinking of software producers. The various commands that may have to be embedded in the text also make the screen look ugly.

Another drawback is that margin settings and instructions for tabulation must be reset for each new document since these are not stored or activated automatically.

Many functions are controlled by unhelpfully named control keys, such as ^OX for releasing margins or ^KD for saving your file and returning to the main menu.

Finally the package does not contain a spelling checker which must be bought separately. Nowadays many competing products throw in a spelling checker for the same price.

Produced by: MicroPro,
33 San Pablo Avenue,
San Rafael,
CA 94903,
USA

References

LANG, Kathy. Ways to Make Wordstar Whizz. *Sixteen Bit Computing*, April 1985, pp 25–8, 30
LANG, Kathy. Text Play. *Business Computing:The Survival Guide,* VNU Business Publications, 1985, pp 50, 51, 54, 55
O'REILLY, Richard. A Painless Way to Learn Software. *Los AngelesTimes*, 30th Oct 1983
TEHAN, Patricia. Training 1:Learning from a Disk. *Apricot User* May 1985, pp 59, 60, 62

XCHANGE

Type:	Integrated Software	
Management Verdict:	Getting started	(2) **
	Ease of use	(3) ***
	General performance	(4) ****
	Documentation	(4) ****
Supplied by:	Psion Systems, 22 Dorset Square, London NW1	
Telephone:	(01) 723 9408	

Xchange ends the floppy disk shuffle. This is familiar to many computer users as they switch in and out of programs that demand different disks. *Xchange* offers the manager just one system for handling several tasks. It consists of four separate modules, each designed to fit together into a coherent whole. You can buy them separately on different disks, or have a single program disk for everything.

There are obvious benefits with an integrated approach. Apart from ending the disk shuffle syndrome, there are economies in learning how the products work and the way to issue instructions.

The price though, is higher not only in money terms, but in added complexity. For example, to prepare (install) *Xchange* to run on your computer involves an elaborate procedure which is not for the beginner.

To run the software requires at least 256K of computer memory and preferably more. *Xchange* uses the disk as a form of instant memory and the amount of actual work space is only limited by disk capacity.

The four modules are a word processor (Quill), a spreadsheet (Abacus), a database (Archive) and a graphics package (Easel). All have a common way of working and present a consistent face to the user with similar screen ideas.

All four modules are linked through the general *Xchange* program which allows information to be swopped between the various modules. So for example, numerical material and a chart from Abacus and Easel respectively, can be incorporated into a report being written on Quill.

DRAWBACKS

Although *Xchange* allows you to jump from one job to another in different modules there is no general window facility for you to look and work at two jobs simultaneously. Nor is it possible, for example, to instruct the package to continue doing one task, such as calculations, while working on another job in a different module.

Of these two limitations the first is more serious than the second and is a curious omission in an otherwise highly professional product.

OTHER GENERAL FEATURES

A useful feature that comes into its own, once you really know the programs well, is the ability to store frequently used sequences of keys, calling them up at will. Not only can it save time, but this permits the package to be tailored to users who have little or no knowledge of the product as a whole.

Explanations of commands are shown at the top of the screen and this facility can be switched on or off as desired. There is also a full help facility which goes to several layers. So, for instance, if you do not understand the advice, it is possible to ask for still more assistance.

Moving information around between one module and another is not as simple as it might be. A separate file must be created which is then incorporated into the place where it is needed.

But to jump from say, word processing to a spreadsheet and thence on to the creation of a graph is merely a case of pressing a special function key to freeze what you are currently doing. When you return to the first task, you arrive exactly where you originally left off.

It is possible to be working on up to eight different tasks spread across the various modules, dipping into and out of each at will. This is a useful facility since it reflects the way that many managers actually work during their normal day.

QUILL

The word processsor is extremely easy to use and although the penalty for this is fewer features than some other products on the market, the package will satisfy most manager's needs.

The cursor movement is straightforward but slow and keyboard wizards may find that they can type faster than the program can respond. A particularly irritating aspect is that the standard (default) setting for a new job is to have the first line of every new paragraph indented. The standard setting cannot be altered except at the start of each new job.

Moving blocks of text around is particularly easy, using a special function key. Also the package usually shows on the screen exactly what will finally appear on the printed page. For example, on the screen text can appear underlined, in italics, highlighted, in bold and any combination of these.

There is a facility for producing standard, personalised letters (mail merge) but strangely no spelling checker which is now standard in most good word processors.

ABACUS

Abacus is a spreadsheet with few surprises. Managers familiar with such products will have no difficulty learning to use it.

It can handle 999 rows by 255 columns, giving over a quarter of a million cells. This is large enough for most management purposes.

To produce calculated figures it is possible to enter formulas using meaningful names instead of grid references. For example, if you want a column called Profit, derived from Sales and Price you just type in Profit = Revenue − Expenditure.

EASEL

This graphics package is fun to use and reflects the producers' considerable experience in devising computer games. You can create instant bar and pie charts, graphs and 3-D charts in a bewildering assortment of colours and patterns.

The speed with which this package works and its ease of use makes it highly attractive as a management tool. Data from the spreadsheet or the database can be fed into the graphics package and raw data does not have to be manually put into tables before being incorporated into charts.

As with most packages of this kind, to produce the results as hard copy on paper it will be necessary to have access to a graphics printer.

ARCHIVE

Archive is the most complex of the four modules and many managers may consider it too sophisticated for their personal needs. It is not meant for a quick look at the database but for solid data analysis work.

To use *Archive* means mastering a special command language. For example, in a database containing information on nations of the world, to find French-speaking African countries you type:

```
select continent$="AFRICA and instr(languages$,"FRENCH")
```

At least the commands are mainly English style statements and not particularly hard to grasp. But *Archive* is demanding of accuracy in giving instructions and a slightly careless entry will produce an error response.

The database is certainly a powerful one but since it is aimed at serious users with a major database application in mind it would be sensible to see a full dealer demonstration. This should involve handling a database of the size and type that will eventually be used.

LEARNING XCHANGE

Integrated software is notoriously harder to learn than more conventional products. This is only partly because they consist of several different products. It is also because the integrated concept involves a more complex process of handling material.

Xchange is mainly easy to use apart from the database which is at the more difficult end of the spectrum. There is a separate tutorial disk which takes the user through each of the four modules and the interchange of information between them.

The tutorial is interactive, that is, the user must respond to the lessons and thus begin to gain familiarity with the product. However, the tutorial is occasionally errratic, leaving the user slightly unsure what to do next when in fact the next screen is due to arrive automatically.

Also, once you start a particular item on the tutorial it is not possible to quit and then, sometime later, return where you left off. Each of the items of the tutorial take around half an hour to complete and the whole induction course lasts about two hours.

At the end of the tutorial the user is at least familiar with some of the main concepts of *Xchange*, but the disk is more of an overview than a real learning instrument.

DOCUMENTATION

Each of the modules comes in a sturdy, injection-moulded plastic container which opens lengthways to show the manual. Pages are held by a ring binder along the hinge edge, with protruding tab guides for each topic.

Because each module is sold separately, the manuals repeat sections on installation, using *Xchange* and the common features. But the specific material on each module is mainly, though not always, easy to follow and produced to a high standard of presentation.

SOFTWARE PROTECTION

It is important to note that this package is software protected, it is not possible to make multiple copies. Without condoning software piracy, the ability to copy one's package for perfectly legitimate reasons is an important one.

To run *Xchange* it is necessary to insert a master disk in a drive before anything else will work. This master disk can then be removed and a data disk inserted.

Master disks are fine while they work. What happens when they wear out? Packages that rely on a master disk concept are also vulnerable to problems like the software producers going out of business.

Xchange's producers seem unlikely to go broke and they promise to replace any master disk within 48 hours. Even so, this could mean an awkward wait in the middle of an important job.

SUPPORT

To adopt an integrated package as a regular management tool represents a significant personal investment in learning what amounts to four or more different packages combined into one.

Help and advice is therefore of critical importance. The producers of *Xchange* have recognised this and offer a user support and maintenance plan. For an annual subscription customers are automatically sent product upgrades free of charge and have access to a telephone hotline service.

References

Xchange. *Which Computer?*, Nov 1984
PIPER,Robert. Getting It All Together. *Apricot User*, March 1985
HAWKINS, A. Look Beyond 1-2-3. *Apricot User*, March 1985

Appendices

SOFTWARE APPLICATIONS

	Database	Diary Systems	Grammar/ Spelling Checker	Graphics	Spread sheet	Training	Project Planning	WP	Other Aids
Brainstorm	**								**
Cardbox Plus	**								
Condor	**								
Datamaster	**	**							
Datebook	**								
Everyman	**								
Files & Folders	**								
Friday!	**								
Grammatik			**						
Lotus 1-2-3	**			**	**				
Hands on Micros	**					**			
Microfile	**								
Milestone							**		
Hands on MS-DOS						**			
Negotiation Edge						**			**
Notebook	**								
Nutcracker Suite								**	
Open Access	**	**		**	**			**	**
Palantir	**	**	**					**	**
QED+	**	**					**	**	**
Snowball						**			
Spellbinder			**	**				**	**
Symphony	**	**		**	**			**	**
Touch 'n Go						**			
Trendisk	**								
Trendisk/2		**							
Ultimate Diary		**						**	
Wordcraft			**					**	
Wordstar			**					**	
Xchange	**			**	**			**	**

GUIDE TO COMPUTER TRAINING AGENCIES

Company	Phone No	Introduction to Computing	Word Processing	Spread Sheets	Data Bases	Integrated Software	Venue	Client Site
ADM Ltd	01-863 0621	*	*	*	*		London	
Adda	01-579 2333	*	*	*	*	*	London	
Anderson Jacobson	0753 821021		*	*		*	Various	*
Arthur Young	01-831 7130	*		*		*	London	*
Bespoke Computer Services	061-236 2552						M'chester	
BIS Applied Systems	01-261 9237	*	*	*	*		Various	*
Business Systems	01-252 1253	*	*	*	*	*	London	*
Byte Shop Training	0480-218812	*	*	*	*	*	Various	*
C/WP Computers	01-828 9000		*	*	*		London	
Centre for IT	0533-551551	*		*			Leicester	
Circuit (UK)	0480-217425	*	*	*	*		Various	
Compower	05435-2511		*	*	*		Cannock	*
Compsoft	04868-25925			*			Surrey	
Computer Factors	0203-555466	*	*	*	*	*	Coventry	
Computer Training	01-585 2322	*		*		*	London	
Computerland	01-379 0855	*	*	*		*	London	*
Computacenter	01-602 8405	*	*	*	*	*	Various	
Data Logic Education	01-486 7288	*	*	*		*	London	*
Datasolve	01-499 7099	*	*	*			London	
Digital	0734-859766	*	*	*	*			

Note that agencies often specialise in one particular package within their general fields; do ensure that your requirements can, in fact, be met by your chosen training agency.

Company	Phone No	Introduction to Computing	Word Processing	Spread Sheets	Data Bases	Integrated Software	Venue	Client Site
Digitus Ltd	01-379 6968	*	*	*	*	*	London	*
Ditec	01-900 1577	*	*	*	*	*	Various	
Drake Computers	01-734 0911	*	*	*	*	*	London	
Edutext	01-937 8633	*	*	*	*	*	London	*
Executive Computer	01-629 9255	*	*		*		London	
Ferrari Software	0784-38811	*	*	*	*	*	Various	*
G&M Software	0293-511855	*	*	*	*		Crawley	*
Granada	01-579 3003	*	*		*	*	London	
ICL Training Services	01-788 7272	*	*				Windsor	
The Industrial Society	01-839 4300	*	*		*		London	
Institution of Industrial Managers	0582-37071			*				
MSS Services Ltd	0903-34755/6	*	*	*	*	*	Various	*
Management Centre	01-242 9201/5915	*	*	*	*	*		*
Matrix Training	0274-736455	*	*	*	*	*	Bradford	*
Micro Advisory Centre	01-928 8989	*	*			*	London	
Microcomputing Tyne & Wear	091-417 6018			*	*	*	Washington	
Microword Services	021-622 4794	*	*	*	*	*	Birm'ham	
NCC	061-228 6333				*		Various	*
Office Systems	01-439 4001	*	*				London	*

Note that agencies often specialise in one particular package within their general fields; do ensure that your requirements can, in fact, be met by your chosen training agency.

Company	Phone No	Introduction to Computing	Word Processing	Spread Sheets	Data Bases	Integrated Software	Venue	Client Site
Owl	044-282 7302	*	*	*	*		Herts	*
P & P Micro	0706-217744	*	*	*	*	*	Various	
Pera	0664-6413 3			*			Leics	
Personal Computers	01-377 1200	*	*	*	*	*	London	*
Pitman IT Centre	01-379 7515	*	*	*	*	*	London	
Planning Consultancy 01-839 8890		*	*	*	*	*	London	*
PPM	0734-595957	*	*	*	*		Reading	
Productivity Systems 0753-68116		*					Herts	
Programs Unlimited	01-487 3351	*	*	*	*	*	London	*
Raindrop Computers	01-734 1091	*	*	*	*		London	
Ranmor Computing	0702-339262		*	*	*	*	Southend	*
Slough College	0753-34585	*	*	*		*	Slough	
Softutor	01-430 1200	*	*	*	*	*	London	*
Stag Terminals	01-977 3288	*	*	*	*	*	Various	*
System Build	0778-344388			*	*	*	Stamford	*
Tecam	07372-42062		*		*		Reigate	
Training International 01-935 4555		*	*	*	*	*	London	*
United Sumlock Ltd	01-250 0505	*	*	*	*	*	London	
Wang Isleworth Educ. centre 01-560 4151		*	*	*	*		Various	

Note that agencies often specialise in one particular package within their general fields; do ensure that your requirements can, in fact, be met by your chosen training agency.

Source: Adapted from PC Management, June 1985

Useful Addresses

AICS,
18, Leicester Street,
London WC2 H7BN.
(01) 437-0678

The Association of Independent Computer Specialists. Write for a list of members who are small consultants, software producers and so on.

Association of Computer Clubs
17 Lowne Park Crescent,
London, SE26 6HH
Tel N/A

Has regional groups. Keen to hear from business microcomputer users who want a good computer club in their area.

Business Microcomputer Users Association
First Chicago House,
90 Long Acre,
London WC2E 9NP
(01) 839-9795

Aims to provide help and advice on financial modelling information systems. Annual membership fee £25.

Computer Services Association
Hanover House,
73/74 High Holborn,
London WC1V 6LE
(01) 405-2171

Advises on software systems, packages, training etc. Free commercial enquiry services.

Computing Publications Ltd,
VNU House, 32-34 Broadwick Street,
London W1A 2HG
(01) 323 3211

Publishers of useful reference books on software. Till 1984 produced Microcomputer Software Directory, subsequently remodelled as The Software Users' Year Book.

CoSira
141 Castle Street,
Salisbury
(0722) 6255

Council for Small Industries in Rural Areas. Offers initial discussion free, technical advice at reasonable rates.

Information Alert
38 Part Street,
Southport,
Merseyside PR8 1HY
(0704) 33596

Produces Micro Alert, an index of literature on microcomputers for home and business.

Planning Consultancy Ltd,
46-47 Pall Mall,
London SW1Y 5JG
(01) 839-8890

A de luxe version of business user group called PLC Club. Has a variety of computers and the £250 membership fee includes training, consultancy, a help line, software lending library etc.

Small Firms Service
Abell House, John Islip Street,
London SW1 4LN

Direct advice by usually retired businessmen at low cost. Source of contacts and literature.

The Arts Council of Great Britain
105 Piccadilly,
London W1V 0AU
(01) 629-9495

Offers an information exchange to advise on computerisation. Has also been involved with developing standards for computer training.

The British Computer Society
13 Mansfield Street,
London W1M OBP
(01) 637-0471

Representative organisation for those working in all aspects of computing in the UK. Various branches in country.

The Computer Services Association
Hanover House,
73-74 High Holborn,
London WC1V 6LE
(01) 405-2171

The CSA is a mixture of computer bureaux, software houses, consultancies etc. There is a free commercial enquiry service.

The National Computing Centre
Oxford Road,
Manchester M1 7ED
(061) 228-6333

Provides general information, advice and consultancy at competitive rates. Is also responsible for the Federation of Microsystems Centres around the country.

Bibliography

BAGSHAW, Eric. Data at Your Fingertips. *Business Computing and Communications*, October 1984, pp 26–8

BAGSHAW, Eric. One for All. *Business Computing: The Survival Guide*, VNU Business Publications, 1985, pp 73, 75–7

BIDMEAD, Chris. Brainstorm. *Practical Computing*, July 1984, pp 80–1

BRIGHT, Peter. Open Access. *Personal Computer World*, June 1984, pp 162–164

BUDGETT, Henry. Having a Brainstorm. *Computing Today*, April 1984, pp 64–5

CHRISTIAN, Charles. Easier Accounts. *Micro Decision*, October 1983

CREEKMORE, Wayne. *Through the MicroMaze*, Ashton Tate, 1983

FORD, J. Milestone: A Program to Aid Project Management. *InfoWorld*, May 1983

FOREMAN, Michael. Triple Attraction of Lotus 1-2-3. *Micro Decision* December 1983, pp 47–50

GLOSSBRENNER, Alfred. *How to Buy Software, The Master Guide to Picking the Right Program*. 1st United Kingdom Papermac, 1984

HAWKINS, A. Look Beyond 1-2-3. *Apricot User*, March 1985, pp 66–7, 70, 72

HERSHEY, William. Think Tank. *Byte*, May 1984, pp 189, 190, 192, 194

HOLMES, Geoffrey. Management data at Your Fingertips: Fast and Painless. *Accountancy*, August 1984, pp 108–10

JADRNICEK, Rik. Symphony, A Full Orchestra Version of Lotus 1-2-3. *Byte*, July 1984, pp 121–3, 372–3

LANG, Kathy. Data Management on Micros Comes of Age? *Sixteen Bit Computing*, July 1984, pp 47–8, 50, 54, 56

LANG, Kathy. Datamaster. *Personal Computer World*, May 1984, pp 242–3, 245–6

LANG, Kathy. Everyman. *Personal Computer World*, 1984, pp 251–3, 256, 258

LANG, Kathy. Files and Folders. *Personal Computer World*, Dec 1984, pp 204–7

LANG, Kathy. Friday!. *Personal Computer World*, July 1984, pp 132, 133–5

LANG, Kathy. Home–Grown Word Processing. *Micro Decision*, June 1984, pp 31–2, 34–6

LANG, Kathy. Watch Out Wordstar! *Sixteen Bit Computing*, March 1984, pp 32, 35, 37

LANG, Kathy. Database Comparison, The Story So Far. *Personal Computer World*, Jan 1985, pp 140–1, 143, 202, 203

LANG, Kathy. Software File, Word Processor Round Up. *Sixteen Bit Computing*, February 1985 pp 37–9, 41–2, 46, 47–8

LANG, Kathy. Ways to Make Wordstar Whizz. *Sixteen Bit Computing*, April 1985, pp 25–8, 30

LANG, Kathy. For the Record, *Business Computing: The Survival Guide*, VNU Business Publications, 1985 pp 63, 64, 65, 66

LANG, Kathy. Text Play. *Business Computing: The Survival Guide*, VNU Business Publications, 1985 pp 50, 51, 54, 55

LEIGH, Andrew. Turn Confusion Into Clarity. *Apricot User*, April 1985, pp 30, 31, 34, 36

LEIGH, Andrew. Time Your Tasks, Move After Move. *Apricot User*, June 1985, pp 50–2, 54

LEIGH, Andrew. The Pocket Money Software Suites. *Apricot User*, July 1985, pp 24, 25, 28, 30

LEIGH, Andrew. Desktops=Integration. QED? *Apricot User*, August 1985, pp 34–7

LEWIS, Mike. Friday!. *Practical Computing*, June 1984, pp 110–1

LIARDET, Mike. Lotus 1-2-3. *Personal Computer World*, Nov 1983, pp 132–5

MYERSCOUGH, Paul. A Database By Any Other Name. *Practical Computing*, April, 1984

O'REILLY, Richard. A Painless Way to Learn Software. *Los Angeles Times*, 30th October 1983

PIPER, Robert. Find Your Facts More Easily. *Micro Decision*, August 1984, pp 47, 48, 50, 52, 54

PIPER, Robert. Putting Your Office on Disk. *Micro Decision*, June 1984, pp 51–2, 56

PIPER, Robert. Getting It All Together. *Apricot User*, March 1985, pp 58–9, 62, 64

POUNTAIN, Dick. All Within Easy Reach. *Business Computing: The Survival Guide*, VNU Business Publications, 1985, pp 78, 80–2

ROBERTS, Liz. On the Menu. *What Micro?*, May 1984, pp 104–6

RODWELL, Peter. Thinking on the Computer. *Sixteen Bit Computing*, Aug 1984, pp 27–8, 30–2

TEHAN, Patricia. User Clubs. *Apricot User*, March 1984, pp 87

TEHAN, Patricia. Training 1: Learning from a Disk. *Apricot User*, May 1985, pp 59, 60, 62

VAIL, Simon. Sniffing Out the Right Formulae. *Micro Decision*, November 1984, pp 126–8, 130

WOOLEY, Ben. Superwriter. *Apricot User*, March 1985, pp 52, 56

WOOLEY, Ben. The Rivals in Friendliness. *Apricot User*, February 1985, pp 36–8, 44–5

As easy as 1-2-3. *Which Computer?*, January 1984, pp 163, 165

Brainstorm. *Which Computer?*, May 1984, pp 134–5

Computer Tutors. *Which Computer?*, June 1984, pp 86–7, 89

Database. *Punch* October 1984, p 100

Database. *Punch* March 1984

Database Packages. *Business Micro*, November 1983, pp 31, 32, 35–6

Datamaster. *Which Computer?*, April 1984

Having it all. *Which Computer?*, June 1984

High Flying Database. *Sixteen Bit Computing*, March 1984

How to Smarten up Your Ideas. *Business Computing and Communications*, April 1984

Integrated Software. *Which Computer?*, July 1984, pp 102–3, 105–8

Lotus 1-2-3. *Which Computer?*, May 1985, pp 57, 61, 64, 66

The Best Spread Sheet. *Which Computer?*, December 1984, pp 99, 101, 103–4, 109, 112, 113

The Best Word Processing Package. *Which Computer?*, February 1985, pp 93, 95–6, 98, 100–1

The Executive Path to Word Processing. *Business Computing & Communications*, September 1984, pp 48–9, 51, 55, 57

Trendisk. *Which Computer?*, Feb 1984

Trendtext/2. *Practical Computing*, March 1984

Word Processing, How to Select Your Software. *Business Micro*, December 1983, pp 45–6, 48–50, 51

Xchange. *Which Computer?*, November 1984, pp 53, 55, 57

Glossary

Alphanumeric
Letters, numbers and symbols which can be processed by machine.

Applications Program
A program specially written to solve a particular problem such as word processing or database management.

ASCII
Short for American Standard Code for Information Interchange; pronounced 'az-key'.Used in virtually all personal computers and data communications, represents keyboard characters, symbols and functions. Allows computers and software to communicate with each other.

Auxiliary storage
Auxiliary storage facility for data held outside the computer's own memory. Usually hard or floppy disk but can be other methods.

Back-up
The process of duplicating a disk or part of it to another storage device, usually a second disk.Essential to insure against possible failure of the hardware or software.

BASIC
Beginner's All Purpose Symbolic Instruction Code. A programming language for beginners.

Booting the system
To load the operating system into memory, usually by inserting a disk with the system on it; the instructions allow more instructions to be loaded.

Bug
Broadly any malfunction in hardware or software. It is said that in the early days of computers a moth or some other insect caused a computer in the American Navy to fail by becoming stuck in the relay circuits.

Byte
A small unit of computer memory that is roughly equivalent to one character but can hold one or two numeric characters.

Cell
A single, uniquely defined location in a spreadsheet; can contain either a single number, formula or piece of text.

Character
A letter, space, number, punctuation mark or symbol.

Chip
An integrated circuit able to perform calculations.

Circuit
An electrical pathway that carries a current.

COBOL
COmmon Business Oriented Language; a computer language suitable for business applications.

Code
Rules that govern how data is to be managed.

Column
A vertical, as opposed to horizontal, grouping of data (see row).

Command
Instructions given to the computer telling it what to do next; usually issued via a keyboard or a computer program

Command-driven
The way a program is controlled by the user, issuing instructions in the form of codes, rather than choosing from a menu of options (see menu-driven).

Compatibility
Ability of one device to communicate with another, or a software program to work with another.

Computer
Electro-mechanical device that automatically performs a set of programmed instructions.

Concurrency
A technical term which in practice means that you can switch rapidly between one software package and another.

Configure
See Install

Copy protected
A method of ensuring that a program cannot be pirated by making illegal copies.

CP/M
Control Program for Microcomputers, an operating system.

CPU
Short for Central Processor Unit, the core of the computer.

Data
Pieces of information.

Data analysis
The process of trying to make sense of the information by classifying, grouping, and generally manipulating it.

Data disk
The disk which contains your data, as opposed to that containing the software program.

Data Protection Act
Introduced in Britain in 1984 and backed by a special secretariat to ensure that personal information held on computers is not abused.

Data Subject
Defined by the 1984 Data Protection Act as someone who has personal information about them recorded on a computer in Britain.

Database
Any collection of information, though usually computerized.

DBMS
Stands for DataBase Management System and is a program for controlling a database so that information can be rapidly entered, sorted, selected and reports produced.

De-bug
To sort out a problem in either hardware or software (see bug).

Default
The value that will be assumed by the computer or any device when you give no other value.

Delete
To remove or erase text or a file.

Desktop
A type of software package that tries to make the computer an extension of the manager's desk. It sits between the operating system and the other regular software so that you can switch rapidly between the two sorts of programs.

Directory
A list of all the files available currently held on disk.

Disk
The medium of storage for most personal business computers; disks can be hard or soft (floppy) and are usually 8″, 5.25″ or 3.5″ in diameter.

Documentation
All the accompanying written material that supports a particular software package. The purpose of it is to help you understand how to use the product, though sometimes you would never guess.

Dongle
Software protection device which plugs into the computer to prevent illegal copying; if not inserted the program will not function.

Drive
A device that moves tape or disk past a read/write head.

Edit
To add or amend existing text, characters, symbols and so on.

Escape
A command key on a computer keyboard; when pressed usually gives the instruction to leave that particular part of the program or to cancel a recently-made entry.

Field
The computer equivalent of the blanks you fill with your name and address and other information when you complete a census return. Strictly it is a specific entry.

Field size
The number of blank spaces needed for information which will be placed in a field.

File
A collection of information held in one place and sometimes made up of a series of separate records.

Floppy
The flexible disk on which data is recorded.

Flow chart
A diagrammatic way of showing, step-by step, a particular activity or series of tasks.

Flying blind
Using a software package for the first time and without referring to the manual or document-ation for guidance.

Form letter
A standard letter prepared using data drawn from a database to enable the letter to be personalised to each recipient.

Format
Preparing a blank disk for use on the computer. Also refers to the arrangement of text on a page or screen so that it is presented as required, for example with left or right justification etc.

Fortran
Stands for FORmula TRANslator and is a specialist type of computer programming language, suited for solving mathematical equations and other complex scientific chores.

Function key
A labelled key on a computer keyboard which allows an operation to be carried out with one key stroke.

Graphics package
A software application which can produce charts, diagrams and other visual displays; draws its data usually from other packages such as a database or a spreadsheet.

Hands-on
Literally getting your hands onto a computer keyboard and making the machine work.

Hard copy
Any printed record a computer makes.

Hard disk
A storage device often sealed inside the computer, which can contain a much larger quantity of information than floppy, removable disks (see also disk).

Hardware
The physical parts of a computer.

Hotline
A phone service to a dealer or software supplier giving instant advice and help with your software problems; sometimes free in the first year after purchasing a product but usually on a subscription basis.

Input
Any way of getting data into the computer.

Install
To tailor your software package so that it can work properly with your hardware.

Integrated software
Software applications that combine a number of facilities that are compatible with each other so that swapping information between them should be relatively simple.

Interactive
Process in which the user and the computer exchange information in a series of steps which are linked together in some kind of logical sequence.

Internal memory
Temporary memory inside a computer controlled by the CPU (see RAM).

Justify
Spacing so that text is aligned on the left or right margins or both.

K
Short for Kilobyte (see Kilobyte).

Keystroke
Action of pressing a key.

Kilobyte
Roughly 1000 bytes of memory. Actually it's 1024 bytes but who's counting? Roughly indicates a computer's horsepower! Thus 48K is 48 x 1024 = 49,152 which is rounded to 48,000 bytes.

Language
Any way of telling a micro what you want done; programs are written using artificial forms of language, some closer to English than others.

Load
To read data or a program into a computer's memory.

Machine language
The detailed gut-level instructions that a micro needs to do anything.

Macro
A stored sequence of keystrokes which thus avoid constantly retyping; initiated using either a special function key or by holding down the control key and typing in a previously arranged character.

Mail merge
A facility in a software package for generating customized form letters; involves merging a list of addresses with a master letter.

Mailing list program
A program which generates address labels and also acts rather like a database management program; will sort records, print out labels based on particular information such as whether the person has ordered recently. More powerful generally than mail merge programs.

Manual
The written instructions accompanying a software product.

Menu
A number of choices that appear on the screen that offer several courses of action to accomplish what you want with a particular program; saves having to remember individual commands.

Menu-driven
One way in which a software package may be controlled by the user, namely by selecting what action should take place next by choosing from a menu shown on the screen and requiring a simple choice. (See also command-driven.)

Micro
Short for microcomputer.

Modem
Electronic device for sending computer information over the telephone and similarly for receiving it.

MS-DOS
Stands for Microsoft Disk Operating System, a product protected by copyright.

Navigational commands
Instructions for moving the cursor around the screen and throughout the current workspace.

NLQ
Short for Near Letter Quality. Refers to achieving a print finish almost as good as that from an electric typewriter but usually using a matrix printer.

Online
When people and hardware are in contact with the CPU; online help is assistance available while you are using a particular program.

Operating system
A mediator between you and the hardware. Takes care of often repeated instructions, saving you time. It is a control program responsible for the overall operation of the computer and any peripherals.

Output
Information created by the computer program and presented to the user; output is concerned with the real world, producing results.

Program
A set of instructions that tell the computer what to do.

Program disk
The disk which holds the software program, as opposed to your own data.

Programmable
Capable of being programmed, that is, following a sequence of instructions.

RAM
Short for Random Access Memory; any cell can be accessed directly; these days just about everything in the computer world has random access so the words do not mean much. RAM is volatile; whatever you put into it vanishes when the power is removed.

Record
A collection of data in a file.

Record
A unit that holds a set of information and which may be one of many such units. Records are sub divisions of a file.

Relational
The connection between a set of information, either in records or between files.

Relational database
A database management system able to link all the records and files to each other without requiring them to have similar structures; treats the database as if it were just one giant record card.

Report
The output from a computer program.

Return
Command given from the keyboard for the computer to take a previously specified course of action. The return key is often shown as a bent arrow like a reverse 'L'. It may also be this shape on the keyboard too.

ROM
Read Only Memory; once its contents are entered it cannot be changed. That's the theory, in practice there are also programmable ROMS.

Row
A horizontal, as opposed to vertical, chain of data (see column).

Screen prompt
Suggestion from the computer program shown on screen that you are now expected to do something.

Search and Replace
Facility for finding a specific piece of information in a file and either manually, or automatically substituting it with some other required data.

Software
The paperwork that makes the computer go. It is not just programs, it is also the document-ation which accompanies it. Software is the instructions for achieving a particular task, not the task itself.

Software package
See applications program.

Source code
The original language in which a program is written before it is converted to machine readable language.To tailor software packages to suit the user it may often be necessary to have access to this code.Software suppliers normally guard it jealously.

Spreadsheet
Anything with rows and columns of numbers; an electronic spreadsheet is a system of auto-matically recalculating numbers in a work sheet that depend on others; the ideal tool for any job requiring arithmetic or calculation (see chapter on spreadsheets).

Stand-alones
Any software application or equipment that works independently of any other.

Storage capacity
The amount of data that can be held in memory or auxiliary storage and usually defined in bytes.

Store
Command usually given during a program to save data on disk.

Support
The help you should be able to receive from anyone who sells you a software package; support is sometimes called backup support and is general advice about using your software, not consultancy about how the software is to be applied to your particular problems.

Tutorial
The part of a software package that teaches the new user how to operate it.

Tutorial disk
A disk that contains one or more teaching modules to help new users learn how to operate a particular software package or some other aspect of computing; can also refer to general training packages.

User-friendly
Increasingly dated term meaning the extent to which a software package helps one to use it.

Windows
Method of splitting up the display area on the screen into two or more portions allowing you to see and work with information in all the separate parts; windows can fill the screen or occupy a tiny space, some can even change shape.

Word processor
A software application which handles text and allows the user to edit, erase and rearrange material and then produce a hard copy via the printer.

Word wrap
Ability of a package to handle text so that words can be typed continuously without the user needing to perform carriage returns. The words 'wrap' around the screen as if they were a continuous line.

Work space
The section of the computer memory reserved for the creation and handling of your data, as opposed to the program. It is the amount of memory remaining after the operating system and the software package program have been loaded.

WYSIWYG
What You See Is What You Get. Indicates that what the user sees on the screen will appear in an identical format or layout when printed.

Index